WHEELER WINSTON DIXON

VISIONS OF THE APOCALYPSE

Spectacles of Destruction in American Cinema

WALLFLOWER PRESS London and New York

WALLFLOWER PRESS
4th Floor, 26 Shacklewell Lane, London E8 2EZ
www.wallflowerpress.co.uk

A catalogue for this book is available from the British Library

ISBN 1-903364-74-4 (pbk) ✓
ISBN 1-903364-38-8 (hbk)

Design by Loaf Design

Printed in Great Britain by Antony Rowe, Chippenham, Wiltshire

"I'm the commander—see, I don't need to explain—I do not need to explain why I say things. That's the interesting thing about being the President. Maybe somebody needs to explain to me why they say something, but I don't feel like I owe anybody an explanation."
— George W. Bush (in Ridgeway 36)

"What we do now is withhold films from most of America, which is shocking. And what do we withhold? The best films. If you live 30 miles out in mall-land, you can't see all the great movies. Same with the rest of the world: we export the crap. And then we wonder why everybody hates us and has a distorted picture of what Americans are."
— Meryl Streep (in King W4)

"We don't always understand what happens to us, or why."
— Olivier Assayas (in Dupont 18)

For Linda Ray Pratt

CONTENTS

List of Illustrations..xi

Acknowledgments..xiii

Introduction: The Tyranny of Images 1

Chapter One: Freedom from Choice.. 21

Chapter Two: Invasion U.S.A... 59

Chapter Three: The Limits of Time 97

Coda: The Copenhagen Defense..130

Works Cited 145

Index 159

LIST OF ILLUSTRATIONS

1. Preview of coming attractions: New York City is vaporized by an atomic blast in *Invasion U.S.A.* (1952). Courtesy Jerry Ohlinger Archives.

2. New York City as atomic wasteland: *Invasion U.S.A.* (1952). Courtesy Jerry Ohlinger Archives.

3. The war of the past: Mutual Assured Destruction. *The Last War* (1961; original title *Sekai daisenso*, 1961). Courtesy Jerry Ohlinger Archives.

4. The Arc de Triomphe is destroyed in *The Last War* (1961; original title *Sekai daisenso*, 1961). Courtesy Jerry Ohlinger Archives.

5. Manhattan, before the collapse of the World Trade Center, is decimated by a nuclear attack in *The Last War* (1961; original title *Sekai daisenso*, 1961). Courtesy Jerry Ohlinger Archives.

6. The city collapses in *Tidal Wave* (1973; original title *Nippon chinbotsu*, 1973). Courtesy Jerry Ohlinger Archives.

7. Airborne firefighters attempt to halt the rampaging fire that engulfs the failing metropolis in *Tidal Wave* (1973; original title *Nippon chinbotsu*, 1973). Courtesy Jerry Ohlinger Archives.

8. Skyscrapers collapse from the intense heat in *Tidal Wave* (1973; original title *Nippon chinbotsu*, 1973). Courtesy Jerry Ohlinger Archives.

9. The end of the world occurs through natural catastrophe in *When Worlds Collide* (1951). Courtesy Jerry Ohlinger Archives.

10. Survivors carry on with the tasks of civilization in *The Bed Sitting Room* (1969). Courtesy Jerry Ohlinger Archives.

11. The city is leveled by earthquake in *San Francisco* (1936). Courtesy Jerry Ohlinger Archives.

12. The ruins of Manhattan in *Deluge* (1933). Courtesy Jerry Ohlinger Archives.

13. Tragedy on a human scale in *The Day the Sky Exploded* (1961; *La Morte viene dallo spazio*, 1958). Courtesy Jerry Ohlinger Archives.

14. The staging of Armageddon; synthetic destruction in *Hooper* (1978). Courtesy Jerry Ohlinger Archives.

15. Transportation becomes superfluous in *The Last Days of Man on Earth* (1973; original title *The Final Programme*, 1973). Courtesy Jerry Ohlinger Archives.

ACKNOWLEDGMENTS

The author wishes to sincerely thank Linda Ray Pratt, Chair of the Department of English, and the members of the Department of English at the University of Nebraska, Lincoln (UNL), for their support during the preparation of this text. As always, Dana Miller's superb skills as a typist made this manuscript possible, and Gwendolyn Audrey Foster assisted in the research for the book, as well as critiquing various drafts of the manuscript. Therese Myers did an excellent job with the copy editing of the manuscript. My thanks also to the staff of Wallflower Press for their help in the final presentation of this book, particularly Yoram Allon and Hannah Patterson. My warmest thanks also go to Dean Richard Hoffmann, whose continuing support of Film Studies at UNL makes projects such as this possible. Dennis Coleman, as always, contributed unique insights in the matter of the production and reception of the dominant cinema. Jerry Ohlinger provided the stills that illustrate this text, and numerous other friends and colleagues helped me shape the material in this book into its final form. Carol L. Inskip provided the index. My thanks to all.

Wheeler Winston Dixon

THE TYRANNY OF IMAGES

This is a book about the end of cinema, the end of the world, and the end of civilization as we know it. The signs are there, waiting to be deciphered. The worldwide proliferation of nuclear arms, including North Korea's decision to resume nuclear weapons production, assures that sooner or later one of these violently destructive devices will be used, either by some sort of constituted government, or by terrorists seeking to gain the upper hand. Natural resources are being depleted, the polar ice caps are melting, "rogue states" pop up with increasing frequency, and international politics are fraught with tension and deception. And other than a few desultory op-ed pieces in the newspaper, or on television, no one is really doing anything about it; embracing instead the fossil fuel culture of the 20th century as our model for what's left of the future. We'd like to care, but it's too much effort. Bombarded by a plethora of competing media sources, contemporary humankind seeks some sort of refuge from the incessant images of destruction that flood our telescreens, without success. The use of the Orwellian word "telescreens" is not an accident; if ever we lived in a zone of perpetual hypersurveillance, we do so now. Images seek to control and dominate us; access to information is strictly controlled. If something doesn't fit into the corporate pattern, it is ruthlessly excised. We have abandoned humanism as a model, and replaced it with the culture of ceaseless "alerts," "bulletins," and "updates," designed to terrorize us into submission to the state. The televised "hate breaks" of Orwell's *1984* have been replaced by omnipresent 24 hour "news" coverage, which isn't *news* at all, but rather a series of carefully crafted press releases designed to favor the ruling elite, and convince dissenters that resistance to this new regime is futile.

Indeed, as a culture, we seem tired with life. As we enter the 21st century, there are signs of exhaustion everywhere. The narrative structures of feature films, as I will discuss, are being shamelessly recycled from one film to the next, and sequels (which have always been a part of movie history) now predominate the box-office. Politics, especially in the U.S., have become so "stage managed" as to divorce themselves from anything remotely resembling democracy or the representation of one's constituents: it's all about money, access to the media, hyperconglomerization and buying up the competition, the better to dominate what passes for public discourse. The media is now so closely controlled by a few corporations that any hope of getting alternative viewpoints to the general public has all but evaporated. Are we interested in the welfare of the general populace? Or do we seek the obliteration of social culture, in which the ever-widening gap between the rich and the poor recalls the gulf between the workers and the ruling class in Fritz Lang's *Metropolis* (1927)? The questions this books thus seeks to address are, "how does the current cinema reflect these concerns?," "what are the forces that have brought us to the brink of social and cultural apocalypse?," and "what assurance do we have that our continued existence is feasible, or even likely?" As the reader will discover, I feel that we are experiencing a global cultural meltdown, in which all the values of the past have been replaced by rapacious greed, the hunger for sensation, and the desire for useless novelty without risk. Indeed, in all our contemporary cultural manifestations as a worldwide community, we seem "eager for the end."

And there is, after all, something comforting in the thought of imminent destruction. All bets are off, all duties executed, all responsibilities abandoned. Contemplating not just one's own mortality, but that of an entire civilization, somehow makes the unthinkable not only palatable, but also vaguely reassuring. If no one will survive, who is to say that any of us ever existed at all? What values will histories of the earth have when the entire planet is destroyed? The people, places, events, wars, cataclysmic upheavals, intrigues, triumphs, and failures of humankind will be obliterated in an instant, leaving no one behind to tell the tale. If we all go together, so to speak, have we ever been here at all? Equality will at last be achieved in the final seconds before Armageddon, when countries, boundaries, and political systems instantaneously evaporate, making a mockery of all our efforts at self-preservation. The absolute destruction of the earth, and all the peoples on it, will create a vacuum only for those who no longer exist. Centuries of art, literature, scientific achievement, the mechanisms of instantaneous communication, all will vanish—including this book and its potential readers. No one will know that we have ever existed. No one will bear witness to our demise.

The cinema has grappled with these questions since its inception in the late 1880s and remains fascinated by them today. Yet each filmic depiction of the apocalypse inherently projects the existence of surviving witnesses, for whom the film has been made. Thus, none of the cinema's numerous attempts to "document" the true end of the world can be held to be truly authentic if only because they require an audience by the very fact of their existence. And yet, as we know, films can easily be destroyed, and 50% of all films made before 1950 no longer exist, the victims of nitrate deterioration, poor preservation, or corporate and/or private neglect. As each film ceases to exist, it takes with it the actors who performed in it, the director who staged their actions, the scenarist who plotted their conflicts, the cinematographer who recorded these staged conceits, and all the other participants in the film's creation into oblivion: merely a line, perhaps, in the Library of Congress catalogue. Memories of surviving actors, technicians, and auteurs, recorded and transcribed by scholars who seek to keep the memory of the particular film in question alive. Testimony shelved in libraries, forgotten, and then eventually purged from the collection, perhaps pulped to create raw material for new texts. But if and when the entire planet Earth ceases to exist, all records of its existence will also cease to exist, and nothing (except for some bits of space junk, and perhaps a plaque on the moon with Richard Nixon's name on it) will remain for any future civilizations to contemplate. This, then, is the true and humbling nature of genuine apocalypse; not an atom of the Earth will remain to bear witness to our birth, life, and death. What makes this appealing is the thought that if none shall survive, then, at last, all class, social, and racial boundaries will have been erased. No more slavery, no more sweatshops, no more prejudice, and no more inequality. As the Earth atomizes into cosmic dust, we will at last achieve the true perfection of nonexistence with nothing but some space debris to bear witness to our passing. We are all, thus, equal in death.

And yet this thought is simultaneously too appalling, too comprehensive for the human psyche to truly absorb. No books, postcards, monuments, videotapes, museums, armies, childhood memories, picnics, wars, riots, strikes, weddings, or funerals to remember? Nothing to mark our time on Earth? The thought is too totalizing for the mind to absorb. Yet perhaps that is why so many people are eager for the end. As an "event," the true apocalypse would cancel out all other occurrences and render the state of human existence absolutely blank. Such a situation is impossible to comprehend, even as our own mortality is incomprehensible to us. We move though life in a fever dream, acquiring objects, pursuing goals, engaging in trysts, and surviving conflicts until that day when a car swerves into the wrong lane and crashes into our vehicle head-on, or a blood vessel in our brain bursts, or a button is pushed, or, after a night's sleep, we just do not wake up. The total embrace of nothingness thus becomes the unstated goal of existence, a headlong rush into the abyss. Simultaneously feared and anticipated, the end of "all" is the defining moment that we all seek. Perhaps this is why the movies are so obsessed with ritual displays of sex (procreation) and violence (death), coupled with myriad cataclysmic explosions to spice up things when the hopelessly recycled narrative slows to a crawl. There is no real difference, for example, between *Jason X* (2001) and *Hollywood Ending* (2002). In the first film, Jason rises from a state of cryogenic suspension to begin, once again, the mute and ritual murder of yet another isolated group of victims, this time on board a spaceship in the 25th century. At the film's end, Jason plunges to Earth (or Earth II, the original having been rendered unfit for human habitation by centuries of relentless pollution) and lands in a replica of Crystal Lake, where the first film, *Friday the 13th* (1980), took place. The film's final shot of Jason's signature hockey mask floating in the water assures us that he will again return to dispatch more victims, only to be momentarily vanquished so that he can once again return from the dead. In *Hollywood Ending*, Woody Allen is once again the stammering neurotic who self-destructs through fear of success, improbably in love with a woman half his age, suffering temporary indignities only to be miraculously rescued in the final reel so that he can return for another installment next year. Both Jason Voorhees and Woody Allen are thus series characters, as Andy Hardy and Vin Diesel, and Julia Roberts are series characters, their fictional personae indistinguishable from their offscreen selves. *Spider-Man* (2002) thus paves the way for *The Hulk* (2003), with director Ang Lee attached to the project; *Spider-Man 2* (2004), in which Sam Raimi again puts Tobey Maguire and Kirsten Dunst through their predictable paces; *X2* (2003), reuniting Bryan Singer with numerous members of the original cast, including Patrick Stewart and Hugh Jackman; as well as future projects *Fantastic Four* (2003), *Daredevil* (2003), and *Sub-Mariner,* all announced from the Marvel Comics stable. Batman and Superman, as characters, seem momentarily exhausted from their labors, but they will no doubt return in the near future, in new and updated digital versions. In the meantime, we can content ourselves with *Star Wars: Episode II— Attack of the Clones* (2002), which at least affords Christopher Lee some work, as well as *Stuart Little 2* (2002), *Men in Black II* (2002), a remake of *Mr. Deeds Goes to Town* (1936), this time titled *Mr. Deeds* (2002), with Adam Sandler as the new millennium's everyman, not to mention *Austin Powers in Goldmember* (2002), the latest Austin Powers film.

Sequels have always dominated genre filmmaking—look at the *Sherlock Holmes* series, *The Bowery Boys, Blondie, Boston Blackie,* and numerous other long-running examples as proof of this phenomenon—but once upon a time, the series films were B pictures, produced by Monogram or PRC or Republic, shown on Saturday mornings along with a newsreel and a travelogue and perhaps a cartoon. Now, the comic book characters have assumed center stage, pushing all humanist concerns off the screen in favor of a diet of perpetual adolescence. The television series *The Osbournes* (2002–?) is the new *Father Knows Best;* whereas the original series ran from 1954 to 1967 and ran on ABC, NBC, and CBS before its demise, *The Osbournes* was designed for one season, although a follow-up season on MTV was eventually negotiated to drag out the wretched spectacle a bit longer. But as the pace of connectivity accelerates, so does burnout; we know people instantly, and then we want something new. Out with the newly old, in with the momentarily new. Decay, collapse, and then regeneration; no wonder William Faulkner observed, "they worship death here [in Hollywood]. They don't worship money, they worship death" (qtd. in Friedrich 237). Only death can presage resurrection. Only death ensures immortality. Only death permits endless repackaging. The past, the present, and the future all melt in one moment, that space when the original vanishes to be replaced forever by the simulacrum. The digital recycling of cinematic icons is so firmly established as an imagistic convention that we no longer blink when the long-dead John Wayne appears in a beer commercial, or Marilyn Monroe or Jack Kerouac appear in print ads for everything from men's slacks to perfume. These faces, these attitudes, no longer belong to their originators. They belong to us, and they long ago forfeited any authenticity they may once have held claim to. Delbert Mann remembered working with Cary Grant on one of his last films, *That Touch of Mink* (1962), and recalled that Grant was

> rather strange. He was always charming; always smiling, warm, and witty, and very likable. But I think he knew he was quite close to the end of his career. He was rather bored with acting by now; he was looking forward to not doing it anymore, and it just did not challenge him or excite him. Maybe it was the role; he was playing someone, I think, essentially rather close to himself; therefore, the role itself didn't offer the kind of stimulation another part might have. His concern seemed more with the physical aspects of the production than with his performance, though in every way he was always totally professional, on time, never caused any problems, knew his lines. (qtd. in Higham and Moseley 264-5)

Already the subject of countless tributes and retrospectives, Grant knew that his image on screen was assured of a fair degree of indestructibility—why expend any more effort on something that had already been accomplished?

Shuei Matsubayashi's *The Last War* (1961; original title *Sekai daisenso*, 1961) confronts these issues more directly than the numerous US and British films that toy with the concept of Armageddon. Films such as *On the Beach* (1959), *Dr. Strangelove or: How I Learned to Stop Worrying and Love the Bomb* (1964), *The Day the Earth Caught Fire* (1961; also known as *The Day the Sky Caught Fire*), *Armageddon* (1998), *The Core* (2003), *Meteor* (1979), *Fail-Safe* (1964), and other Dystopian fantasies either hold out the promise of false hope or treat the prospect of global annihilation as a matter of grim amusement. *The Last War*, in contrast, posits a world without a future, in which the inexorable buildup of nuclear weapons in the East and West leads inevitably to nuclear holocaust. Japan positions itself within the film's narrative as a neutral observer, unable to influence the events that bring about world destruction. Although the two world powers in the film are thinly disguised depictions of US and former Soviet Union forces, thus placing the film firmly within the context of the Cold War era, unlike its closet US counterpart, the television movie *The Last Day* (1975), *The Last War* offers no hope of a return to normalcy. Throughout the film, minor world crises keep both sides on edge, and numerous false alarms occur due to mechanical malfunctions and border disputes. An uprising in Korea along the thirty-eight parallel nearly precipitates world destruction, but through last-minute diplomacy this crisis is revolved.

In the end, what triggers global nuclear destruction is human error rather than aggression. Two airplanes from the rival superpowers accidentally collide in midair over the Arctic, and both sides, fearing imminent attack, launch their entire fleet of missiles; this time, there is no reprieve. As the surprisingly downbeat press book for *The Last War* details, the film's final reel depicts nothing less than the entire destruction of the planet, beginning with a huge nuclear firebomb over Tokyo, illuminating the night sky for one last, irrevocable instant. The film's synopsis concludes with these stern words:

> And then, the end. In colossal, blinding explosions the urban areas of the world are leveled to dust, while rural populations are left to die by agonizing degrees from radioactive fallout. Thus man, through stubbornness and blind stupidity, has wrought his own destruction. (*The Last War* press kit)

In a series of brutal wipes, Paris, New York, Moscow, and other foreign capitals are obliterated in an instant. A few vessels at sea hold a minuscule number of survivors, who, realizing the hopelessness of their situation, decide to return to their homes to die. The film's final images depict the planet as a nuclear wasteland thanks to Eiji Tsuburaya's superb predigital effects.

The Last War, produced by Toho, the company that spawned *Godzilla, King of the Monsters!* (1956; original title *Gojira,* 1954), *Mothra* (1962; original title *Mosura,* 1961), *Rodan* (1956; original title *Sora no daikaijû Radon,* 1956), *Monster Zero* (1970; original title *Kaijû daisenso,* 1965), and numerous other post-Hiroshima monster films, is not an entertainment. Along with a few other films, such as Peter Watkins's *The War Game* (1965), the mock documentary film

7

that depicted the effect of a nuclear attack on Great Britain, *The Last War* is an earnest plea for nuclear disarmament, one that was, unfortunately, unheeded. With such postapocalypse films as the latest version of *The Time Machine* (2002) and a TV movie remake of *On the Beach* (2000), it seems that despite the collapse of the decades-old East/West dynamic, the threat of global annihilation is as great as ever. At this writing, after the events of September 11 in the United States, Iraq is supposedly developing long-range nuclear missiles and "dirty bombs" for terrorist use in large metropolitan centers, while war rages unchecked in the Middle East. Films such as *Black Hawk Down* (2001), *We Were Soldiers* (2002), *The Sum of All Fears* (2002), *Collateral Damage* (2002), and other jingoistic texts recall the propagandistic excesses of World War II, even as a steady stream of escapist comedies and romances, such as *The New Guy, Deuces Wild, 40 Days and 40 Nights, Ice Age, The Scorpion King,* and *Snow Dogs* (all 2002) seek to satiate and distract the contemporary viewer. What comes next will probably be a curious revival of the noir cycle, unrelated to the spate of so-called neo-noir films such as *Wild Things* (1998), *Red Rock West* (1992), *L.A. Confidential* (1997), *The Usual Suspects* (1995), and *Bound* (1996), this last film the first feature by Larry and Andy Wachowski, who went on to create *The Matrix* (1999).

The hallmark of neo-noir film is a certain manic energy that keeps these films moving with effortless assurance through a bewildering series of double crosses and betrayals, in contrast to the slightly more restrained narrative pacing of the classic noir. But the neo-noir, operating in the shadow of nuclear oblivion as a fact of existence rather than a new phenomenon (as the classic post-1945 noirs did) treat the unthinkable as a commonplace, rather than an omnipresent threat. When the flag-waving and escapism of the current conflict is cleared away, in some unimaginable fashion, and after how many wasted lives, the postnoir will be distinguished by its somberness. The nihilistic dread of Arch Oboler's *The Arnelo Affair* (1947), in which the conscienceless John Hodiak draws Frances Gifford into a web of lies and murder, or the cold calculation of José Ferrer as he hypnotizes Gene Tierney to do his bidding in Otto Preminger's *Whirlpool* (1949), will prove a better model for the 21st century postnoir. In *Wild Things,* the audience is invited to unravel the puzzle presented by the film's protagonists; *Red Rock West* and *L.A. Confidential* are so luridly aggressive in their characterizations and events that they qualify for near-camp status. Nothing in neo-noir films is real, or pretends to be; all is exaggeration. There is no real threat, nothing truly at stake; we are conscious that we are watching a recreation and often a period piece at that. *The Arnelo Affair* and *Whirlpool* take place in the domain of the living dead, utilizing truly vulnerable women (Gifford and Tierney) juxtaposed with vicious, unscrupulous leading men to create a vision of utter hopelessness. There is no escape from the world of the true noir, just as there will be no escape from the postnoir. As in Basil Dearden's underrated *The Man Who Haunted Himself* (1970), in which Roger Moore's doppelgänger gradually takes over his existence until the copy replaces the original in the affection of his family and friends, the classic noir spins a tale of chronic alienation so complete that it is a totalizing experience: the death of the soul.

As Abel Gance observed, "Abandon All Hope, Ye Who Enter the Hell of Images" (qtd. in Virilio, *War and Cinema* 31). Virilio goes on to note that by World War I,

> the cinema became the major site for a trade in dematerialization, a new industrial market which no longer produced matter but light, as the luminosity of those vast stained-glass windows of old was suddenly concentrated into the screen. "Death is just a big show in itself" said Samuel Lionel Rothapfel [...] inventor of the first cinema to be baptized a cathedral, the Roxy. (Virilio, *War and Cinema* 32)

The "hell of images" Gance refers to thus refuses to release its dead, forcing them to repeat, and repeat again, past situations and poses, endowing them with real, not phantom, agency. In many ways, *Star Wars: Episode II—Attack of the Clones* is the perfect exemplification of this phenomenon in that the line between the real and the constructed has been completely obliterated, and the film itself was produced entirely without conventional motion picture technology. A digital creation from first to last, except for its transfer to 35mm film for final projection in most theaters, *Attack of the Clones* is a moving image construct in which the actors are overwhelmed by the hypertechnology of the enterprise that surrounds them. *Attack of the Clones* is the perfect postfilm movie; it lacks soul, inspiration, originality, and style. As A. O. Scott observed in his appropriately scathing review of the film, *Attack of the Clones* possesses "all the spontaneity and surprise of an election day in the old Soviet Union." Scott continues:

> while *Attack of the Clones* is many things—a two-hour-and-12-minute action-figure commercial, a demo reel heralding the latest advances in digital filmmaking, a chance for gifted actors to be handsomely paid for delivering the worst line readings of their careers—it is not really much of a movie at all, if by movie you mean a work of visual storytelling about the dramatic actions of a group of interesting characters. (B1)

More tellingly, Scott argues that "Mr. Lucas [...] has lost either the will or the ability to connect with actors, and his crowded, noisy cosmos is psychologically and emotionally barren" (B20). Indeed, the actors in the film seem to have been cut adrift in *Attack of the Clones* without any concern for the consistency of their performances; as Scott observes, only the endlessly dependable Christopher Lee (still energetic and involved at age 80) manages to convey any authority in his performance (see Edelstein 3, 17). A viewing of the electronic press kit for the film confirms Lucas's lack of emotional connection to the project. Left to their own devices, the actors deliver their lines in robotic fashion, helplessly seeking some credibility in the text that does not exist. In contrast, Lee treats Lucas far more brutally during the shooting of the film, demanding to know precisely where his "eye-match" is, complaining when the proposed blocking will not work, and drawing on his inner reserves as an actor in the classic British tradition to give his Count Dooku at least some semblance of motivation and believability. Lee also brings a welcome dash of gravitas to Peter Jackson's *The Lord of the Rings: The Fellowship of the Ring* (2002), demonstrating again that even in an age dominated by high-tech effects, the human element is still indispensable. As Jackson comments, "in front of the camera he has to do something to his eyes [...] they suddenly glaze over and then gleam in a very chilling way; it's as if he turns on an internal light. When you've got your shot he turns it off and he's back to [his normal self]" (Edelstein 17). In short, Lee's presence is more than enough to hold the viewer's attention; he has no need of external artifice.

Which leaves us with the much-heralded digital special effects. The human aspect of *Attack of the Clones* having been so handily disposed of, what about the visual sheen of the film? No problem there: they are the essence of manufactured perfection, immaculately conceived and executed, devoid of any human agency, a testament to the film's essential inhumanity and hollowness. But the effects are merely a landscape, a backdrop, marvelous in their evanescent syntheticity, but scrupulously devoid of any defect that might render them fallible, authentic, organic. Lucasfilm officials have complained in the press that the "twenty-first century" films of George Lucas are being presented with "nineteenth-century technology." As the president of Lucasfilm, Gordon Radley, noted shortly before the release of *Attack of the Clones,* "we've proselytized about this for years. So, it's disappointing to think that it continues to take digital cinema longer to come to fruition than it should" (qtd. in Di Orio, "Clones" 1). But technology is the driving force here, not creativity. And when the final episode of the *Star Wars* saga is finally released, what more can Lucas possibly offer us? The Adbusters Media Foundation reminds us in a broadside that "corporations are legal fictions that we ourselves created and must therefore control" ("Organized Crime"). In such a nonhumanist atmosphere, actors become little more than props within the scenes they nominally inhabit, to be used for effect rather than for dramatic motivation. Diane Lane recalled during the shooting of Adrian Lyne's *Unfaithful* (2002) that:

> There was [...] one morning when Adrian surprised me. He was waiting for me in my trailer before I'd even had coffee. He said, "I got this great idea: I think we should do this scene naked, except you're wearing Oliver's combat boots."
>
> What do you say? You slowly, graciously whittle it down to, "Maybe that's not the greatest idea." (Kehr, "Aiming for More" B6)

In such an atmosphere of exploitation and strategic situations, motivation is lost in a parade of artificial constructions. Also lost in the media blitz surrounding the film is the fact that *Unfaithful* is a remake of Claude Chabrol's *The Unfaithful*

Wife (1969; original title *La Femme Infidèle*, 1969), something that most reviewers of the film failed to realize.

And yet, in the contemporary cinematic marketplace, who has time for history? For all its artistic nullity, the *Star Wars* franchise is the benchmark for the new cinema, as confirmed by producer Sean Daniel, whose film *The Scorpion King* created a new action star in The Rock, a former professional wrestler, and is itself part of the new *Mummy* franchise, which recycled the 1932 original and its 1940s successors into a new series beginning in 1999, which continues with no end in sight. "You really have to look at the success of *Star Wars* as one of the signature enterprises in this trend," said Sean Daniel, a producer of *The Scorpion King* and a former studio production chief. "Truly, that series was—and is—the envy of everybody. As the movie culture becomes more global, there is an added value to making movies that are part of a series or attached somehow to some title or brand that already has market recognition" (qtd. in Lyman, "Spinoff" B1). In addition to the aforementioned franchise films, we see new versions of *Halloween,* more *Harry Potter* films, more *American Pie* sequels, *The Fast and the Furious 2* (the "original" itself was a thematic remake of a 1954 film by legendary exploitation producer Roger Corman), and the list goes on and on. As Rick Lyman comments:

> Warner Brothers, now leading the way in this franchise frenzy, is preparing to revive the *Batman, Superman, Conan, Terminator* and *Exorcist* franchises, as well as creating new ones with *Wonder Woman, Looney Tunes* and remakes like *Westworld* and *Charlie* [not *Willy Wonka] and the Chocolate Factory.* Universal Pictures is hard at work on *The Hulk, The Cat in the Hat, Red Dragon* (featuring the movies' favorite serial killer, Hannibal Lecter) and a Coen Brothers remake of the 1960's caper comedy *Gambit.*
>
> New Line Cinema has remakes of *The Texas Chainsaw Massacre* and *Willard* in the works; MGM wants to bring *The Outer Limits* television series to the big screen and has teamed with Miramax on a remake of Akira Kurosawa's classic *Seven Samurai;* DreamWorks is hoping to jump-start a new franchise based on the Matt Helm spy books that spawned a Dean Martin series in the 60's; Sony is working on a new version of

Peter Pan; Miramax is starring Roberto Benigni as *Pinocchio*; Paramount is beginning a remake of *The Warriors*, a 1979 teenage-gang thriller; and RKO, the long dormant Hollywood studio, is reviving its name and hoping to capitalize on remakes of movies drawn from its vaults, like *Suspicion* and *Beyond a Reasonable Doubt*.

"It's much harder these days to get anyone's attention," said Ted Hartley, RKO's chairman. "You only have about 10 seconds to grab them. And to get somebody to react positively to some new idea, some new title, takes a lot more than 10 seconds. So we all love starting with something that's already known." ("Spinoff" B10)

Or, as producer Mark Abraham succinctly comments, "Everybody is trying to establish a brand and exploit it" (Lyman, "Spinoff" B10).

The reason for all this recycling is simple: money. Traditionally, sequels underperformed the financial success of their predecessors; now, increased brand awareness makes subsequent films in a series more profitable than the original. The first *Austin Powers* film, released in 1997, grossed a mere $54 million; the first sequel, *Austin Powers: The Spy Who Shagged Me,* generated $205 million in rentals in 1999. *Rush Hour* (1998) did a respectable $141 million in business, but *Rush Hour 2* (2001) made $226 million (Lyman, "Spinoff" B10). Is it any wonder that invention or originality has become curiously passé? As another Hollywood executive noted, "If you have a movie that is not differentiated, that does not fit into one of these categories, it really has to be spectacular to carve out a spot in the marketplace today" (Lyman, "Spinoff" B10). With the ever-increasing cost of movie production and distribution, what chance does a small, thoughtful film have with the general public? Eric Rohmer's *The Lady and the Duke* (2001; original title *L'Anglaise et le duc,* 2001) is the veteran director's own initial foray into digital technology. Set during the French Revolution, the film uses extensive "green screen" work to place the actors within a series of paintings that suggest the locations of the era, but also depends heavily on the performers to contribute to the success of the project, creating a sort of cinema verité video record of a vanished time and place (see Mackey 20). In contrast to the digital universe posited by George Lucas, Jerry Bruckheimer, and their mainstream cohorts, Rohmer's film is at once spectacular yet intimate, deeply connected to the human drama of the state in crisis. Rather than armies of anonymous clones or robotic battleships, Rohmer uses the new digital tools to create a small, intimate film, very much in the spirit of his earlier films. Yet Rohmer's film was screened at the New York Film Festival for only a few screenings and then opened to desultory bookings in New York and a few major cities in 2002 without any hope of a national release. Increasingly, it seems that audiences do not wish to be entertained; they want to be bombarded by an assault of light and sound. Imagine *Marty* (1955) winning an Academy Award for best picture in the current climate, a modestly budgeted film about the forlorn love life of a Bronx butcher. It just is not possible.

It is astonishing to think that as late as 1951, a modest western such as Philip Ford's *The Dakota Kid* (1951) could be shot in seven days on a budget of $52,471 and be assured of a theatrical release. The film's single biggest expense was the cast—$8,761—and the film used only 23,000 feet of 35mm film to create a 60-minute feature. One year earlier in 1950, John Ford's *Rio Grande* was shot in 32 days, with a total budget of $1,214,899, using a mere 80,000 feet of film to complete the 105-minute film. The stars included John Wayne, Maureen O'Hara, Ben Johnson, Victor McLaglen, and numerous other stalwarts of the Golden Age of Classic Cinema. Their combined salaries for the project totaled just $318,433 (McCarthy and Flynn, "Economic Imperative" 26, 29). Such figures are impossible to replicate a half a century later. Certainly, even after allowing for factors such as inflation costs, which must have necessarily risen since the post-World War II era, the simple fact is that a level of human craftsmanship has been sacrificed in the contemporary cinema for the sake of synthetic spectacle. Who could imagine completing a film in seven days now? Perhaps only James Toback, who shot the modestly successful *Two Girls and a Guy* (1997) in one week in Robert Downey Jr.'s loft, using Downey, Heather Graham, and Natasha Gregson Wagner to create a compellingly intimate tale of two women vying for the same man. *Two Girls and a Guy* actually received a national release, solely on the basis of its star cast and modest budget, but such films are now a rarity. With the average production cost of a Hollywood film nearing the $60-million mark, plus another $30 million for prints and advertising, to say nothing of promotional budgets to finance talk-show appearances by the film's stars, who can afford to bet on an untried commodity? We have become a culture of sameness in which conformity dominates, and everything is equally replaceable.

What drives all this conformity is, of course, the fear of the new—not new technological developments, which are eagerly embraced by capitalist culture as tools to increase their dominion over international consumers—but rather new ways of interacting with one another, departures from the hyperconglomerized new order now firmly established, anything that threatens to upset the status quo. The current political and social climate, particularly after the events of September 11, ensures that all deviations from what are perceived to be normative values will be immediately censured. The entertainment conglomerates—AOL Time Warner, Vivendi Universal, and Rupert Murdoch's News Corporation—create a virtual monopoly on all that we see and hear with increasingly infrequent interruptions. All of these corporate entities are undergoing internal turmoil in the wake the dot-com crash and the broadband glut, but eventually they will survive, refigured in another form. These nation-states, entities whose realm is international, specialize in misinformation, repetition, and titillating scandal, all in an attempt to satisfy an increasingly bored and restless public, unsure of where their next meal is coming from, unable to escape the cycle of grinding poverty that supports these media giants.

And to whom can they turn for the truth? Certainly not their supposed leaders. The Nixon White House serves as an excellent example of the complete lack of integrity in government. When George Wallace was shot, Nixon told his aides to start a rumor that Wallace's attacker "was a supporter of McGovern and Kennedy. [...] Say you have it on unmistakable evidence." He suggested that the famous photograph of a young Vietnamese girl running from a US napalm attack was faked. He described protesters against the conflict in Vietnam as "a wild orgasm of anarchists sweeping across the country like a prairie fire." And when Billy Graham told Nixon that he believed that Jewish interests had a "stranglehold" on the media, Nixon responded "Oh boy. So do I. I can't ever say that, but I believe it." Indeed, in a mood of exasperation, Nixon rhetorically inquired of his aide Bob Haldeman, "What the Christ is the matter with the Jews, Bob? What is the matter with them? I suppose it's because most of them are psychiatrists" (all qtd. in Slansky 43). All of these excerpts are culled from tapes Nixon himself made during his tenure at the White House, as if he were possessed of a compulsion to document his own destruction. Andy Warhol accomplished much the same function with his silent screen tests, compiling a silent, visual record of his numerous associates during his most prolific period as an artist. As Jonathan Jones describes these 100-foot, 16mm black-and-white static films:

> Warhol's *Screen Tests* are his best works on film, closest to the severe dignity of his painted portraits. [...] They are elegiac too, even though most of the people filmed are younger than Warhol. The youthful and vulnerable pass before his camera, are loved by it, and then vanish. Each black-and-white film ends with a silvery fade-out, the face slowly dissolving in a burst of light, as if the Bomb had just been dropped. This ghostly effect could not more explicitly make us think of mortality—and of film as a fragile defense against it. Hollywood specialises [sic] in immortality, but Warhol's use of film is more material. At the end of each film, you see the texture of the celluloid itself. These people could easily have been dead for centuries, the films found rolled up in a Ballardian desert necropolis. ("Candid Camera")

Thus, as many of his subjects died, Warhol's cinematic portraits remained as mute testimony to their brief, incandescent existences. In the 1950s, 1960s, and 1970s myriad movies addressed the human desire for self-immolation, including the forgotten *Ladybug, Ladybug* (1963), *The Earth Dies Screaming* (1964), and *Damnation Alley* (1977), along with a number of sensationalized "documentaries" purporting to depict humankind in the last days before Armageddon, the most famous of which is perhaps *The Late Great Planet Earth* (1979), cobbled together from stock footage and some hastily recreated sequences and narrated by a transparently desperate Orson Welles.

All of these enterprises—the deceptions, the recreations, and the staged immolations—have one thing in common: they contain the seeds of their own destruction. Nixon was clearly eager to see himself implode, at some level, in front of an international audience. Warhol's desire for self-publicity is justly legendary. Not surprisingly, Hollywood eagerly grabbed the baton of willful self-destruction and ran with it, imagining a world in which destruction is not something to be avoided, but the desired object of all ambition. One could argue that the very act of construction anticipates destruction, as E. B. White famously pointed out in his 1949 study, *Here Is New York.* At the conclusion of the text, after celebrating the city's multicultural heritage and magnificent urban sprawl, White sounded a note of warning:

> The city, for the first time in its long history, is destructible. A single flight of planes no bigger than a wedge of geese can quickly end this island fantasy, burn the towers, crumble the bridges, turn the underground passages into lethal chambers, cremate the millions. The intimation of mortality is part of New York now; in the sound of jets overhead, in the black headlines of the latest edition.

> Of all targets, New York has a certain clear priority. In the mind of whatever perverted dreamer might loose the lightning, New York must hold a steady, irresistible charm. (qtd. in Frank 9)

Thus, long before the prophets of disaster turned Armageddon into a pop culture pastime, the author of *Charlotte's Web* and *Stuart Little* had a perfect fix on precisely what makes Manhattan so alluring: its vulnerability. Even something so illimitable as the Internet has an "end," appropriately titled, "The Last Page of the Internet." When one arrives at this cyberdestination, the viewer is confronted with these words: "Attention: You have reached the very last page of the Internet. We hope you have enjoyed your browsing. Now turn off your computer and go outside and play." This is followed by a hyperlink to take the viewer back to the "boring old Internet"; appropriately enough, it is a dead link (1112 Networks). Even hyperspace has a putative end; although it increasingly lacks imagination, Hollywood continues to churn out new, eminently exploitable product. *The New Guy* offers us yet again the story of the geek turned cool; *About a Boy* (2002) presents us with the unlikely spectacle of Hugh Grant in a film that might well be titled *One Man and a Baby,* practically a remake of the Adam Sandler vehicle *Big Daddy* (1999), which has itself been remade many times before. *The Bourne Identity* (2002) is a remake of a 1988 television movie based on the book by Robert Ludlum, starring Richard Chamberlain; now Matt Damon takes his place. *Scooby-Doo* (2002) recycles the long running Hanna-Barbera cartoon series as a live action/digital animation hybrid. Steven Spielberg serves up yet another dose of predictable action in *Minority Report* (2002), a futuristic thriller in which Tom Cruise plays a police officer framed for a murder he did not commit, interspersed with the visual spectacular leaps and structures audiences have come to expect from a "summer movie."

The Powerpuff Girls make their big-screen debut in *The Powerpuff Girls* (2002), while the Spy Kids are back for more predictable misadventures in *Spy Kids 2: The Island of Lost Dreams* (2002). *The Tuxedo* (2002) presents us with the unlikely pairing of Jennifer Love Hewitt and Jackie Chan in one of Chan's trademark action comedies (the sole difference being that, even in middle age, Chan still does his own stunts, thus lending a welcome touch of verisimilitude to the endless succession of doubles who normally populate such films). *Eight Legged Freaks* (2002) once again trots out the menace of gigantic killer spiders on the loose, redolent of *Tarantula* (1955), *Them!* (1954), and *Earth vs. the Spider* (1958). *Insomnia* (2002) is a remake of a superb 1997 film of the same title from Norway, starring Stellan Skarsgård as a dysfunctional detective investigating a murder case. In the new version, Al Pacino replaces Skarsgård in the lead role, the action moves to Alaska, and Christopher Nolan, who did such a good job with his initial film *Following* (1998), takes over the director's chair. Certainly Nolan is an appropriate choice for such dark material, but why is he doing a remake when he has shown himself capable of brilliant work as an original auteur? Mel Gibson stars in M. Night Shyamalan's *Signs* (2002), another film about crop circles and UFOs. Nothing new, nothing original; all is the same. Is there no alternative to this endless procession of prefabricated blockbusters?

Agnès Varda's *The Gleaners & I* (2000; original title *Les glaneurs et la glaneuse,* 2000), is one alternative vision to the current glut of cynically calculated Hollywood remakes. The film opened in 2001 in New York City in a limited commercial release. In *The Gleaners & I,* Varda documents the activities of a group of French social "outsiders," who scavenge food, appliances, housing materials, and other essentials from the trash that others create. Shooting with a small, handheld digital video camcorder, rather than a conventional 35mm film camera, Varda demonstrates that it is possible to create a compelling alternative to the mainstream Hollywood film with the simplest of equipment. Near the conclusion of *The Gleaners & I*, Varda focuses on a young man who has jettisoned a promising career to become a dedicated recycler of society's cast-off goods. He lives in a homeless shelter and teaches English to some of the émigré inhabitants in his spare time. Varda offers us a view of the high and low in French society; the landowners and magistrates who are not too sympathetic to the gleaners' activities, and the gleaners themselves, unshaven and unkempt, living in trailers without running water or electricity, but still possessed of both generosity of spirit and the faith that life is worth fighting for.

However, millions of people will never see Varda's film, even at an art house. For the most part, we have lost our access to the vision of filmmakers from other cultures and other countries. Only large metropolitan centers such as New York, Paris, London, and Amsterdam offer the public any real choice in the films they see. As Uberto Pasolini, the producer of *The Full Monty* (1997), a surprise hit, bitterly noted even after that film's success:

> Distribution, distribution, distribution—that's the issue [...] the whole business of people saying to European producers that you just need to make films audiences want to see is complete crap. There are American movies that should not be in 100 theaters, ghastly movies with terrible reviews that no one cares about, but because a major has the muscle they get them onto those screens. (qtd. in Miller, Govil, McMurria, and Maxwell 148)

The Full Monty became a box-office bonanza only after 20th Century Fox, sensing a certain appeal in the film's rough-and-tumble sexuality, decided to pick up the negative for international distribution. As Miller, Govil, McMurria, and Maxwell report, other films have not been as lucky. Ken Loach's *Riff-Raff* (1990) was pulled from UK theaters to make way for Ron Howard's *Backdraft* (1991), even though the latter film had already performed dismally in the United States.

Similarly, Louis Malle's *Damage* (1992; original title *Fatale*, 1992) lasted only a week in UK theaters before it was taken off to accommodate a prearranged release date for a Hollywood film (Miller, Govil, McMurria, and Maxwell 148). Without the imprimatur of a major distributor, most overseas films languish in the limbo of big city bookings ("now playing in selected cities"), on DVD, or cable. And as we have seen, if the film is not in English, dubbing or subtitling will no longer suffice. The film must be remade to accommodate US audiences, with American stars, and then exported, in most cases, to the same country that the original film was produced in. Thus Hollywood's hyperconglomerate vision colonizes the world, even as those members of the public who know that an alternative cinema exists are denied access to it. Such is the current tyranny of images that informs moving image production, distribution, and reception in the contemporary dominant cinema.

CHAPTER ONE

FREEDOM FROM CHOICE

Before the proliferation of electronic media made possible the distribution of films at minimal cost through DVD, cable, and the World Wide Web, world cinema and Hollywood cinema coexisted on a relatively equal basis. Each country's films had a different theatrical distribution system within the United States, depending on language, point of origin, and the perceived artistic merit of the film in question. British films, such as *The Loneliness of the Long Distance Runner* (1962), *The Knack* (1965), *Carry On Nurse* (1958), *Tom Jones* (1963), and others required no subtitles and generally were accorded a wide release. French films usually appeared in major metropolitan centers with subtitles and in outlying districts with a dubbed version. Italian films such as *Open City* (1945; original title *Roma, città aperta,* 1945), *La Dolce Vita* (1960), *Juliet of the Spirits* (1965; original title *Giulietta degli spiriti,* 1965), *Big Deal on Madonna Street* (1958; original title *I soliti ignoti,* 1958), *8 1/2* (1963), and other films designated "instant classics" by US critics were generally subtitled, whereas titles such as *The Day the Sky Exploded* (1961; *La Morte viene dallo spazio,* 1958), *Black Sunday* (1961; original title *La maschera del demonio,* 1960), *Hercules in the Haunted World* (1964; original title *Ercole al centro della terra,* 1961), *My Son, the Hero* (1963; original title *Arrivano i titani,* 1961), and other more commercial fare were routinely dubbed. This general pattern of "quality" versus "commercial appeal" governed the linguistic fate of most non-US films. When *Yojimbo the Bodyguard* (1962; original title *Yojimbo,* 1961), *High and Low* (1963, original title *Tengoku to jigoku,* 1963), *Woman in the Dunes* (1964; original title *Suna no onna,* 1964), *Kwaidan* (1964; original title *Kaidan,* 1964), and other "quality" Japanese films appeared in the United States, they were subtitled; the *Godzilla* films, on the other hand, suffered from atrocious dubbing, usually done by the Titra Sound Studios in New York, which specialized in dubbing foreign imports.

Indian films remained, for the most part, within the boundaries of their own nation, except for the films of Satyajit Ray, which were always subtitled; Ingmar Bergman, for many years the sole representative in the United States of Swedish cinema, was also scrupulously titled. German films generally were subtitled, unless they were cheap programmers in the long-running Edgar Wallace mystery series, in which case they were dubbed. The same fate befell Hong Kong action films in the 1970s; an extremely slipshod, often asynchronous dubbing job ensured that films would reach only grind house audiences. The dubbing or subtitling of a film often determined its critical fate, as well as its commercial destiny. Dubbed films were almost universally excoriated by the critics and thus by the audiences who read their reviews; subtitled films, on the other hand, were usually afforded a modicum of respect. International coproductions were guaranteed an even warmer reception at the US box office, particularly if they featured an American star. Hammer Films used this strategy in its early British films of the 1950s, casting Tom Conway, Brian Donlevy, Alex Nicol, Hillary Brooke, and other fading stars to ensure US release. Occasionally, a film made outside the United States would be afforded a measure of commercial viability through its choice of director, as in the case of British director Thorold Dickinson's *Hill 24 Doesn't Answer* (1955; original title *Giv'a 24 Eina Ona*, 1955), which dealt with the turmoil surrounding the early days on the state of Israel. *Hill 24 Doesn't Answer* received solid distribution in both the United States and Great Britain, but hedged its bets by being shot in English (using British star Edward Mulhare as one of the leads), although the film was officially classified as an Israeli production.

Thus, even through the early 1970s, when Roger Corman's New World Pictures functioned as one of the last surviving conduits of foreign theatrical distribution in the United States, most famously coproducing and distributing Ingmar Bergman's *Cries and Whispers* (1972; original title *Viskningar och rop*, 1972) when no other US distributor would touch it, non–US films had a chance to crack the US market, albeit an increasingly slim one as the decades rolled on. With the introduction of pay television, however, in the mid- to late 1970s, theatrical distribution was no longer a financial necessity, and the number of "art" houses in the United States began to dwindle. In the first part of the 21st century, they have almost completely vanished—not only in the United States, but in Europe and Asia as well. At the same time, the number of repertory theaters also declined. Audiences could no longer see the classics of the past in their original 35mm format.

I remember the first time I saw Charles Crichton's *The Lavender Hill Mob* (1951) in a revival house in 1961 on a double bill with Robert Dhéry's just-released *The American Beauty* (1961; *La belle Américaine*, 1961), allowing me to see both films on equal terms—the then-current and the classic projected in their proper formats. The experience, of course, was overwhelming and nothing at all like the off-the-cuff, "background noise" effect of viewing a film on DVD on a television, no matter how gargantuan the screen. A very real argument can be made that all films that originated in 35mm should be screened in that format alone if one wants to approximate anything like the original viewing experience available to audiences when the film was first produced.

As another example of this phenomenon, in early 2002 I traveled to Los Angeles for a series of screenings at the American Cinematheque, coordinated by Dennis Bartok. On the bill that week were screenings of Val Guest's *The Day the Earth Caught Fire*, with its original color prologue and epilogue intact, and Mario Bava's *Planet of the Vampires* (1965; original title *Terrore nello spazio*, 1965), the latter presented in a brand new 35mm print. Both films are readily available on video and shown constantly on television; *The Day the Earth Caught Fire,* which is in CinemaScope, has even been screened on commercial television in letterbox format. Both films sit on my shelves in DVD format, but nothing prepared me for the shock of seeing them projected again, for the first time in nearly 40 years, on a large screen with first-rate International Alliance of Theatrical Stage Employees (IATSE) union projectionists in front of an appreciative audience. Rather than viewing the films as a solitary spectator, I was allowed to experience them as part of an audience, as a social and communal act.

Subtle touches that would have drifted past my eyes on the small screen—a sudden optical effect, a striking composition, a deftly edited dialogue sequence—appeared anew to my eyes, seen in the proper size and format again. These films were never meant to be seen on the small screen; they were spatially and emotionally designed for a heroic canvas. Thus, as the director Roy Ward Baker has commented, although you can "inspect" a film in DVD/televisual format, you cannot really judge its effectiveness or participate in it on an emotional or artistic level of any real consequence. The DVDs we buy are mere *aides de memoire* of experiences we once shared with others and now are unable to authentically recall. In an interview with this author in 1994, Baker discussed his own film, *A Night to Remember* (1958), perhaps the best of the *Titanic* films. Having just seen the film in a retrospective of his work, Baker noted that

> I had seen *A Night to Remember*, obviously, several times on television since I made it, but I made it, after all, in 1958. And since that time, I'd never seen it on a big screen. [...] And the effect of seeing it again on the big screen, after all this time, it shows you the whole difference between movies and television. [...] You see, when you see a film on television on a small screen, you're not in the film at all. You inspect it. You can look at it. You can enjoy it to a certain extent, but you'll never be involved in it. You can judge it; you can say, "Well, that was a good movie." But it's an entirely objective judgment; it's not subjective because you're not being subjected to the film. (qtd. in Dixon, *Collected Interviews* 156-7)

It's almost like viewing a photocopy of a Caravaggio painting; no copy can ever do the original justice. What makes this all the more frustrating is that economics, not artistic forces, is driving the current digitization of the cinema, even as studio heads and archivists pay token homage to cinema's past. Thus, when one speaks of a particular film being "available" on DVD or another home video format, one should more correctly say that an inferior copy of the original is available for viewing, rather than the film itself. An even more insidious factor is that although the American Film Institute and other organizations celebrate the heritage of the moving image, contemporary Hollywood studios are busily strip-mining the past (as we have seen) to create "new" product. In doing so, many production entities consciously engage in legal maneuvering to keep the source film off the market, even in 16mm and 35mm formats, in the ostensible hope that newer audiences, unaware of the original film, will be unaware of its existence. An example of this is the remake of Norman Jewison's *Rollerball* (1975; remake 2002). Although the first film was deeply flawed, its vision of a future world without war, dominated by violent recreational sport, carried a direct political message to the audience. The remake, which centers only on the game of Rollerball itself as an extreme sport, eschews the theme of global corporate domination entirely. Does one really need to ask why?

At the same time, a great deal of evidence exists that contemporary audiences recognize the recycled quality of the current cinema—and reject it. They would go to see something else if they had the choice, but they do not. As Rick Lyman noted:

> Something profound is happening at the megaplexes, and it has little to do with what appears on the screen. Rather, it is about how those movies are being seen.

> The summer hits of 2001 are making about as much money as hits from previous summers, but they are making it quicker, making more of it than ever on opening weekend.
>
> Movies are opening on more screens, generating staggering grosses and then plummeting off the radar. Many executives in Hollywood see this trend, which they call "front loading," as a fundamental change in the way summer movies are being watched. [...] In the future, when digital distribution comes and movies are shipped electronically rather than on metal reels, these trends will only be magnified, as they will when studios become more adept at opening films not merely all over the country but all over the world on the same day. ("Blockbusters" A1, A12)

Lyman goes on to demonstrate how newer films open in 3,000 theaters simultaneously to avoid Internet piracy and gain as much audience penetration as possible before negative word of mouth sets in. This strategy, originally created by James Nicholson and Samuel Z. Arkoff of American International Pictures (AIP) in the mid-to-late 1950s, was originally dubbed "saturation booking." Nicholson and Arkoff had no illusions about AIP's product; they knew that what they were selling was commercial junk and that only a hit-and-run booking pattern would reap maximum return on their investment. Whereas major studios in the 1950s often "platformed" their films, opening them in

25

major cities in "road show" engagements at higher ticket prices before releasing them throughout the United States and subsequently foreign territories, AIP's smash-and-grab tactics gave the company a solid cash flow to produce new product, essential in what was a very thinly capitalized operation. Such AIP films as *I Was a Teenage Werewolf* (1957), *I Was a Teenage Frankenst*ein (1957), and *Ghost of Dragstrip Hollow* (1959) have become exploitation classics, films that accurately pegged audience expectations and delivered what the majors at the time refused to do: adolescent entertainment. Made on six-day schedules and budgets in the $100,000 range, AIP's films constituted a genuine threat to the majors, which had just been deprived of their guaranteed theatrical outlets with the advent of the consent decree of 1948. AIP offered exhibitors advantageous terms, immediate delivery, and splashy ad campaigns designed to appeal to the widest possible audience.

By the 1970s, when AIP was absorbed into Filmways, the majors had caught onto AIP's strategy and began aggressively duplicating it. In 1975, *Jaws* opened in 409 theaters in the United States and did spectacular business. The budget was higher, the advertising costs greater, the number of prints more than AIP could ever have afforded. In 1983, *Star Wars: Episode VI—Return of the Jedi* opened in 1,002 locations. In 1996, *Mission: Impossible* opened in 3,000 theaters; in 2000, *Mission: Impossible II* opened in more than 3,500 theaters. *The Mummy Returns* (2001) started in 3,401 theaters; *Shrek* (2001) in 3,587 theaters; and *Rush Hour 2* in 3,118 theaters (Lyman, "Blockbuster" A12). By the summer of 2002, *Spider-Man* was able to open in 3,615 theaters simultaneously on as many as 7,500 multiplex screens. In the film's first three days, it grossed $114 million (Di Orio, "Spider's" 1). But how long it can hold on to that kind of audience is a real question. *Planet of the Apes* (2001) opened to $68.5 million, but fell by 60% in its second week at the box office. *The Mummy Returns* fell 50% in its second week; *Pearl Harbor* (2001) fell 50% in its second week; *Lara Croft: Tomb Raider* (2001) fell 59% in its second week (Lyman, "Blockbuster" A12). People rush to the theater on the week a film opens, but then just as rapidly desert it when the next blockbuster comes along. Studios are delighted with this phenomenon because opening weekend contracts typically stipulate a 90/10 split of the profits, with 90% of the first week's profits going directly to the production entity. The theater makes its money on the concession stand, as it always has, and by the second week, an 80/20 split, again favoring the studio, usually kicks in. But by this time, another film comes roaring out of the gate, and the game starts all over again, week after exhausting week (Lyman, "Blockbuster" A12). Internet piracy only adds to the urgency in getting a film out to as many paying customers as quickly as possible; in the three days before the opening of *Planet of the Apes,* a complete version of the film, pirated from a stolen 35mm print, was circulating on the Web. AIP in the 1950s and 1960s would play their films territory by territory across the United States until every last dime had been extracted from the audience. The majors in the 1970s and 1980s could afford far larger "breaks," increasing the chances that regardless how bad the reviews were, the film would be a hit. In the days before the Internet, the studios could also follow the seasons around the globe, opening a summer film in Australia in December, typically the warmest time of the year down under. No more. With piracy, the ubiquity of the Web, and the complete interconnectivity of contemporary audience and fan base, a film must open everywhere, all over the world, simultaneously.

As foreign markets open up (China will probably be the last to fall before Hollywood's onslaught), the number of prints distributed will increase. Soon, releases of 5,000, even 7,000 prints will be commonplace, and then, film will vanish entirely. With the coming of digital distribution, the entire cinematic landscape will be altered forever. Movies will be shipped on disc, or, for better security, downloaded from a satellite directly into the hard drive memory of the projector. The theater owner will then flick a switch, and the "film" will appear on the screen. Still at issue, of course, is who would control the final distribution of any given title to a certain number of screens. Theater owners want the ability to shift nonstarters to fewer or less prestigious screens (with fewer seats) within the multiplex; they want flexibility. The studios, however, are unlikely to grant this. In one possible scenario, the heavily encrypted movie will be downloaded from a satellite to a dedicated projector for a limited number of runs, in one theater only. Studios would thus be able to guarantee a certain number of screens and seats for their product. As always, because the studios create the product, thereby offering a "pipeline" of continuous entertainment to the various theater chains, they will be able to dictate the terms that are most favorable to their interests. Finally, by producing films such as *Spider-Man* and other fare aimed strictly at teens on a constant basis, the majors have done away with the potential threat that an upstart independent producer, such as AIP, might cause. When and if audience tastes change and some new genre becomes the flavor of the month at the multiplexes, the majors will instantly adapt because all of the films they produce are the result of exhaustive market research (see Rosenbaum, *Movie Wars*, for more on this subject).

Where does this market research come from? Surprisingly, the Dutch firm Verenigde Nederlandse Uitgeversbedrijven (VNU), or United Dutch Publishers, generates most of the data. This seemingly innocuous company has a truly astonishing global reach into all areas of consumers. VNU owns, among other holdings, the National Research Group (NRG), which conducts audience preference surveys throughout the United States. These surveys, conducted for the most part by poorly paid temporary employees who must generate a large pool of interviewees designed to reflect the public's taste, govern the production of nearly every feature film now made in the United States and Europe. As Miller, Govil, McMurria, and Maxwell outline, the NRG is merely a small part of VNU's vast surveillance empire:

> [...] the NRG is just one of seventeen market research subsidiaries operated by VNU USA's Marketing Information Services Group (MIS). VNU has long been an important business information provider through professional newsletters, trade magazines, directories and trade shows and a publisher of telephone directories and consumer magazines in Europe, Japan, South Africa and Puerto Rico. It owns several financial data services, a film distributor in the Netherlands, where it is building a chain of television stations, and the largest consumer magazine publisher in the Czech Republic. Its marketing research operations span North America and Europe, and it holds 85 per cent of ORG-MARG, the leading market research company in India. Its most prominent magazines include Editor & Publisher Magazine and those published by VNU USA's subsidiary, BPI Communications, Hollywood Reporter, Adweek and Billboard magazines, among others. BPI also manages the Clio Awards, which celebrate and

promote good will toward the advertising industry. [...] By 2000, VNU USA had become one of the leading business information and service providers in the world, largely through its control over the principal commercial and consumer surveillance companies in North America. VNU USA's 1997 acquisition of NRN from Saatchi & Saatchi was followed in 1999 by its US$2.5 billion purchase from Dun & Bradstreet of both Nielsen Media Research (television and Internet audience measurement) and a majority share of Nielsen NetRatings (Internet user measurement), giving it leading audience and consumer tracking companies for film, television and the Internet. In 2000, as part of an anti-trust settlement following the Nielsen purchases, VNU sold Competitive Media Reporting—the biggest advertising tracking service in the US and the leader in Internet usage surveillance—to the world's fourth-largest market research company, Taylor Nelson Sofres, which already dominate media tracking in Europe, in particular through its UK Tellex and French TNS Secodip operations. [...] Soon thereafter, VNU completed its absorption of the old Nielsen empire with the US$2.3 billion purchase of A.C. Nielsen Corporation, the world leader in consumer behaviour surveillance and analysis. [...] Among VNU's remaining holdings in surveillance are Claritas, Scarborough, Spectra, and National Decision Systems. (188)

Producer Mark Horowitz agrees: "everybody in the industry, the ones who are really in the game, looks at this stuff" (Miller, Govil, McMurria, and Maxwell 184). And as always, US films continue to drive the marketplace forcing other countries to accede to their demands. The rash of "run away" productions to Canada is yet another symptom of the globalization of US cinema production. Crews are less expensive in Canada, tax incentives abound, union regulations are easier to circumvent, and the water and air are relatively free of pollution. In many ways, the current flight abroad (for production only; the actual decision-making apparatus remains firmly entrenched in Los Angeles) mimics the move to Hollywood from New York in the early part of the last century as independent producers sought to escape the interference and monopolistic threats of the Edison trust. However, in the contemporary model, we have no cinematic pioneers trying to create a new industry free from conglomerate restriction, but rather the tentacle of twenty-first century megaconglomerates reaching out to colonize new international territories for cheaper production.

And yet the new international entertainment states are also highly vulnerable if only because of their massive size. AOL Time Warner lost $54 billion in spring 2002, due primarily to the loss of advertising revenue on its American Online service. Shares of the corporate giant plummeted from a high of $60 per share to less than $20, even as the film, television, publishing, and music sectors of the company continued to show a profit (Goldsmith 1). AOL Time Warner banked on the continual expansion of the Internet, but, as we have seen, this is not the case. Increasingly, Internet users are logging on, finding the information they need, and then logging off, rather than spending hours aimlessly trolling through the Web. Although no one can deny the impact of the Internet on daily communications and information storage and retrieval, the medium has also been grossly overvalued as an investment commodity.

Jean-Marie Messier, the former head of Vivendi Universal until his board of directors ousted him in July 2002, was embroiled in a series of fractious corporate wars as he attempted to force the French/US media giant to adhere to the US entertainment business model. "Vivendi is French by birth, European by nature and global by vocation" (Vaucher and Klaussmann 41), Messier stated at a stockholder's meeting of the megaconglomerate on April 24, 2002, but his constituents were not convinced. Messier clearly wanted Universal and Canal+ to take over a larger sector of the US market. Although Vivendi's US publishing and film operations remain profitable, the European sector of Vivendi Universal has traditionally supported the creation of more individualistic, less commercial films, and Messier clearly saw no point in continuing down that road. Addressing his constituents, Messier proclaimed that "we want to be the No. 1 global media group, bringing the best content to the most consumers, all the time on screens of every kind" (Vaucher and Klaussmann 41). Such an overwhelming goal is, of course, impossible. Under Messier's model, Vivendi Universal was set to lower the bar of quality even further in their output by pursing the US business models of lowest common denominator appeal and least offensive programming.

The days when Luis Buñuel's *The Young and the Damned* (1950; original title *Los Olvidados*, 1950) could win the grand prize at the Cannes Film Festival in 1951 have altogether vanished. At the festival in 2002, Woody Allen's lightweight comedy *Hollywood Ending* was the opening night gala event, conspicuously shown "out of competition." The films in actual competition included a good deal of conventional Hollywood product, such as Paul Thomas Anderson's *Punch-Drunk Love* (2002), starring Adam Sandler, a decidedly mainstream project. Although films by Mike Leigh, Olivier Assayas, Amos Gitai, Robert Guédiguian, Manoel de Oliveira, and Abbas Kiarostami were also under consideration for the Palme d'Or, new films by major feminist filmmakers, particularly Claire Denis, Catherine Breillat, and Tonie Marshall were missing from the competition list (Elley and Vaucher 38). In addition, there was a screening of the new animated feature from DreamWorks, the family-themed *Spirit: Stallion of the Cimarron*, (2002), and a 20-minute preview of scenes from Martin Scorsese's long-awaited *Gangs of New York* (2002). In the midst of all this commercial cross-pollination, the festival's artistic director Thierry Fremaux blandly announced, "the only thing we care about is the quality of the film. Last year we had *Shrek* (2001), when for years the Cannes Film Festival didn't welcome animated films" (Elley and Vaucher 38). In the meantime, the main festival buzz concerned rumors that *Attack of the Clones* might receive a surprise screening at the festival. (Lucas eventually did make an appearance at the Cannes Film Festival with *Attack of the Clones*, which was screened digitally to an audience that was momentarily impressed by its special effects, but ultimately unimpressed with the film itself.) For the first time, the Palais at Cannes was equipped with state-of-the-art projection equipment in conventional 35mm and digital video formats, another sign that commercial use of digital distribution is only a few years away. Indeed, four films in the competition category were shot entirely on video: "Abbas Kiarostami's *10*, Michael Winterbottom's *24 Hour Party People*, Aleksandr Sokurov's *Russian Ark* and Jia Zhangke's *Unknown Pleasures*" (Elley and Vaucher 38). As a barometer of hyperconglomerate artistic temperament, the Cannes Film Festival succeeds brilliantly. The US films are brought in as crowd pleasers, the most high-profile among them screened out of competition to avoid any potential embarrassment, while the rest of the films are dutifully screened, prizes are awarded, and the nonmainstream films sink rapidly into oblivion.

The success of *Shrek* (both at the Cannes Film Festival and at the international box office) is yet another indication of the juvenilization of contemporary cinema. The aforementioned *Spirit* (this year's replacement at the Cannes Film Festival for *Shrek*) is being advertised as "a motion picture experience for everyone." Indeed it is if watching an updated version of *Bambi* (1942) is one's ideal of an optimal night at the cineplex. Parents, desperate for a film to which they can take their seven-year-olds, have contributed to the stampede toward G- and PG-rated films such as *Spirit, Shrek,* and *Lilo & Stitch* (2002). The manner in which Spirit is being hyped is remarkable: DreamWorks executive Jeffrey Katzenberg has flatly declared that the film has been made "literally for every audience, every age group—every human being will be able to see it [...]" (JamMovies). *Ice Age,* as another example, has done extraordinary business because of the emotional climate in the United States and other countries. In times of uncertainty, people retreat to simpler and safer material. How else to explain the success of *Snow Dogs,* in which James Coburn is actually presented to the viewer as Cuba Gooding Jr.'s long-lost father in the background story of this formulaic children's comedy?

Not that an uncertain social and political milieu is the sole force propelling these films to box-office success. *Shrek,* for example, spent $57 million to generate a $268 million domestic gross; *Monsters Inc.* (2001) spent $41.5 million to create a $253 million payday. Even with a strong presales factor, *Harry Potter* spent a not inconsiderable $36.3 million to generate $317 million in domestic rentals, proving that even the most merchandisable commodities still need a hefty promotional boost ("Grabbing the Auds," A4). As Peter Adee, president of marketing at Universal Pictures comments, the biggest challenge in selling a movie in the twenty-first century is "being able to shout loud enough. It's more and more difficult to make sure your audience hears about your movie [...] and that's not easy when there are a lot of big event titles" (A4). Most of these advertising dollars are spent on television ads and the creation of an effective trailer to announce the film in theaters. But in addition to a comfortable ad budget, audience research and favorable word of mouth can ensure a big opening week for a film.

In Los Angeles, the appropriately named Girls Intelligence Agency (GIA) focuses on "girls" ages 6 through 20, who represent a demographic that spends $67 billion a year on entertainment and other nonessential items. GIA founder Laura Groppe is admirably direct in her pursuit of her chosen target. "Word of mouth is the No. 1 driver for filling up movie theaters. We need these girls, they are the trend setters, their opinions matter" (Feiwell A4). Consulted for the marketing of both *Harry Potter* and *Spirit,* Groppe asserts that a film's appeal to this core audience is essential for its success:

> With such a booming female youth market, marketers can't afford not to target girls. If this alpha girl fails to find a piece of herself in the film, her attention is lost. At the end of the day, this girl may have only 25–50 bucks in her wallet; what's stopping her from heading straight to the jewelry store instead of a Cineplex? (Feiwell A4)

Where does GIA get its information? Jill Feiwell states that:

> [...] the firm's strong relationships with thousands of on-call secret agents (girls from across the country) [is a key factor in the information gathering process]. Using such strategies as nationwide slumber parties—where they screen a film or test a trailer—shopping trips and an online chat room at PlanetLaLa.com, GIA is given a front-row seat in the minds of their target audience. (A4)

With a direct line to their target audience's innermost dreams and desires, films can be shaped and reshaped to appeal not only to young women, but also other desirable groups.

As Jack Valenti, president and CEO of the Motion Picture Association of America commented, "the Hispanic population is the heaviest in movie-going, with a per capita viewing of 9.9 films per year, and represents 15% of admissions" (Hispanic Broadcasting Corporation A5). Other niche markets are targeted in similar fashion, selling their audience through newsprint ads, radio spots, television commercials, and promotional tie-ins. To promote *Scooby-*

Doo, promotional tie-ins were arrayed with Breyer's Ice Cream, Tater Tots, Kraft Lunchables, Dairy Queen, Coca-Cola, Kibbles and Bits, and numerous other products (Cohen A6). The list goes on and on, and as one views the entire process from a distance, one becomes aware that the film being thinly promoted and marketed is itself a commercial, promoting not only its future sequels or prequels, but also the various products, performers, and social values encoded within the body of its text. Does anyone really believe that *Spider-Man, Scooby-Doo, Men in Black II,* and the forthcoming remakes of *Hawaii Five-0, Foxy Brown*, and *Billy Jack* are inspired by anything other than the thought of commercial gain? The original *Billy Jack* (1971; itself a sequel to *The Born Losers,* 1967) was touted for its counterculture values in the spirit of *Easy Rider* (1969) and other antiestablishment films of that era. In *Easy Rider,* Dennis Hopper portrayed a coke-snorting outlaw on a coast-to-coast quest of personal rediscovery; today, Hopper lounges serenely in front of an oversize swimming pool, promoting Gap jeans in a series of ubiquitous television spots. In *The Limey* (1999), Hopper's costar in *Easy Rider,* Peter Fonda, has been transformed from a cultural rebel into a corporate music executive, who comments at one point that, "the 60s weren't all that great." And indeed they weren't if *Easy Rider* is any measuring stick. Greeted by rapturous reviews when first released, the film is really a carefully constructed pastiche of technique borrowed from experimental films of the period, backed up with a wall-to-wall rock-and-roll soundtrack. Perhaps the most telling incident in the film comes when Fonda's character, in a symbolic moment, takes off his Rolex watch and throws it in the dust as a gesture of his rejection of conventional values. But when the camera cuts to Fonda's discarded timepiece lying in the road, it has been magically transformed into a cheap Timex watch (Givens 53, 54). In short, nothing of any consequence is truly abandoned; all is commerce—and deceit. The heroes of one generation become the commercial spokesmen for a new era, and the seeds of the shift were there all along.

Think the magazine in your hand is the product of an independent vision? Guess again. As just one example of the hyperconglomerization that typified the print industry: *Vogue, Architectural Digest, Glamour, Bride's, Modern Bride, Self, GQ, Vanity Fair, Gourmet, Bon Appétit, Traveler, Allure, House & Garden, Wired,*

Lucky, and *The New Yorker* are all published by Condé Nast. What hope does an original point of view have in such a wilderness of potential conflicts of interest? Does anyone seriously think that any of these publications would directly oppose the interests of its brandmates, or, for that matter, of its parent company? The answer is obvious. Not only has an artificial consensus been established through the mechanics of hyperconglomerization, but dissent also has been banished to the margins of social discourse.

Little wonder, then, that of all graduate degrees awarded in the United States in 2002, an MBA had the most market value, boosting the typical graduate's salary from $45,000 to $80,000 after attaining an MBA, an increase of 78% in take home income (Haran). Even the World Trade Center attack on September 11 exists to be marketed. ABC devoted an entire day's programming on the events of September 11; exactly one year to the day of the attack, on September 11, 2002, with "more than 50 pieces" of programming and commercials "tastefully" interspersed throughout (Offman 4). As the fabric of everyday existence becomes fodder for corporate programming and nations themselves become marketing zones rather than sovereign territories, just as in the original *Rollerball*, it makes sense that each corporation should devise its own anthem, a hymn to the corporate culture. The accounting firm KPMG, for example, openly boasts in its corporate anthem of its global reach, power, and aggressiveness:

> KPMG, we're strong as can be
> A team of power and energy
> We go for the gold
> Together we hold onto our vision of global strategy.
> KPMG, we're strong as can be
> A dream of power and energy
> We go for the gold
> Together we hold onto our vision of global strategy.
> We create, we innovate,
> We pass the ones that are la-a-ate.
> A global team, this is our dream of success that we create.
> We'll be No. 1, with effort and fun,

Together each of us will run for gold,

That shines like the sun in our eyes. (qtd. in Shearer 7)

Clearly, the corporate culture knows no boundaries—and values no allegiances—focusing solely on the bottom line. The Enron and WorldCom debacles, the near collapse of AOL Time Warner, and the Arthur Andersen scandals are more proof, as if any were needed, that the human factor is rapidly evaporating from global commerce, to be replaced by the quest for profits at any cost. In previous works, I've discussed Hollywood's desire to create the perfect synthetic star to sell their films and ancillary products; the failure of *Final Fantasy: The Spirits Within* (2001) at the box office is regarded as little more than a blip in this quest. In *Simone* (2002), yet another synthetic star is "created" to merchandise the various wares of the corporate interests. If the past is any reliable index of probability, we can expect a fully realized virtual "star" within the next decade, eternally yours, eternally perfect, ready to perform on command, and not subject to the whims of unions or strikes. Erasure of the human is thus the true goal of every corporate entity, except, of course, as consumers.

Perhaps not surprisingly, churches are also following this trend toward hyperconglomerization with the creation of "megachurches," such as Robert Schuller's Crystal Cathedral. However, even that opulent edifice pales next to the new generation of mass-market houses of worship, such as the Southeast Christian Church in Louisville, Kentucky, a 50,000-square-foot facility that contains a gym with 16 basketball courts, as well as restaurants, stores, schools, banks, and of course, a church (Brown D1). The Glendale, Arizona, Community Church of Joy boasts 12,000 members and has a "school, conference center, bookstore and mortuary on its 187 acre property"; a hotel, water-slide park, and convention center will soon be added to the amenities offered to parishioners and visitors (Brown D6). The Brentwood Baptist Church in Houston, Texas, has its own McDonald's. David Kinnaman, vice president of Barna Research, is part of a consulting service that assists churches in reaching the greatest customer base. "People are looking at churches with a similar cost-benefit analysis they'd give to any other consumer purchase. [...] There is little brand loyalty. Many are looking for the newest and the greatest" (Brown D6). At the same time, consumers at home are becoming ever more dependent on new electronic storage and retrieval devices, allowing you to access not only 500 television channels from your couch, but also

> virtually every song you have ever heard of, your favorite movies and series episodes, and 20 albums' worth of family photos. [...] Entertainment servers are making their way onto the rack next to the television. These various devices—game systems, audio centers, set-top boxes and digital video recorders—have four common attributes: a microprocessor, networking capability, a graphical user interface and a huge hard drive. (Rothman E1)

Why should you ever go out? And if you do, why not go to a 24/7 location—such as one of the new megachurches—where all your needs can be met without walking or driving around? Operating in such a phantom zone of perpetual desire and instant gratification, who can tell where the real ends and the simulacrum begins? After the destruction of the World Trade Center, numerous proposals were put forth for the rejuvenation of the property, but before any of the new physical structures could be built, six designers (architects Richard Nash Gould, John Bennett, and Gustavo Bonevardi; artists Julian LaVerdiere and Paul Myoda; and lighting designer Paul Marantz) created a $500,000 virtual memorial to the World Trade Center using 88 searchlights, aimed at the sky in block formation to create two gigantic towers of light (Dunlap A23). So popular was the installation that, even though it was designed as a temporary tribute, many New Yorkers protested when the proposed end date approached—they had become accustomed to the phantom towers, as if they represented an actual structure. Eventually the light sculpture was dismantled and put into storage, but the question remains. Which "towers" were more "real"? Did the World Trade Center constitute an invitation to destruction, as E. B. White postulated in 1949? What new structures will replace the World Trade Center? And what will any of this matter to the thousands of people who lost their lives in the attack? Memorials are for the living, not the dead. The faces, voices, and lives of those who perished in the collapse of the twin towers are not memorialized

guilt one might have concerning the appropriation of Native American land in a spectacularly inauthentic recreation of past history, whereas *Edison Newsreels: San Francisco Earthquake Aftermath* (1906) documents a genuine tragedy with crisp, dispassionate objectivity. Roy Disney's "I Like Ike" campaign spots for the 1952 election offer two one-minute animated promotional spots for the first candidate to make extensive use of television as part of his bid for the White House, and *English Children: Life in the City* (1949) documents the daily life of British families cleaning up after the Blitz. *Escape* (ca. 1940s), produced by the US Air Force, offers tips on how downed air pilots might escape from prisoner of war camps, whereas *Exercise and Health* (1949), another offering from Coronet, demonstrates how physical fitness will make you successful in life. This is just a small selection of the films available at the Prelinger Archives Web site. Taken together, these films offer an invaluable overview of the social structures and value systems that shaped the United States in the first half of the 20th century. Indeed, one might argue that these sponsored films, for all their contrivance and compromise, reveal more about the United States' past than they might superficially seem to do. The attitudes, the clothing, the lighting and sets, the person-on-the-street interviews, and the primitive film stocks and equipment (making synchronous sound a luxury) all conspire to present a previsual America before television's ubiquitous gaze made us all media conscious. Were it not for Prelinger's zeal in literally rescuing these titles from destruction, we would not be able to see any of the images these films contain. Furthermore, the films in Prelinger's archive serve as a totemic marker for the thousands of other films, sponsored or commercial, that have vanished from public view.

Budd Boetticher's tense police drama *The Killer Is Loose* (1956), with a mesmerizing portrayal by Wendell Corey as an obviously psychotic bank robber bent on revenge after a violent prison escape, is a superb 73-minute film that has been all but forgotten. Part of the reason for this is that the film is unavailable in either film or video format and exists only in the memory of those fortunate enough to have seen it; the negative for it has rested unseen and unscreened for decades. Boetticher's film joins a long list of works to which the public has been deprived access because the current owners of the copyrights of these works deem them uncommercial. But, as we have seen, the commercial shelf life of a moving image construct is based directly on the aggressive marketing and distribution of that work, which Kino Video proved when it resurrected the even-more obscure *Strange Impersonation,* directed by Anthony Mann for Republic in 1946, from archival limbo. Released on DVD in a superb transfer, the film was a significant sales success for the distributor and demonstrates conclusively that a market exists for these "unknown" films if only someone will take the time and effort to properly promote them.

Numerous non–US films have also fallen into the public domain, at least until the inception of the General Agreement on Tariffs and Trades (GATT), which essentially restored foreign copyrights to formerly public domain films with the stroke of a pen. The reasons behind this move were ostensibly to placate the then-nascent European Union as a part of a series of trade agreements, but what GATT essentially does is limit US distribution of these films because the former (and now reinstated) copyright owners have no interest in promoting the properties they now reown. An entire subculture of public domain distributors in the United States has grown up around these other classic films, making them available on VHS and DVD formats long after the original distributors and/or producers had abandoned them. Diverse films such as *Mill of the Stone Women* (1960; original title *Il mulino delle donne di pietra,* 1960), *Boudu Saved from Drowning* (1932; original title *Boudu sauvé des eaux,* 1932), *School for Scoundrels* (1960), and numerous other titles that used to be readily available in 16mm rental libraries have now become all but unavailable, except to those who might find a copy in a studio archive. For all the publicity surrounding restored films, the studios themselves have proven remarkably inflexible when deciding which films to offer to the general public. Orson Welles's films are generally considered a safe bet, but what about the works of Jean Renoir? Less than half of Renoir's considerable output is now available for public distribution, a lamentable situation when one considers his place in the cinematic pantheon. And if Renoir cannot find a market niche in the current digital landscape, what hope do Fred F. Sears, Joseph H. Lewis, Ted Tetzlaff, R. G. "Bud " Springsteen, Kurt Neumann, and Ralph Nelson have, American auteurs all?

Interestingly enough, classic films are marketed in video rental and sales outlets not only by director name and genre, but also by theme. Ray Milland, much better known as an actor than a director, directed several films during the course of his long career. *A Man Alone* (1955) is a routine western; *Lisbon* (1956), a stock tale of foreign intrigue; *The Safecracker* (1958), a curious mixture of World War II British patriotism and lowbrow slapstick. Only one of Milland's directorial efforts, however, still pops up regularly on television and is thus readily available to the average consumer. The film in question is his bleak *Panic in the Year Zero!* (1962), cheaply produced by AIP in black-and-white CinemaScope. At first glance, the project would seem unmarketable by conventional standards. Milland, although he won the Academy Award for best actor in 1945 for Billy Wilder's *The Lost Weekend* (1945), is no longer a box-office draw. Milland's costars in the film, including Jean Hagen, Mary Mitchel, and then-teen-idol Frankie Avalon, also lack the necessary promotional angle for a typical video release. What, then, drives the film's current popularity? Perhaps it is because the film, concerning the efforts of Milland and his family to survive in the aftermath of a nuclear attack, serves as a thinly disguised endorsement for the National Rifle Association and feeds into the current climate of hysteria and paranoia in the United States.

In *Panic in the Year Zero!* the Baldwin family are going on a fishing trip when Los Angeles is destroyed by a nuclear terrorist attack. As the Baldwins make their way across the country, they encounter looters, rapists, and killers, all of whom predictably seek the family's destruction. Only guns can help the Baldwins as society collapses, and Milland and Avalon are not shy about doling out gun-barrel justice to all who cross their path. In one particularly brutal scene, a gang of young toughs rape the Baldwin daughter. In retaliation, father and son track the young men down and kill them in cold blood. The film's narrative closure occurs when the family, out of ammunition at last, is cornered by a phalanx of machine-gun–wielding strangers, who are eventually revealed to be soldiers from the Army patrolling the district, which has now been placed under martial law. "Thank God!" Milland exclaims, "It's the Army!" After a brief interrogation, the soldiers determine that the Baldwins are "some good ones" and let them pass through to an area unaffected by the nuclear attack. No mention is ever made of their murderous acts or the fact that during their escape from Los Angeles, Mr. Baldwin intentionally causes a freeway pile up using an exploding tank of gas so that the family can cross the road in safety. Car after car piles up as a result of his sabotage, but no matter: "the good ones" have made it out of apocalyptic wasteland, thanks to the guns they carry and their willingness to use them at the slightest provocation. Seen on conventional television, the film is shoddy, garish, and cheap. Screened only in pan-and-scan format from a CinemaScope original, indifferently photographed and directed, and further compromised by an ineffective music score by Les Baxter that was originally intended for another film (!), *Panic in the Year Zero!* survives not because of its merits, or lack of them, but rather because it suits the current political climate. It lacks even that most primitive prerequisite of contemporary commercial exploitability: the black-and-white cinematographer is drab and grimy in contrast to the all-color format today's audiences demand as a prerequisite for viewing.

At the same time, the Sonny Bono Copyright Term Extension Act, recently affirmed by the US Supreme Court, extended the existing regime of copyright by an additional 20 years, making it even less likely that "noncommercial" copyrighted films will ever again see the light of day, regardless what their artistic ambition might be. Lawyers at the Berkman Center for Internet and Society briefly summarize the impact of the Bono Act on its Web site, *Openlaw: Eldred v. Ashcroft*, explaining how hyperconglomerates have successfully lobbied the US government to extend copyright into near perpetuity, solely to protect the interests of a few large and highly influential corporations.

> Under the copyright regime existing before the Sonny Bono Act, works created by individuals, say J. D. Salinger or Elvis Presley, enjoyed protection for the life of their creators plus an additional 50 years. Works created by so-called "corporate authors," such as Disney and the New York Times, received protection for 75 years from the date of their creation.
>
> The Sonny Bono Act adds 20 years to both terms of protection, giving individual authors protection for life plus 70 years and corporate authors protection for 95 years. Thus, a symphony created by a 5-year-old modern Mozart who lives to be 85 will not be available in the public domain for the first 150 years of its existence. The Bono Act was the 11th extension of copyright terms in the last 40 years. (Openlaw Web site)

The Bono Act is a matter of considerable import to the Walt Disney Company, for example, who would have seen the copyright to *Steamboat Willie* (1928), the first Mickey Mouse sound cartoon, expire in the early years of the 21st century much to the company's chagrin. The *Washington Post* took notice of this situation in an editorial appropriately titled, "Copyright Forever?" In part, the editorial noted that:

> The Supreme Court has indicated that it will weigh a challenge to a 1998 law that lengthened copyright protection by 20 years. The bizarre and unhealthy state of copyright law is indeed a situation overdue for scrutiny, though the high court may not be the best venue for fixing it. The 1998 law was the latest in a series of congressional moves that have gradually expanded the protection for copyrighted works—originally 14 years—to nearly a century. Under current law, works created by an individual author are protected for 70 years after that author's death; works created by a corporation, such as Disney's Mickey Mouse, are protected for 95 years. The law was pressed by an assortment of influential and deep-pocketed copyright owners, most notably Disney, whose copyrights to key properties (including Mickey) were soon to expire. The ostensible reason was to bring American copyright law into harmony with that of the European Union, which uses the longer terms. But the resulting terms are far too long to cordon off works that should long since have entered the public domain, to mingle with, be reshaped by and enrich the general culture. (A18)

But the Supreme Court predictably disagreed, and now we have, indeed, "copyright forever" (see Greenhouse, A22, for more on this). Frances Hodgson Burnett's *The Secret Garden* has been the source for numerous adaptations for the screen and television since it entered the public domain in 1987, including Agnieszka Holland's entrancing version, produced in 1993. Before the novel fell into the public domain, it had been filmed only three times, in 1919, in 1949, and in 1975 as a television movie. Almost as soon as the copyright restriction vanished, *The Secret Garden* became a 1987 television movie and later a musical on Broadway. Although one can easily argue that Burnett's estate did not benefit from any of these new versions, only the collapse of the copyright barrier allowed fresh interpretations of her work to be presented to the public (Opposing Copyright Extension Web Site). When Sir Arthur Conan Doyle's character Sherlock Holmes entered the public domain, a similar surge in production occurred, particularly the superb teleseries with the late Jeremy Brett as Holmes. As the works of Gilbert and Sullivan entered the copyright-free zone one by one, numerous new versions of their classic operettas were mounted, as well as a remarkably vivid account of the composers' long collaboration, Mike Leigh's *Topsy-Turvy* (1999). In contrast, Sidney Gilliat's *The Story of Gilbert and Sullivan* (1953; also known as *The Great Gilbert and Sullivan*) offers a fancifully sanitized version of Gilbert and Sullivan's often-fractious relationship, yet gives no real insight to the circumstances surrounding the creation of their best work. The works of Dickens, Twain, Austen, Shakespeare, and many other authors have been available in the public domain for some time, resulting in an explosion of new versions of their works for stage, screen, and television. One of the reasons that so many Shakespearean adaptations are produced is that the play scripts are both royalty free and heavily presold. Actors, recognizing the brilliance of these classic texts, clamor to appear in new versions as a validation of their skills as actors and so are willing to participate for minimal fees. Michael Almereyda's version of *Hamlet* (2000), as one example, boasted a cast that included Ethan Hawke, Kyle MacLachlan, Sam Shepard, Bill Murray, Liev Schreiber, Jeffrey Wright, Paul Bartel, and Casey Affleck. The film, made for a minimal budget, nevertheless recouped its expenses at the box office because all the actors in it agreed to appear for scale wages rather than the exorbitant fees they usually command for more commercial projects.

An additional argument may be made against perpetual copyright protection as well and that is the matter of *avowed existence*. Movies that have fallen into the limbo of nondistribution are fairly easy to track. A glance at the Library of Congress Copyright Catalogue, or perhaps an older text of film history, theory, and criticism, and these works become tantalizingly alive, driving the reader on to seek out the films themselves. In short, one knows of their existence, despite their phantom availability. But what of books that have never been adapted for the screen, of which no record remains other than the long-forgotten volumes themselves, or perhaps in long out-of-print volumes of the reference work *Books in Print*. As Mark Lemley usefully points out, 10,027 books were published in 1930. As of late 2002, only 174 of these titles remain in print (qtd. in Associated Press, "High Court"). For the rest, what are the titles of these lost works? How will we know them? Once again, we are confronted by the straitjacket of canon, which seeks to enforce a proscribed list of the "classics," whatever the medium, on viewers who have been trained to be wilfully ignorant.

In cinema the 1930s have been reduced to a handful of gangster films and musicals; the 1940s to *Casablanca* (1942), *Citizen Kane* (1941), *The Big Sleep* (1946), and a few other immediately recognizable works. Oldies stations play an increasingly tight list of classic rock and roll, eschewing the more adventurous popular music of the rock and roll era. Big band music, for aficionados of the genre, has almost vanished from the radio dial. So, too, has serious classical music, replaced by the "lighter classics," show tunes, and soundtracks from hit films. All of the material presented, of course, is rigidly controlled by copyright, and, in the case of newer films, from one large music company's catalogue, resulting in a virtual monopoly on our shared cultural heritage. No matter the format, most AM/FM radio stations today are merely retransmitting substations for a national feed that serves hundreds of outlets or markets around the country. The days when an individual station could "break" an artist, as was the case with Elvis Presley in the 1950s and The Beatles (on WABC and WINS in New York) in 1960s, have vanished forever. In their place, prepackaged bands and solo acts such as 'N Sync, Britney Spears, and the Backstreet Boys rule the charts. Nothing is spontaneous. Nothing is original. Nothing is left to chance. Slickly choreographed, the new pop acts depend on smooth dance routines, onstage pyrotechnics, and multimedia saturation via the Internet, cable, radio, and broadcast television to market their prefab goods to the public.

And yet, in all fairness, they know nothing else because they are given no access to alternative media, except through low-wattage college radio stations and public access television, and even there, the audience's choices are more rigidly circumscribed than ever. It is more than being denied access to a particular performer, or song, or movie; by refusing to acknowledge the existence of alternative, noncanonical works, the mainstream hyperconglomerates postulate their virtual nonexistence. Covering the Darklight Digital Film Festival in Dublin in November 2001, Karlin Lillington, who interviewed Lawrence Lessig, John Perry Barlow, and others, argued that:

> Copyright laws in the United States are placing the control of material into an increasingly "fixed and concentrated" group of corporate hands. [...] Five record companies now control 85 per cent of music distribution, for example.

> Because copyright law now also precludes "derivative use" of copyright material, people cannot develop new material based on copyrighted work without permission. Lessig said this radically changes how human culture will evolve, since "the property owner has control over how that subsequent culture is built."

> This restriction also stymies technological innovation, as developers cannot follow the long-established practice of taking existing code and enhancing it to produce something new, he said.

> Because companies in industries such as music, publishing and film routinely demand that artists hand over copyright on their creative work, "kids don't own their own culture," said Electronic Frontier Foundation founder John Perry Barlow, who also attended the conference.

> "The period of copyright primacy is going to end up as a huge hole in the cultural record."

> Lessig said a major problem is the fact that copyrighted material simply vanishes because corporations aren't interested in keeping all that they copyright commercially available. Such material "falls into a black hole where no one will have access to it," he said.

Another threat to the availability of cultural material such as older films, books and music is that it can be difficult or impossible to establish who owns the rights to a work if the company that once owned it goes out of business. "If a corporation goes bankrupt, we're going to lose access to our culture," Lessig said.

But digital and Internet technologies have the potential to create a more diverse and open culture, he believes.

"Digital production and the Internet could change all this, so that creative action and the distribution of these arts could be achieved in a much more diversified way than before," Lessig said. This would allow for a "production of culture that doesn't depend on a narrow set of images of what culture should be."

As the reach of the Internet continues to grow, alternative visual and aural constructs continue to seep through the cracks. In the past several years, a new phenomenon in popular music, the "mash-up," has begun to dominate the underground music scene. *Mash-ups* are digital recordings made by combining the vocals from one track with the bass line of another and the melody of yet another composition to create a new, hybrid work. In essence, this is very much like "sampling," using preexisting snippets of earlier songs in newer works, which can be traced back to the novelty "tape collage" 45 RPM singles of the 1950s and 1960s in which segments of current pop singles were physically spliced together to create a new Top 40 hit. But mash-ups are far more sophisticated, combining elements of the works of up to 100 artists into a single end product. Most mash-ups are frankly illegal, but as with all new trends where money is to be made, the entertainment industry is rapidly jumping on the bandwagon. In mid-2002, Island Records in Great Britain released a legal mash-up, combining chunks of 1980s synth pop star Gary Numan, rhythm and blues singer Adina Howard, and the girl–pop band the Sugababes. As critic Neil Strauss argues:

The growing scene is a result of two colliding technological forces that have been revolutionizing music-making and the record business: cheap computer software, which makes it possible for a teenager with no musical or studio knowledge to create professional-sounding productions at home, and Internet film-sharing services, which provide a quick way to gather and share music.

All users need to do is download or buy software programs like Acid (which automatically synchronizes the rhythms of different tracks). Then they can scour a file-sharing service for a cappella versions of songs, which record companies sometimes include on promotional singles for club disc jockeys. Then, using a program like Acid, they can combine the material into a new song. [...] "If you take two or three or four great records and mix them together, you should end up with a superior product," said Steve Mannion, a co-editor of *Boom Selection* (www.base58.com), a Web site documenting the do-it-yourself remix, bootleg and sampling movements. "The best bootlegs don't sound like bootlegs. They work at a profound level, and actually sound like they are the original record." (12)

This approach to the use of found materials has its precedents in the films of Bruce Conner, Craig Baldwin, Robert Nelson, Joseph Cornell, and other "collage" filmmakers of the 1940s to the present to create entirely new films, often without any regard for copyright restrictions. Craig Baldwin's films *Tribulation 99: Alien Anomalies under America* (1992), *Spectres of the Spectrum* (1999), *Sonic Outlaws* (1995), and *O No Coronado* (1992) are all composed entirely of stock footage from other films, as is Bruce Conner's *A Movie* (1958) and *Crossroads* (1976), as well as Joseph Cornell's *Rose Hobart* (1936). In creating *Tribulation 99*, Baldwin used segments from now-forgotten films such as *Journey to the Seventh Planet* (1962), *This Island Earth* (1954), *The Mysterians* (1957; original title *Chikyu Boeigun*, 1957), *The Hideous Sun Demon* (1959), and *The Flying Serpent* (1946), as well as clips from newsreels, classroom films, and "industrials" to create a hellish vision of the earth destroyed by an attack from outer space. *O No Coronado* "documents" the career of one of the most spectacularly unsuccessful Spanish conquistadors,

49

using a mix of instructional films from the 1940s through the 1970s to illuminate the life of the film's putative subject. *A Movie* consists entirely of segments from old Castle "year in review" newsreel films and other home-movie short subjects; *Crossroads* is comprised of stock footage of the same atomic bomb blast repeated inexorably from a variety of angles, set to a soundtrack composed by Terry Riley. *Rose Hobart* contains reedited material from the 1931 film *East of Borneo* as its sole source material. Cornell found a print of *East of Borneo* at "a warehouse in New Jersey that was dumping useless footage" (Hauptman 88) and cut down the film to a 20-minute meditation on the star of the film, Rose Hobart. My own film *Serial Metaphysics* (1972) is recut entirely from early 1970s television commercials to create a vision of the world as viewed through the eyes of the corporate sponsor with a target audience always in mind. All of these works are mash-ups in their own right; now, with the capability of swapping image and sound files on the Web with relative impunity, we may be witnessing the dawn of a new era of "found film" collage works. As Craig Baldwin is fond of observing, "copyright infringement is your best entertainment value" (Craig Baldwin Web Site), and with the past of film becoming simultaneously inaccessible and yet tangentially available to avid recyclers of images, this cheerfully sardonic witticism may well be the true wave of the future.

Government and corporate interference with the free trade of ideas, images, and speech is, of course, nothing new. In 1963, the Federal Bureau of Investigation (FBI) tried to stop the production of Walt Disney's *That Darn Cat!* (1965), which was based on a novel by former FBI agent Gordon Gordon. In an internal memorandum dated August 14, 1963, an FBI operative noted that the proposed film, which might cause damage to the FBI's reputation, should be closely monitored. The memo concluded with the notation that:

> This is just another instance where Gordon Gordon is trading on his former affiliation with the FBI to further his own personal motives. Certainly, any production or book authored by Gordon is not going to do the Bureau any good. Therefore, every effort will be made through the Los Angeles office to protect the Bureau's interest in this proposed movie.

The Crime Records Division will continue to follow this matter closely through the Los Angeles Office to insure that if the proposed movie is made the Bureau's interests are protected. (FBI memo)

If a trivial matter such as the production of a mildly critical, comic film by former FBI operative Walt Disney (see Eliot for further details on this) upset the Bureau, then one must reasonably wonder what sort of activities are not under surveillance. As shows such as *The Osbournes* (three months in the life of a rock star's family, edited down to a season of profanity-free, MTV sanitized half-hour "reality" programming), *Big Brother, Survivor,* and other hypersurveillant spectacles proliferate, the big question is not whether Big Brother is watching you, but rather, "are you getting paid for it?" As the plethora of television trash talk shows such as *Jenny Jones, Sally Jesse Raphael, Jerry Springer,* and other series demonstrated in the 1990s, people expect to be watched and are disappointed when their activities, no matter how quotidian, go unnoticed. As Orwell predicted, telescreens are now installed in every room of every house. But now, instead of trying to avoid them, we desperately seek to attack the surveillance camera's lens.

With the advent of DVD, VHS became obsolete, as did its near-universal translatability. VHS tapes were either PAL/SECAM or NTSC, that is, European or US standard. Tapes were easily converted from one format to another with only minimal loss in quality. However, with the introduction of DVDs, the world was split into six zones, most notably Region 1 for US DVDs and Region 2 for Europe. This region coding was an attempt by Hollywood to hold onto the exclusivity of its product for a longer window of release time before allowing it to be disseminated to the rest of the globe. Significantly, many European films that are hits on DVDs in their home countries are never released in the United States either because the producers/distributors feel no market exists for it or they want to prevent territorial overlap with respect to underlying rights. To combat this, DVD player manufacturers began to create a new breed of all region DVD players designed to play any region DVD on one player without interference. This strategy worked, and as collectors and scholars became aware of the limitations of region coding, sales of the all-region players skyrocketed.

However, Hollywood again fought back to regain control of its unruly universe of images with the creation of regional coding enhancement (RCE). This new double coding system is designed to defeat the all-region capability of the universal DVD players, and Warner Brothers, New Line Cinema, and Columbia Pictures have enthusiastically embraced the double coding system on their newer releases. Tellingly, RCE has only one objective: to make Region 1 discs only unplayable in foreign territories on all region machines. For the most part, the films being given the RCE treatment are mainstream box-office hits, such as *Charlie's Angels* (2000), *Ghosts of Mars* (2001), *Hollow Man* (2000), and other highly commercial titles. European films are generally unaffected, but if a Region 1 DVD with RCE is put into an all-region DVD player, explanatory messages will appear. For Warner Home Video (WHV) releases, the viewer will see this warning, in appropriately stentorian capital letters:

> This DVD player may have been altered and is unable to play this disc. There is nothing wrong with this disc. DVD players and discs are designed to work in certain regions. This disc is not compatible with this player. Please contact your local retailer or player manufacturer for additional information. We apologize for any inconvenience.

Columbia offers this slightly less draconian version:

> This disc is intended for play on non-modified Region 1 players only. There is nothing wrong with the disc. To assure playback you should purchase or rent a disc designed specifically for your region.

But for both companies, the objective is the same, as evidenced by the text of this internal memo from WHV:

> WHV will start applying the RCE to discs scheduled for release in the US market beginning in late October [2000]. At this time, the RCE will only be applied to Region 1 versions of titles. At least one other studio (Columbia TriStar) will also be releasing discs with the RCE during the 4th quarter.

The program has two objectives. (1) Discourage the export of Region 1 discs to other regions and (2) discourage the sale of DVD video hardware that has been modified to "region free" [...].

With the online retailers, we must discuss the need to properly notify consumers outside the Region 1 territories that the disc may not play in their player before the disc is purchased. The customer dissatisfaction and returns risk is significant if this is not done. At this time there is no plan to send out a press release on this program. (*DVD Talk Web* site)

Typically, the program is not only invasive, but also secret. Thus does corporate culture mask its true intent: to limit viewer choice still further while never publicly admitting to the fact. Furthermore, several DVD manufacturers have suggested that the modification of DVD players to be all region is illegal, as if their region coding system constituted some sort of internationally binding trade agreement. But no, it's just the media hyperconglomerate's last-ditch attempt to limit sales zones, thereby further controlling what the viewer sees and hears. Nevertheless, within the precincts of the megaconglomerates themselves, RCE and region coding have assumed the status of phantom legality, a doctrine to be enforced.

As consumer frustration with corporate media control increases, so do the number of ways to circumvent it. Napster and other free MP3 file sharing services were shut down in 2001, but a variety of MP3s, legal and illegal, still proliferate on the Internet. Significantly, the free MP3s download with much greater frequency than the pay-to-listen MP3s because people are tired of paying too much for their entertainment. Indeed, some MP3-like formats, such as Liquid Audio, are designed to be played only on the computer that downloaded them. Without serious file modification and a good degree of technical sophistication, these Liquid Audio files can be listened to as streaming audio and then must be erased. When one site for MP3s is closed or shuts down, numerous others appear in its place, ensuring a constant supply of free music to listeners. The same is true with online video, whether streaming video played through Real Player, or downloaded in MPEG DivX, QuickTime, and other formats. The free downloads outnumber the paid downloads, regardless how aggressively the for-sale product is marketed. As we've seen with the numerous setbacks at America Online (AOL), not everyone is thrilled to hear, "You've got mail!" Most of the e-mail messages are advertisements, "spam," solicitations, notices of renewal for expiring software. The real treasures of the Web are those that lie beyond the domain of corporate control, created by artists, philanthropists, and visionaries who view the Web as it was intended to be, a medium for the free exchange of ideas and images, free from hyperconglomerate influence.

And there are also signs that media saturation and technological overload are short-circuiting consumer's desire to keep up with the next wave of electronic hardware. In Japan, NTT DoMoCo Inc. has introduced its new 3G cell phone, a handset "packed with high-speed video and audio functions [...] part personal digital assistant, part portable entertainment center" (Belson 13). Despite the phone's capability to receive and display movies and audio, as well as e-mail and traditional phone messages, however, Japanese consumers are not rushing to buy the 3G, at least not in its current configuration. One potential customer, Mikio Fukai, a salesman for the Compaq Computer Corporation in Tokyo, allowed that she was "extremely interested in the functions on the 3G phones. But the critical problem is that the screens are not spacious enough to read letters, and the buttons are too small" (Belson 13). Nevertheless, the technology exists and will doubtless be improved. DVDs will soon be the wave of the past; we will be able to have feature length films beamed to our cell phones, which may in the next few years will have somewhat larger screens. For the moment, Japanese consumers seem content to use their cell phones for talking with clients and friends, and sending the occasional brief, urgent e-mail. Indeed, another high-tech Japanese consumer, Yukiko Asaoka, works for a small technology company that purchased two DoMoCo videophones. Yukiko finds the phones intriguing, as does Mikio, but agrees that on the whole, the technological advantage is overrated. She used one of the new phones for a videoconferencing session, but found that the novelty soon wore off. The new phones cost roughly $500 apiece, and for Yukiko, the new technology is not worth the cost. "It's out of the question," she says (Belson 13).

Indeed, even as the media become more a part of our lives, the more a portion of our being seems to resist them. We've become justifiably cynical, waiting on hold for services that never materialize, dealing with corporate customer service representatives who present new obstacles rather than solving problems, and coping with an increasingly unresponsive technological matrix that wants to know everything about us, but that is unwilling to divulge even the slightest bit of information regarding its own motives. IBM is developing a new handset that photographs "non-English words, transmits them for translation and then superimposes the results on the image" (Eisenberg 12). Wouldn't it be simpler to ask someone to translate the sign in question, rather than relying on an IBM InfoScope to do the work for you? Then, too, the human interaction is lost. We are all, in the future world, divided by, advised by, and governed by machines.

Perhaps this is why a show such as *The Osbournes* is so appealing. As Scott Lyle Cohen observed, "reality TV shows like *Survivor* and *The Real World* make ordinary people into celebrities, but *The Osbournes* has flipped that formula and made celebrities—[Ozzy Osbourne] and his family—into ordinary people" (Cohen, *Ozzy* 63). Unlike their predecessors in family reality television, the Louds, who were the putative stars of the PBS series *An American Family*, first televised nationally in 1973, attained a sort of ersatz celebrity almost overnight. All of the Louds got some "burn" from the media spotlight, and, for added drama, Pat and Bill Loud (the husband and wife of this very 1970s nuclear family) divorced during production of the series. Shot by Alan and Susan Raymond, who created the "reality" format with their pioneering ½" reel-to-reel Portapack video production *The Police Tapes* (1977), prefiguring *Cops* by more than two decades, *An American Family* began as more than 300 hours of 16mm film shot over a seven-month period, which was eventually whittled down to 12 hour-long, unscripted episodes. But the biggest surprise of the series, by 1970s standards, was the "coming out" of Lance Loud, the eldest son of the Louds. In the series, Lance moved out of the house, took up residence at the Chelsea Hotel in New York, and embraced the bohemian lifestyle of Manhattan. Brimming with confidence, Lance started a punk band, Lance Loud and the Mumps, did a few pieces for Andy Warhol's *Interview* magazine, and generally enjoyed his 15 minutes of fame. But when he died, Lance Loud seemed, according to those who knew him, to be unsure that he had accomplished anything. Succumbing to Hepatitis C at age 50 in an AIDS hospice in December 2001, Loud called the

Raymonds and asked to be interviewed one last time. As Alan Raymond put it, "He could have asked for a priest or a minister. But he called for his filmmakers" (Woodward 20).

A child of the media to the last, Lance Loud in the end had only his public image to cling to, even as his life came to a close. The Raymonds produced a retrospective program on the series for PBS, *An American Family: The Final Episode*, dealing for the most part with Lance Loud's final illness. In photographs from the publicity packet for the series, the Louds seem stiff, uncertain of the public personae, ill at ease in the media spotlight—all except for Lance. As with so many instinctive performers, Lance Loud knew how to seduce the camera, and thus the viewer, into accepting his vision of the world as both authoritative and real. The Louds were the first family of reality television, and although they are nearly forgotten, their trials and heartbreaks are as immediate and compelling today as when they were first broadcast if one can find a copy. But here, of course, is the crux of the matter. You cannot find a copy because the series was broadcast before home VCRs were even a hypothetical possibility, and only the 16mm original materials and some ancient 2" video masters remain. To gain access to the world of the Louds, one must again become an archivist, searching through the detritus of the past. And, of course, one must know that the series is there in the first place. Otherwise, like so many other cinematic sepulchers, it will have vanished into the dim light of memory, stored somewhere in a mountain of film cans, outtakes of people who are dead, divorced, grown up, and married— people who have lived a life outside of the film itself. Even the medium used to create the film speaks to its era: 16mm film. When one looks at the grainy images produced by the Raymonds for the series, or encounters the PBS promotional materials that accompanied it, one might as well be looking at a daguerreotype from the 1880s, so remote are these images to the contemporary viewer.

In contrast, *The Osbournes*, recorded in vibrant, scratch-free video by a willing family of participants who retained complete control over the final cut, is an altogether different matter. Ozzy's career was fading, but he was still good copy; the notorious incident of biting a head off a bat, and then at a news conference, a dove, conferred on Ozzy Osbourne a certain kind of irrevocable notoriety. Daughter Kelly and son Jack, both eager to launch their own careers (Jack is already a talent scout for Epic Records) had no objections, and wife-manager Sharon saw the MTV deal as a godsend. No cost, total control, excellent publicity for an already admittedly eccentric rock star, and the possibility of rejuvenated fame. As everyone now knows, the series was an overwhelming success, and Ozzy Osbourne is now a household name to a whole new generation of fans who were not even born when Black Sabbath (with Osbourne as their lead singer) made their debut in the waning years of the 1960s. As Scott Lyle Cohen declares:

> From a business standpoint, the TV show's given Ozzy's musical career a kick in the ass. The week after it debuted, his latest album, *Down to Earth* [Epic], jumped 52 places on SoundScan's Top Current Album chart to number 93. And next week *The Ozzman Cometh: Greatest Hits* [Epic] will be number four on Billboard's Top Pop Catalog Albums chart. ("Sharon" 62)

And from the standpoint of personal privacy, one has to ask, what personal privacy? The Osbournes seem ready-made to step in front of the camera. Their enormous mansion serves as a backdrop as effective as anything conceived for *Dallas* or *Dynasty*. Sharon, by her own admission "a spendaholic" (Cohen, "Sharon" 62), manages to be both funky and glamorous as she parades around the house in her robe and slippers, complaining about housework, the dishes, the children, and the pressures of high-level domesticity. "Martha Stewart can lick my scrotum," she says at one point, momentarily defeated by a mountainous stack of dirty dishes. But minutes later, she's chucking the dirty plates, pots, and pans into the dishwasher, musing to the camera, "Do I have a scrotum?" Jack is spoiled, as one might expect from the child of a superstar with a powerful mother as an ally, and Kelly, while just as foul-mouthed as the rest of the family, radiates an inner sweetness even as she "borrows" Sharon's credit card to go on a semi-illicit spending spree and then almost loses it in the bargain.

But what is missing? According to Sharon, precious little:

> There were a couple of things that were taken out of context that we've changed, but stuff like Ozzy being stoned and family arguments, we kept it all in there, because there's no point in doing it otherwise. I mean,

there's shit where I'm picking my knickers out of my ass, where Ozzy's stoned and I've got bed head. What more can you say? My husband is a recovering alcoholic who slips from time to time, I'm a spendaholic, and we live the way we want to. Do people think that we have an Asian boy hidden in a fucking closet that we both screw? (Cohen, "Sharon" 62)

And thus we have the new spectacle of domestic normality in the 21st century; people being documented for a series whose entire aim is publicity and product promotion, but with an added twist. *The Osbournes* makes the bizarre seem deeply ordinary, and Ozzy's pose as Prince of Darkness has been replaced by his new status as the ultimate father and family man for a new generation. MTV makes money and collects the best ratings of its entire corporate career, the Osbournes sell a hell of a lot of records and further consolidate Ozzy's fame, and Sharon and Jack get a jump start on their own careers, appearing (among numerous other media manifestations) as the stars of a cover story in Andy Warhol's *Interview*. Not even the spectre of Sharon's colon cancer in the second season can halt the family's march to stardom; now the Osbourne's have attained the status of perpetual martyrdom, fodder for the tabloids. Warhol himself may be gone, but *Interview*'s legacy is the same as when he was the magazine's publisher. Anyone can become a celebrity, given the right amount of airtime, the right kind of promotion, and, of course, final cut of their onscreen personae, even Anna Nicole Smith.

CHAPTER TWO

INVASION U.S.A.

The defining moment for 21ˢᵗ century US cinema remains, however, the attacks of September 11, 2001, on the World Trade Center in Manhattan and the Pentagon in Washington, DC. Not since the height of the 1950s Cold War hysteria has the United States lived in such an atmosphere of fear and repression, even as we significantly embrace the concepts of social, sexual, and racial equality. For all intents and purposes, the United States is now in a state of perpetual emergency readiness, braced for the next terrorist attack against a nuclear power plant, a major metropolitan area, or another corporate skyscraper. The heightened attempts at security in the United States, as well as abroad, cannot possibly hope to contain all possible future threats. Eventually, someone will get through. And thus, in an atmosphere of mutual fear and hatred—the West pitted against the Arab world, Christian against Muslim, black against white, Jew against gentile, Protestant against Catholic—the cinema of the 21ˢᵗ century operates in a climate of distrust and cynicism as audiences search for reassurance and an ideal past in a world of pain and cynicism. The remake of *Mr. Deeds* is no accident, nor is the desire for a return to the small-town America of Frank Capra's imagination, a world that never really existed except in that filmmaker's imagination. We want our innocence back, but we know that is not going to happen. And so, we while away the time with sentimental paeans to a fictive, halcyon past, interspersed with digital spectacles of violence, retribution, and destruction.

Whatever may come in the next decade or so, the events of September 11 will inform the US cinema for much of the foreseeable future, unless the horror of that day is eclipsed by an even greater cataclysmic upheaval that renders the disruption in New York and Washington, DC, merely a prelude to a wider war. Just as Pearl Harbor shaped the cinema of the 1940s, so September 11 will serve as the template for the new 21ˢᵗ century conflict. And as that conflict consumes more and more of our time and energy, America's cinematic response to this new war will colonize the globe, wherever Hollywood films are shown. Already, with the near-election of Jean-Marie Le Pen in France and the assassination of far-right xenophobic Dutch politician Pym Fortuyn, Europe is joining the United States in a march to the political right. The fear of the other made manifest in the relentless and invasive assaults on personal privacy that come with the "war on terrorism," such as increased airline security, postal inspections, random house searches, and aggressive deportation policies, only exacerbates an already tenuous situation by dividing the world's populace neatly into two opposing camps—"them" and "us."

Thus construction of forced consensus, already apparent in the orchestrated public display of grief occasioned by the death of Diana Spencer in the late 1990s, as well as events such as the *Challenger* disaster and the Gulf War, created the groundwork for the lockstep society in which we are forced to live. Dissent, although tolerated, is not encouraged. As in the 1950s with the Cold War threat, a newly nuclear Russia cast an ominous shadow over US social and commercial interests. It is the "team" ethic that is most valued, the desire to be part of a simplistic world in which good and evil are readily identifiable and discreet. *We Were Soldiers* , for example, celebrates the much-debated conflict in Vietnam from the viewpoint of "duty, honor and country" (according to the film's director, Randall Wallace; see Hatty 12) without ever once allowing for the notion that those who opposed the war and sought its end might have been motivated by the very same emotions. In the immediate wake of Vietnam, a wave of films critical of the conflict emerged, most notably *Apocalypse Now* (1979, reissued with restored footage in 2001), *The Deer Hunter* (1978), *Platoon* (1986), and *Hearts and Minds* (1974), as well as numerous low-budget exploitation films depicting returning vets as sociopaths and violent misfits whose lives and minds were irreparably damaged by the war. In the aftermath of World War II, a few films emerged that addressed the iniquities of the war, such as *Home of the Brave* (1949), which depicted the plight of an African-American soldier (played by the now-forgotten James Edwards), who suffers more from the racism in his own outfit than from the attacking enemy forces, and suffers a nervous breakdown as a consequence. John Huston's docudrama *Let There Be Light*

(1946) documented the effects of battle fatigue and psychological trauma on returning soldiers. Made while Huston was an officer in the US Signal Corps, it was subsequently banned for more than two decades as a potentially subversive tract, as was Huston's *The Battle of San Pietro* (1945), one of the most shattering documents of actual combat ever created in the cinema. Shot by battleground photographers during an actual ground assault, *The Battle of San Pietro* depicts war as a brutal, unforgiving affair in which men fight and are killed without any of the sentimentality and fraudulent pyrotechnics that marred Steven Spielberg's revisionist *Saving Private Ryan* (1998). *Till the End of Time* (1946) dealt with three former Marines trying to fit into postwar society with varying degrees of success, as did William Wyler's celebrated *The Best Years of Our Lives* (1946). All of these social commentaries were mild compared to European films made in the wake of World War II, such as Vittorio De Sica's *Shoeshine* (1947; original title *Sciuscià*, 1946), Roberto Rossellini's *Paisan* (original title *Paisà*, 1946), and Wolfgang Staudte's *The Murderers Among Us* (1946; original title *Die mörder sind unter uns*, 1946), all of which dealt with the crime, poverty, despair, and corruption of the postwar European social economy. Yet none of these films seriously questioned the underlying reasons behind the conflict in which millions of soldiers, noncombatants, and Jews, Poles, and Gypsies lost their lives, either in combat or in concentration camps. A war against Hitler and Hirohito had a clear moral objective; the enemy was easily identifiable—if not so easy to eradicate. More than half a century later, the wounds from that global conflict are still healing, with each side feeling compelled to justify their own actions in the war or ask for atonement for the atrocities they committed.

In contrast, a film such as *We Were Soldiers* represents an attempt to reconstruct the conflict in Vietnam as an equally clear-cut case of response to outside aggression. Although the film was in production long before the events of September 11, in publicity for the film, both the director (Randall Wallace) and the film's star (Mel Gibson) were at pains to relate the film to American's contemporary shadow war. According to Wallace, "noble impulses led us [to Vietnam], the American spirit was wounded in that war. [...] September 11 reminded us in America there is such [a] thing as evil in the world. [...] I don't think of myself as making war stories; I think of myself as telling love stories.

War puts love in context" (Hatty 12). Agreed Gibson, "I wish no one should ever, ever have to go to war. I would hate to send my children to war. I would hate it. If it's for a just reason, so be it." (Hatty 12). Wallace further stated that he made *We Were Soldiers* to "help heal the wounds left by that war. [I hope] those healed the most will be those wounded the most—the soldiers and the families of the soldiers who fought there" (Hatty 12). But what about the Vietnamese soldiers who, from their perspective and that of their families, fought with equal bravery to defend their homeland? Nowhere in the film are the opposing forces given any real agency or identity; the film dehumanizes the Vietnamese as much as Ray Enright's *Gung Ho!* (1943) extols the virtues of a group of American fighters who "don't like Japs" (in the words of one actor in the film) as they fight their racially segregated way through the war in the Pacific.

Hollywood is reactive, rather than proactive. As late as 1939, the Hollywood studios were afraid to produce any films critical of the Nazi regime for fear of offending Hitler and losing the lucrative German market for their films. Besides, with Hitler on the march in Poland and the former Czechoslovakia, would these territories, too, not be potentially at risk for American films? The war was progressing rapidly. As Mark Lewis documents:

At 6:30 A.M. on 1 September 1939, Germany invaded Poland. The last organized Polish resistance collapsed at the beginning of October. On the Western Front there followed six months of inactivity, dubbed the Phoney War. In April 1940, Hitler invaded Denmark and Norway, and on 10 May he unleashed his Blitzkrieg in the West. By September 1940, the tide of war had washed across Western Europe. Denmark and Norway had been occupied, the Low Countries overrun, France humiliated and the British Expeditionary Force bundled out of Europe. Massive Luftwaffe bomber formations droned across the English Channel daily as the Battle of Britain neared its height. (9)

A 1939 Gallup poll "revealed that although 84% of Americans wanted an Allied victory, 96% of them wanted the USA to stay out of the conflict" (Lewis 9).

Hollywood had good reason to follow the same line toward the war in Europe, albeit for strictly economic factors. As Lewis comments:

> The USA remained neutral, but events in Europe had a serious effect in Hollywood, closing 11 countries to American films. In Belgium and Holland about 1,400 cinemas had been immediately closed, representing a loss of about $2.5 million in annual revenue for American film companies. By the end of the year, with the exception of Sweden, Switzerland and Portugal, the whole of Continental Europe was closed to American films, slashing Hollywood's revenue by over a quarter. (9)

Furthermore, Joseph Goebbels, the Third Reich's propaganda minister, was an avid movie fan, as his diaries readily attest. Rather than leaving the work of censoring American films to his minions, he set up his own private screening room, where he would run Hollywood films in marathon viewing sessions, alternatively complimenting the major studio films on their technical skill, while mercilessly winnowing out all but a few B films for exhibition in Germany and the newly occupied territories. In view of this, Hollywood had good financial reason to be cautious in its criticism of the Reich, even as it evaded its clear moral imperative.

Anatole Litvak's *Confessions of a Nazi Spy* (1939) was one of the first films to criticize the new regime openly and was predictably banned by Goebbels as a result. Indeed, the Roosevelt administration pressured Warner Brothers, producer of the film, not to produce any similar movies. But in April 1940, reports reached Hollywood that several Polish theater managers had been publicly lynched in lobbies of their cinemas for screening the film (Lewis 9). Jean Renoir's *Rules of the Game* (1950; original title *La règle du jeu*, 1939) was another film critical of the Nazis, although in a subtler manner. As Alfred Brockman comments:

> Although on the surface it told of the interaction between guests and domestic staff at a weekend house party, [*Rules of the Game*] was an allegory about life and living and the current sorry state of the world.

Renoir, who had written the screenplay, also appeared in the film as an onlooker commenting on events and their implication.

Blatantly anti-Fascist, it was shortened by its distributors after public protests on its initial release. When war broke out, the censor banned it. Later the Germans destroyed all prints they could lay their hands on, including the original negative. After the war, a new copy was assembled from odds and ends, and in 1962 many international critics proclaimed it the third greatest film ever made. (450)

By the time the United States finally declared war on Germany and Japan after a decade of isolationism, the floodgates opened and a seemingly endless wave of propaganda films were produced with assembly-line frenzy.

In the wake of the Japanese attack on Pearl Harbor, Hollywood shifted into high gear, dividing its output between jingoistic war dramas, tales of home-front heroism, and frankly escapist entertainment. Films such as *Hitler—Dead or Alive* (1942), *The Hitler Gang* (1944), *Hitler's Children* (1942), *Hitler's Madman* (1943), and numerous other B films detailed Nazi atrocities with thinly disguised relish, while Charles Chaplin spoofed Hitler himself in *The Great Dictator* (1940). Germany, too, began producing propaganda films of its own, all centering on anti-Semitism, particularly *The Eternal Jew* (1940; original title *Der ewige Jude*, 1940), all of which depicted an international Jewish conspiracy as the underlying cause of the world's ills. In an attempt to develop a South American market for its films, Hollywood promoted Carmen Miranda in vehicles such as *Down Argentine Way* (1940) as part of "a concerted export drive" (Lewis 13) to open up the new territory for US product. *I Wanted Wings* (1941) and *Dive Bomber* (1941) were clearly militaristic films, whereas *Sergeant York* (1941) detailed a young Tennessee farm boy's conversion from pacifist to war hero when in 1918 he captured 132 Germans single-handedly during World War I and became a national hero (Lewis 61). As the war progressed, Hollywood alternated between frankly commercial entertainment, such as *Honeymoon for Three, Bachelor Daddy, Charlie Chan in Rio, Playmates, Double Date*, and *The Invisible Ghost* (all 1941), and all-out war films, such as *Bataan, Air Force, So Proudly We Hail, Corvette K-225, Action in the North Atlantic, The Strange*

Death of Adolf Hitler, and *Five Graves to Cairo* (all 1943). By 1944, the tide of war was inexorably turning against the Axis Powers, and the Allied victory in 1945 should have opened up Europe once again for US film exports were it not for the machinations of Joseph Stalin, one of the Allied Powers in World War II. Seizing the opportunity to liberate numerous Eastern European countries from the Nazis and then bring them into the Soviet orbit, the end of the war brought about not a sense of peace, but rather one of disillusion. The atomic bombs dropped on Hiroshima and Nagasaki may have brought the conflict in the Pacific to a close, but they simultaneously opened the door on the nuclear era and with it the Cold War and the East/West arms race.

The new mood in the United States manifested itself immediately in the creation of a new genre, film noir, which accurately summed up the exhaustion, failed dreams, and cynicism of the post-World War II generation. In *Act of Violence* (1948) a wartime veteran who betrayed his comrades is stalked by one surviving member of his unit, bent on revenge. *Behind Locked Doors* (1948) presented psychiatry as a racket in one of many 1940s films that were suspicious of psychoanalysis. In *Bewitched* (1945), an evil spirit posseses a helpless young woman, which forces her to kill her fiancé. *The Big Clock* (1948) presents a withering picture of hyperconglomerate journalism as a young man (Ray Milland) fights to clear himself of a murder charge when his megalomaniacal employer (Charles Laughton) is, in fact, the real killer. *The Blue Dahlia* (1946), scripted by hard-boiled author Raymond Chandler in a blind-drunk stupor (see Houseman 7-23 for more on this curious working method), depicted the unhappy homecoming of war veteran Johnny Morrison (Alan Ladd) and his badly wounded compatriot, Buzz Wanchek (William Bendix). When Johnny's unfaithful wife Helen (Doris Dowling) is murdered, suspicion falls first on Johnny and then Buzz. Buzz was, in fact, to have been the murderer (he has returned from duty with a large metal plate in his head and is subject to frequent blackouts), but the War Department vetoed the idea, and Chandler had to come up with another killer. In the final, rather arbitrary scene, Dad Newell (Will Wright), a house detective who has been skulking around various apartments throughout the film, is revealed as the true killer, and so Buzz's character avoided the fate of being one of the screen's first psychotic killer veterans.

Noir proved an enormously popular genre, tapping into the collective unconscious of a deeply disillusioned postwar America, and lasted into the late 1950s as a durable format before it collapsed in the 1960s, only to be reborn in the 1990s as neo-noir. But another kind of film was captivating the public consciousness toward the end of the 1940s as a result of Stalin's duplicity during the war. The Red Scare film, now thoroughly discredited and an object of near-camp veneration among film buffs, nevertheless presented a significant articulation of American fears in the face of the Stalinist war machine. For the most part, they were poorly directed, featured B players who were unable to get work in A productions, and many of them were created by Howard Hughes, the mysterious tool-and-die manufacturer who acquired control of RKO Pictures (and its theater chain) for a mere $9 million in 1948. Hughes immediately demanded that all of his employees sign loyalty oaths, prompting most of his staff to flee. For those who stayed, Hughes embarked on a typically erratic production schedule of hysteria-driven anti-Communist films, the most famous of which is probably *I Married a Communist* (1949).

By 1954, Hughes had run the studio into more than $40 million worth of debt (he later resold it to Desi Arnaz for the home base for Desilu Productions), but although the films produced at RKO, Republic, MGM, and other studios had little artistic merit, they fueled a tidal wave of public anxiety. J. Parnell Thomas's 1947 investigation of Communist infiltration into the motion picture industry was only the curtain raiser for a full-scale blacklist, aimed for the most part at leftist Democrats, which consumed the public's attention through the early 1950s. This ban finally collapsed when blacklisted screenwriter Dalton Trumbo, one of the most famous of the Hollywood Ten, a group of writers, producers, and directors who were sentenced to jail for refusing to testify before the infamous House Un-American Activities Committee (HUAC), finally received screen credit for his work on *Spartacus* (1960) and *Exodus* (1960). But it was too little—and too late. Before the HUAC Blacklist ended, hundreds of actors, directors, technicians, producers, and screenwriters had been forced out of the industry to its eternal detriment. A few lucky exiles, such as director Joseph Losey, found new careers in England. Others, such as Trumbo, worked under a variety of pseudonyms. Trumbo wrote the story for *The Brave One* (1956) under the pseudonym of

Robert Rich; the film won an Academy Award for "Rich," much to the chagrin of the Hollywood community. The seeds of the Blacklist remain. Elia Kazan, who was honored by the Academy of Motion Picture Arts and Sciences and received an Honorary Award, was one of the key "friendly witnesses" for HUAC, naming J. Edward Bromberg, Paula Strasberg (née Miller), Clifford Odets, Art Smith, and Morris Carnovsky as "fellow travelers." More than a quarter of a century later, Kazan remained convinced that he had done the right thing. Other friendly witnesses included writer Martin Berkeley, who named Gale Sondergaard, Dorothy Parker, Howard Da Silva, Carl Foreman, Dashiell Hammett, Lillian Hellman, Robert Rossen, Lionel Stander, Budd Schulberg, and more than 100 others as Communists. Berkeley was followed in the witness chair by Lloyd Bridges, Lee J. Cobb, Edward Dmytryk (who first refused to testify on October 29, 1947, but recanted on April 25, 1951, naming 25 associates as Communist Party members, including director Jules Dassin), Roy Huggins, Frank Tuttle, and many others (see Vaughn 275-92). In addition, celebrities such as actor Robert Taylor and producer Jack L. Warner appeared before HUAC to commend its investigation of the motion picture industry.

In this climate of hypersurveillant paranoia, Hollywood responded with a wave of films that reflected the new public mood. In *Conspirator* (1949), wife Elizabeth Taylor discovers that husband Robert Taylor is an undercover Communist operative; in *Invasion U.S.A.* (1952), one of the most spectacularly violent films of the era, Manhattan is leveled by an atom bomb blast; and *Big Jim McLain* (1952) finds John Wayne in Hawaii sleuthing for the HUAC with the assistance of *Gunsmoke*'s James Arness. *My Son John* (1952) was one of the more prestigious entries in the series, in which college graduate Robert Walker becomes a Communist agent, much to the chagrin of his mother and father (Dean Jagger and Helen Hayes). *The Girl in the Kremlin* (1957) starred Zsa Zsa Gabor in an unlikely tale of espionage and intrigue. With the collapse of the Soviet Union, largely as a result of the influence of US televisual and radio programming, as well as an abundance of consumer goods, convincing the average Russian citizen that even a compromised sort of democracy is preferable to Communism, the balance of power changed, with China and Cuba the only holdouts. At the same time, however, relations in the Middle East between the Palestinians and the Israelis became increasingly strained, and generally unobserved; a network of terrorists began to draw their plots for an attack on the United States.

The September 11 films are deeply reminiscent of the films of both the 1940s and 1950s with regard to their political agenda; they seek to create a sense of unity out of deeply disparate factions. But in the current conflict, the enemy is far more elusive, spread out over a number of countries and financed by a network of digital transactions that move funds from one bank to another with a few keystrokes. Here, we find no clear objective to be hit, no easily identifiable target to be eradicated. The Taliban and Al Qaeda forces are difficult to track; additionally, they have their own network of communications to support their purposes, headed by Al Jazeera, the Arabic news station that serves as the focal point in this new propaganda war.

Al Jazeera broadcasts a mix of sensationalist propaganda and hate speech at an audience of some 35 million "Arabic speaking viewers," as Fouad Ajami comments, and although Al Jazeera "may not officially be the Osama bin Laden Channel [...] he is clearly its star." Ajami continues:

> The channel's graphics assign him a lead role: there is bin Laden seated on a mat, his submachine gun on his lap; there is bin Laden on horseback in Afghanistan, the brave knight of the Arab world. A huge, glamorous poster of bin Laden's silhouette hangs in the background of the main studio set at Al Jazeera's headquarters in Doha, the capital city of Qatar.

> On Al Jazeera (which means "the Peninsula"), the Hollywoodization of news is indulged with an abandon that would make the Fox News Channel blush. The channel's promos are particularly shameless. One clip juxtaposes a scowling George Bush with a poised, almost dreamy bin Laden; between them is an image of the World Trade Center engulfed in flames. Another promo opens with a glittering shot of the Dome of the Rock. What follows is a feverish montage: a crowd of Israeli settlers dance with unfurled flags; an Israeli soldier fires his rifle; a group of Palestinians display Israeli bullet shells; a Palestinian woman wails; a wounded Arab

child lies on a bed. In the climactic image, Palestinian boys carry a banner decrying the shame of the Arab world's silence. (48, 50)

Al Jazeera presents all of this for maximum visual impact. When a particularly violent piece of footage comes along, the viewer can count on Al Jazeera's willingness to air the clip repeatedly. An Al Jazeera "documentary" on the life of Che Guevara skips through the details of Che's career as a Marxist rebel to dwell on extended footage of his bloody corpse (Ajami 48), as if his martyrdom were more important than any other aspect of his existence. US attempts to counteract the wave of propaganda coming from the Al Jazeera studios are feeble at best. As Ajami puts it, "the enmity runs too deep" (51). Even as US and Israeli diplomats and spokespersons appear on Al Jazeera with increasing frequency to combat the station's obvious bias,

> the station will pursue its own oppositional agenda. Al Jazeera's reporters see themselves as "anti-imperialists." These men and women are convinced that the rulers of the Arab world have given in to American might; these are broadcasters who play to an Arab gallery whose political bitterness they share—and feed. In their eyes, it is an unjust, aggressive war they are covering in Afghanistan. Watching Al Jazeera makes all of this distressingly clear. (Ajami 51)

Furthermore, Al Jazeera's reach is rapidly becoming global. In addition to beaming its signal to viewers in at least 20 Arab nations via satellite dish downlinks, Al Jazeera is offered as a premium cable channel in Great Britain and to roughly 150,000 subscribers in the United States as part of a package of Arabic programming (Ajami 52). One of Al Jazeera's most popular programs is a Larry King–style talk show ominously entitled *The First of the Century's Wars*, in which the host, Montaha al Ramhi, offers strident anti-American and anti-Israeli propaganda interspersed with commercials for Western consumer goods, such as Hugo Boss Deep Red perfume (Ajami 78). Other Arab television stations have far wider audiences, including the Middle East Broadcast Center (MBC) based in Saudi Arabia, and Lebanese Broadcasting Corporation International (LBCI)

(Ajami 78). Both are far more restrained in their coverage of events in the Middle East and are hugely popular with audiences. Yet Al Jazeera's slickly packaged programming captures the most international attention precisely because of its inflammatory nature. The Voice of America has begun an aggressive campaign of radio broadcasts featuring Arab pop music mixed with pro-US public service announcements, but most observers perceive this strategy as being too little, too late. As long as Al Jazeera maintains its current status as a putative voice of the disenfranchised, it will continue to remain a high-profile antagonist, broadcasting its message of intolerance in a 24-hour stream to a populace with few resources to alternative media outlets.

The United States' own response to the events of September 11 has been decidedly mixed, as if the entire affair is, at some level, incomprehensible. And portents were clearly present. Microsoft's *Flight Simulator* video game, in fact, allows its players to pilot virtual jet planes through the skies of the United States, and if they so desire, to crash into various landmarks as they attempt to land. As Nicholas Lemann describes it:

> Part of the fun of *Flight Simulator* is that, in addition to simulating flight, it lets you crash, which has the peculiar appeal that comes from playing out a universal fear without consequence. [...] You can crash into the runway, or you can crash into buildings, including the World Trade Center. You aim for one of the towers, it looms larger and larger through the cockpit window, finally filling it, and then there is a flash and the screen fades out. (37)

When Kabul fell to Allied forces, Western journalists noticed that among the items strewn about in the wreckage of the Al Qaeda safe houses were instructions on how to operate the *Flight Simulator* game. Indeed, as Lemann points out, one has "only to encounter a professional flight simulator to see how little difference there is between it and the P.C. [home use] version" (37). The HBO television movie *Path to Paradise: The Untold Story of the World Trade Center Bombing* (1997) documents the 1993 World Trade Center bombing and demonstrates exactly how easy it was for the bombers to gain access to the building (see Battaglio 25, 31). A frustrated terrorist utters the now-prescient final line of dialogue in *Path to Paradise* as he looks at the World Trade Center towers: "Next time, we'll bring them both down." The film makes clear that the terrorists' battle for the world's attention is far from over, and repeat assaults on the twin towers can be counted on as a natural consequence of world events (Busch and Laski 46).

Spectacles detailing the destruction of Manhattan and the 1930s version of the World Trade Center and the Empire State Building are as old as *King Kong* (1933). Films such as *Independence Day* (1996) and *Deep Impact* (1998), to name just two of many examples, reveled in the destruction of vast metropolitan centers, whereas *The Siege* (1998) depicts what might happen in the aftermath of conventional bomb attacks in Manhattan: martial law, concentration camps for Arab nationals, and the dictatorial abuse of powers. The prophetic nature of *The Siege* in light of current events is just one of the many ways in which Hollywood has flirted with the concepts of invasion, destruction, and the collapse of Western civilization, ideas that were a staple of the Cold War 1950s. Indeed, the Communist regime in Russia provided the background for any number of hyperparanoid films from the 1920s onward, including *The Red Dance* (1928), a tale of the Russian revolution; *Red Danube* (1949), in which a ballerina (Janet Leigh) is pursued by Soviet agents; *The Red Dragon* (1945), yet another Charlie Chan series entry involving the search for plans of a secret weapon; *The Red Menace* (1949), in which a returning war veteran inadvertently becomes entangled with Communist spies; the astounding *Red Planet Mars* (1952), in which God is discovered to be alive, well, and living on Mars, broadcasting anti-Communist messages to scientist Peter Graves; *Red Salute* (1935), in which socialite Barbara Stanwyck's suitor (Hardie Albright) spouts Communist propaganda as a bizarre comic relief figure; and *Red Dawn* (1984), a typically heavy-handed John Milius project, depicting the invasion of the United States by Soviet paratroopers with an enormous amount of violence. But when the Soviet Union collapsed, Hollywood needed a new menace. Where was this new foe to be found? As Jim Hoberman suggests, the enemy is now "everywhere."

For Hollywood, this "unspecified enemy," in Deleuze and Guattari's phrase, was variously visualized as Euro-terrorists in *Die Hard* (1988),

71

narco-terrorists in *Die Hard 2* (1990), neo-Nazi terrorists in *Die Hard with a Vengeance* (1995), homegrown terrorists in *Under Siege* (1992), "international" terrorists in *Under Siege 2* (1995), extraterrestrial terrorists in *Independence Day* (1996), microorganic terrorists in *Outbreak* (1995), dino-terrorists in *The Lost World: Jurassic Park* (1997), Russian terrorists in *Air Force One* (1997), Bosnian terrorists in *The Peacemaker* (1997), and Islamic terrorists in *True Lies* (1994), *Executive Decision* (1996), and *The Siege* (1998). ("All as It Had Been" 110)

Hoberman goes on to point out that in the aftermath of September 11, a number of forthcoming terrorist dramas had to be shelved or reedited, including *Collateral Damage* (2002); *Deadline*, a hijack film written for director James Cameron that never made it past the script stage; *World War III*, a proposed Jerry Bruckheimer film in which terrorist invaders drop nuclear bombs on Seattle and San Diego; *Big Trouble* (2002), a Tim Allen "comedy" centered on a bomb on a passenger jet; and *Nose Bleed*, a Jackie Chan comedy in which the veteran action star would have stopped "a terrorist plot to blow up the WTC" ("All as It Had Been" 110). Nor does the list stop there. As Hoberman continues:

A new self-censorship was in place. The CBS show *The Agency* dropped a reference to Osama bin Laden. *Sex and the City* trimmed views of the twin towers; Paramount air-brushed them from the poster for *Sidewalks of New York* [2002]. Sony yanked their *Spider-Man* trailer so as to eliminate images of the WTC and similarly ordered retakes on *Men in Black II* that would replace the WTC with the Chrysler Building. DreamWorks changed the end of *The Time Machine*, which rained moon fragments down on New York. ("All as It Had Been" 110)

And at least one Hollywood veteran saw all of this as nothing more or less than a prophecy fulfilled. Director Robert Altman told the Associated Press in an interview shortly after the World Trade Center attack that movies such as the ones discussed in the preceding lines "set the pattern, and these people have copied the movies. Nobody would have thought to commit an atrocity like that unless they'd seen it in a movie. [...] I just believe we created this atmosphere and taught them how to do it" (qtd. in Hoberman, "All as It Had Been" 110). Indeed, Altman has a point. Abu Zubaydah, the chief of operations for bin Laden's terror network, told investigators that he was thinking of blowing up "the statue in the water" (the Statue of Liberty) as well as "the bridge in that movie," referring to the 1998 *Godzilla* remake, in which the monster is finally trapped in the cables of the Brooklyn Bridge ("Al-Qaida Got Ideas" 3A).

Not surprisingly, once the images of the September 11 disaster were an accomplished fact, duly videotaped from a variety of angles by both professional and amateur video recorders, they became fair game for a new series of pornographic disaster videos, not unlike the notorious *Faces of Death* series. CNN, CNBC, Fox News, and other US outlets broadcast and rebroadcast the images of the twin towers being hit over and over again like a porno loop, but in China, enterprising entrepreneurs went one step further, creating such instant DVD disaster movies as *The Century's Great Catastrophe* (2001), *Surprise Attack on America* (2001), and *America's Disaster: The Pearl Harbor of the Twenty-First Century* (2001) (Hessler 83). These hybrid productions, freely mixing pirated news footage with equally illegal clips from conventional Hollywood disaster movies, appeared fewer than 72 hours after the World Trade Center collapse. The tag lines on the DVD boxes were appropriately sensationalistic:

Several planes attack America!
The World Trade Center totally destroyed.
The Pentagon and Capitol Hill attacked by planes.
White House Capitol Hill continuous Explosions. [sic]
Who is the murderer? It's still unknown. (qtd. in Hessler 83)

The tapes freely mix fact and fiction with an almost Vertovian abandon. Images of Osama bin Laden and George W. Bush are mixed with the appropriated names and faces of Tom Hanks, Ving Rhames, and Jerry Bruckheimer, as well as the corporate logos of Touchstone and Columbia Pictures. The theme from *Jaws* plays on the soundtrack as the twin towers collapse. Clips from *Wall Street* (1987) and the US remake of *Godzilla* are intertwined with actual newsreel footage to create an ersatz Manhattan landscape, at once elegant and treacherous (Hessler 84), while a stentorian narrator comments on the soundtrack that:

> Terrorists are not happy with superpowers like America. There are many reasons for their dissatisfaction, and the most important one is that the powerful nations push their principles on other countries. (Hessler 84)

While Hollywood has been juggling its release schedule and trimming and/or scrapping potentially controversial projects in the wave of PG "family" films that have dominated the box office since September 11, another genre also deserves our attention: the war film. *Windtalkers* (2002), a film covering the work of Navajo "code talkers" during World War II starring Nicolas Cage, retreats to the past with sentimental ferocity. At first reluctant to become involved with the Navajos because of his racist attitudes, Cage grudgingly learns to respect his fellow Americans for the espionage work during the last "good war." The Tom Clancy thriller *The Sum of All Fears* (2002) deals with a band of terrorists who blow up the a football stadium in Baltimore during the Super Bowl and attempt to fix the blame on the new Russian government "in the hopes of rekindling the Cold War" (Busch and Laski 49). No doubt Clancy would prefer it this way: things were so much simpler then. The trailer for the film, as is the norm in the contemporary marketplace, gives away most of the film's plot twists (hence, a presold narrative with few surprises) and features graphic footage of the bomb attack itself as its visual centerpiece. Although some industry analysts such as Mark Gill of Miramax feel that "the violent action genre will go away. It will probably be better in the long term. Films will be more like Hitchcock and less like a 1980s shoot-'em-up" (Busch and Laski 53); the anecdotal evidence seems to suggest otherwise. Although several violent projects have been scrapped (a particularly egregious example being *WW3.com*, in which a Boeing 767 crashes on Broadway and slides into Central Park during a Simon and Garfunkle concert, wreaking predictably spectacular carnage; Busch and Laski 53), numerous other exceedingly brutal films are making it to the screen and doing excellent business.

In 2001 audiences were offered violent thrillers such as *Pearl Harbor, Black Hawk Down*, and *Apocalypse Now Redux.* In 2002, *Charlotte Gray, Behind Enemy*

Lines, No Man's Land, and *Dark Blue World* have been released, along with *We Were Soldiers* and *Hart's War* (Fuller 122). There was also talk for a time of a new version of *Hogan's Heroes* starring Russell Crowe, which may still come to fruition because, as Graham Fuller argues, the genre of the war film is as relevant in 2002 as it was in 1918:

> Whereas westerns, gangster films and musicals are made rarely these days because they became outmoded by cultural and historical change (respectively, the receding of the frontier, the receding of prohibition, and the advent of rock 'n' roll), the war genre never disappeared because war didn't—and because war has made for timelessly kinetic movies in the hands of such directors as King Vidor (*The Big Parade*, 1925), Lewis Milestone (*All Quiet on the Western Front*, 1930), Samuel Fuller (*The Big Red One*, 1980), Francis Ford Coppola (*Apocalypse Now*, 1979), Oliver Stone (*Platoon*, 1986), Terrence Malick (*The Thin Red Line*, 1998) and Steven Spielberg (*Saving Private Ryan*, 1998). (122)

Fuller continues with an apt comparison between Ridley Scott's *Black Hawk Down*, in which a group of US soldiers is besieged by a vastly superior number of combatants in Mogadishu on October 3, 1993, with severe casualties as the predictable result. Throughout Scott's film, the Somali soldiers are depicted as little more than ignorant savages and, in the best war film tradition, dehumanized and stripped of individual identity. The ferocity of the gunplay in *Black Hawk Down* may indeed be a reasonable facsimile of the real event, but Fuller is not far off the mark when he tellingly compares the film to Cy Endfield's *Zulu* (1964), a deeply colonialist film in which a group of outmanned British soldiers attempts to hold on to a small African outpost of the then–British Empire. As Fuller comments:

> *Zulu* unfolds on the same land mass as Black Hawk Down—America's humanitarian nation-building in Somalia the U.N.-sanctioned equivalent of Britain's empire-building in South Africa—and trades in the same kind of white hubris and jaw-dropping heroics. Assegais stand in for rocket

launchers, but British private Henry Hook's famous comment that he and his fellow soldiers at Rorke's Drift "were pinned like rats in a hole" evokes exactly the experience of the downed American pilot played by Ron Eldard in *Black Hawk Down.*

Seventeen British and Natal soldiers were killed at Rorke's Drift; 18 Americans at Mogadishu; approximately 500 Zulus and 500 Somalis died. But whereas the Zulus saluted the British soldiers' bravery from a hilltop at the end of *Zulu*, the Somalis who let the last defenseless Americans scurry out of Mogadishu look on with hatred. History comes back to haunt itself, but the fury of nations made to feel inferior by others only grows. (122)

What Americans view as a paean to patriotism, other nations view as a deliberately hostile enterprise. The very absence of motivation and characterization is what makes *Black Hawk Down* so disturbing; although it is a spectacular display of pyrotechnics coupled with equally adroit editing and computer-generated effects, it is as resolutely racist and oblivious to its own internal contradictions as the most blatantly inflammatory film from World War II. At the beginning of Lambert Hillyer's 1943 serial *The Batman* (the first screen incarnation of Bob Kane's famous character), an alarmed narrator informs us that "a wise government has rounded up all the shifty eyed Japs and put them into relocation camps, where they belong," as the viewer witnesses scenes of a deserted back lot San Francisco Chinatown. What follows seems risible to a contemporary viewer, as the evil Dr. Tito Daka (J. Carrol Naish) and his Fifth Column agents set out on a campaign of sabotage to cripple the Allied Powers' war effort, using outlandish devices such as a "zombie helmet" and assorted Oriental torture devices. Yet no one thought anything of it at the time; if anything, such absurdist propaganda was welcomed by the White House. Tellingly, these lines of dialogue have been removed from new copies of the serial on DVD, as Hollywood once again seeks to erase its own past. But the rest of the serial, which was rereleased uncut theatrically in 1966 as an exercise in camp to a surprisingly good reception at the box office, gives ample evidence of the film's true propagandistic intent. *Zulu*'s continuing popularity (traceable, in part, to the participation of a young Michael Caine in the film) strikes me as profoundly disturbing given the film's outrageous racism and devotion to the concept of global imperialism. Perhaps we will look back in 2050 and wonder how we ever allowed films such as *Black Hawk Down* to be made, or *We Were Soldiers*, or *Hart's War*, and why they were so popular with audiences of the first part of the 21st century. Then again, we may see them as authentic artifacts of a time and period when such saber rattling was a necessary tonic for a jaded public, weary of the responsibilities of peace, satiated only by the phantom violence of video games and hyperviolent filmic spectacles, and eager for genuine conflict.

Such 1950s and 1960s Red Scare relics as the Yugoslavian film *Atomic War Bride* (1960; original title *Rat*, 1960) and the resolutely American *This Is Not a Test* (1962) depict a world in which nuclear annihilation is inevitable; all one can do is wait for the coming conflagration. One could dismiss these feature-length oddities as exploitational aberrations were it not for the existence of numerous government and private promotional films that deliver essentially the same message. The consequences of such an attack, however, were greatly minimized. In *You Can Beat the A-Bomb* (1950), a family survives Armageddon by closing the windows and hiding under the furniture. Soon, dad tells his obedient family that they will be able to go upstairs to "see what happened." The film also dispels "nuclear myths" such as the danger of looking directly into an atomic bomb blast because it may cause blindness, "but this will only be temporary." In addition, any danger of damage to reproductive organs is also a "myth"; the atomic bomb will "absolutely not affect your ability to have children." Significantly, this last comment is addressed to an audience of visibly relieved men; women are seen as being able to open and close curtains and gather blankets to protect the family from the dangers of fallout, but nuclear preparedness is clearly a masculine pursuit in these films. The grade school training film *Duck and Cover* (1948) presents the cartoon character Bert the Turtle, who knows what to do when he sees an atomic blast. Just "duck and cover," with your hands placed tightly over the back of your head. You can hide under your school desk, or in a doorway, or in a Civil Defense shelter; all of these methods supposedly provide excellent protection in the event of a nuclear attack. *Survival Under Atomic Attack* (1951) depicts much the same scenario; find an appropriate doorway or closet, and you'll get through without too much difficulty. Just remember to put cardboard or blankets over the windows. Similarly, farmers are advised that a few bales of hay in front of the barn windows will protect livestock; and, of course, everyone should build his or her own personal fallout shelter. The outright mendacity of these "educational" films is astounding. When Peter Watkins directed the classic docudrama *The War Game* in 1965 depicting what would really happen in the event of an all out nuclear attack on Great Britain, the BBC refused to run it, asserting that it would disturb their viewers. Although not a single sequence in the film is authentic, the 47-minute featurette won an Academy Award for Best Documentary in 1967, a tribute to its gritty cinéma vérité appearance. In Watkins's film, which set the standard for the numerous depictions of nuclear conflict that were to follow, the bomb kills millions immediately, sets houses on fire, and sentences the rest of the population to a lingering death from radiation poisoning. In stark contrast to the "preparedness" films of the 1950s, Watkins demonstrates that no matter what precautions one takes, the loss of life will be enormous, governments will collapse, cities will crumble, and civilization as we conceive it will cease to exist. If one is suspicious of contemporary government pronouncements regarding the effects of terrorism in the United States, perhaps it is due in part to the legacy of these films, which deliberately sought to mislead the public into believing that nuclear war is a viable tactical option. But in the current political climate, particularly after the revelations concerning the intelligence failures surrounding the attack on the World Trade Center, politicians are taking the opposite tack. Far from holding out the false hope that we can survive an attack, administration officials are now predicting that terrorist attacks are inevitable and will be more devastating than the events on September 11.

These pronouncements come in the wake of a series of rumors surrounding September 11 that have kept the public in a perpetual state of anxiety. Not surprisingly, these rumors and hoaxes proliferated rapidly through the Internet, so much so that several sites were created to debunk them. One of the most vicious rumors claimed that "4,000 Jews Did Not Go to Work On Sept. 11," as "reported" on the US Web site *Information Times.* According to reporter Bryan Curtis, this slanderous accusation, implicating the Israeli government in the World Trade Center attacks, first surfaced in a television "report" on Lebanon's

Al-Manar television network on September 17. Since that time, it has been picked up and recirculated by anti-Israeli groups throughout the Internet, and has, for some, assumed the false status of "fact." Curtis details the genesis of this particular lie and its long afterlife:

the first mention of Israeli involvement in the attacks came in a Sept. 17 report on Lebanon's Al-Manar Television. *The Los Angeles Times* reports that the terrorist group Hezbollah has free access to Al-Manar's airwaves, and the station's Web site claims that the station exists to "stage an effective psychological warfare with the Zionist enemy."

The next day at 6:26 A.M., the American Web site *Information Times* published an article headlined "4,000 Jews Did Not Go to Work At WTC On Sept. 11," and credited it to an "Al-Manar Television Special Investigative Report." This was not the first time that *Information Times* had pointed the finger at Israel. The day after the attacks, it warned in an article that the "terrorist government of Israel [...] cannot be ruled out" as a suspect.

Within days, the story appeared in newspapers around the world. A remarkably similar version appeared under the byline of Irina Malenko in Russia's *Pravda* on Sept. 21. *Pravda* removed the article from its Web site a few hours after posting, calling it a "great and foolish mistake" [...]. On Sept. 21, the *Chicago Tribune* reported that a Pakistani paper, which it did not name, had published a similar account. In his Sept. 23 *Slate* "Dispatch" from Islamabad, Peter Maass reported that a local pro-Taliban politician repeated the 4,000 Jews claim at an anti-US rally. On Sept. 26, Pakistan's *Business Recorder* printed the story about 4,000 Jews in language almost identical to the original Al-Manar article as a letter to the editor under the name "Hakeem." The same day, *The New York Times* reported that the allegation had appeared in a newsletter published by an Islamic charity and in lesson plans prepared by Egyptian middle-school teachers. On Oct. 4, *The Chicago Tribune* spotted the allegation in a Saudi paper, which it did not name. In the Oct. 8 issue of *Time*, Tim McGirk reported from Pakistan that the story had swept through the country's mosques and Urdu newspapers.

On Sept. 28, *USA Today* repeated the claim in the context that "Muslims the world over" had tried to pin the attack on Israel. USA Today did not explain the origin of the charge. *The Village Voice* did the same on Oct. 2. The hoax-debunking site *Snopes.com* assailed the story, as well. With the Web as a weapon, a lie spreads quickly and easily. With the Web as a corrective tool, the same lie becomes much easier to bat away. (Curtis)

The rumors include the patently ridiculous assertion that Osama bin Laden owns *Snapple*, the popular soft drink; that the "face of Satan" could be seen in the smoke emanating from the twin towers before their collapse; that "a firefighter or policeman (depending on [the] version) survived the collapse of one of the WTC towers by 'surfing' the rubble as it fell from the 82nd [or in some versions, the 83rd] floor," and that Nostradamus predicted the World Trade Center attack (he did not, but some of Nostradamus's quatrains were rewritten after the attack to prove the point; *Urban Legends and Folklore*, "Rumor Watch, Part III"). Perhaps the most elaborate hoax perpetuated on the public is the purported existence of a "last photo" from atop the World Trade Center building, depicting a tourist with a backpack staring into the camera, as a jetliner approaches the building from the back of the shot (*Urban Legends and Folklore*, "Tourist Guy"). The accompanying text in the original e-mail attached to this photo claims that the photo

is a picture that was taken of a tourist atop the World Trade Center Tower, the first to be struck by a terrorist attack. This camera was found but the subject in the picture had not yet been located.

Makes you see things from a very different position. Please share this and find any way you can to help Americans not to be victims in the future of such cowardly attacks. (*Urban Legends and Folklore*, "Tourist Guy")

Shortly after the message appeared, however, members of the media analyzed the photo and dismissed as a fake for a number of obvious reasons, including the speed of the plane, the fact that the North Tower has no rooftop observation deck, and other inconsistencies. Another rumor claimed that CNN faked footage of Palestinians "celebrating" the attacks, recycling footage of a 1991 festival to create a news story. The footage, however, was "shot by a Reuters crew in East Jerusalem on September 11," as both Reuters and CNN authenticated (*Urban Legends and Folklore*, "Rumor Watch"). More bizarre rumors, however, appear to be authentic. Wreckage from the World Trade Center disaster was offered on eBay for ghoulish souvenir hunters, but eBay immediately put a stop to it. The cover art for a CD by a pop band called The Coup did indeed depict the twin towers exploding behind the group in a fake photo created two months before the attack, scheduled for release in mid-September. Needless to say, the group immediately pulled the offending cover art and released the CD with another graphic design shortly thereafter (*Urban Legends and Folklore*, "Rumor Watch").

In such an atmosphere of rumor and speculation, paranoia seems to be the most politically effective strategy. Fallout shelters, those 1950s relics, are making a comeback with numerous Web sites offering prefab or custom-built shelters aimed at high-income families. Other sites, which offer detailed instructions—including scale blueprints and material sources—for building a do-it-yourself shelter, are available for those with less income. On one such site, author Cresson H. Kearny explains that:

> Having a permanent, ready-to-use, well-supplied fallout shelter would greatly improve millions of American families' chances of surviving a nuclear attack. Dual use family shelters—shelters that also are useful in peacetime—are the ones that Americans are most likely to build in normal peacetime and to maintain for years in good condition for use in a nuclear war.
>
> The longer nuclear peace lasts, the more difficult it will be, even during a recognized crisis, to believe that the unthinkable war is about to strike us and that we should build expedient shelters and immediately take other protective actions. The lifesaving potential of permanent, ready-to-use family shelters will increase with the years. ("Permanent Family Fallout")

In short, one can use the fallout shelter as a recreational facility before one is forced to inhabit it on a continuous basis as the result of a nuclear attack. The shelter will, of course, contain a year's supply of food, which must be kept fresh at all times. In fact, it is "a good idea" to start eating some of this survival food now to prepare for the coming nuclear onslaught.

> The emotional shock of suddenly being forced by war to occupy your shelter will be even worse if you have to adapt suddenly to an unaccustomed diet. It would be a good idea to occasionally practice eating only your survival rations for a day or two, and to store in your shelter a two- week supply of canned and dry foods similar to those your family normally eats. Then it will be easier if war forces you to make the changeover. (Kearny, "Permanent Family Fallout")

Kearny has, indeed, made quite a mark in the home fallout shelter industry with several associated products, such as the Kearny Fallout Meter, marketed under his brand name (*Two Tigers*).

Indeed, several observers feel that more fallout shelters should be built in the United States immediately. The *NewsMax* web site featured an article on February 15, 2002, decrying the fact that "fallout shelters fall short in the U.S.," while noting that:

> In a 1999 survey by the Pew Research Center, 64 per cent of those polled stated that they thought a major terrorist attack on the U.S. involving biological or chemical weapons would happen sometime over the next half century. [...] In the meantime, some Americans are voting with their pocketbooks and digging up their backyards just like the good old days of the Cold War. "They are treating me less like a crazy woman than they did before," Dr. Jane Orient of Tucson, Ariz., who promotes home shelters as head of Doctors for Disaster Preparedness, told *NewsMax.com*. If [Dr. Orient] had it her way, the U.S. would be more like the Russians, Chinese or Swiss. The Moscow subways double as shelters, equipped with blast doors. Much of the population of Beijing could be evacuated underground in about 10 minutes. And Switzerland has shelter for 110 per cent of its population in private homes and public buildings. (Eberhart)

Figure 1 Preview of coming attractions: New York City is vaporized by an atomic blast in *Invasion U.S.A.* (1952)

Figure 2 New York City as atomic wasteland: *Invasion U.S.A.* (1952)

Figure 3 The war of the past: Mutual Assured Destruction. *The Last War* (1961; original title *Sekai daisenso*, 1961)

Figure 4 The Arc de Triomphe is destroyed in *The Last War* (1961; original title *Sekai daisenso*, 1961)

Figure 5 Manhattan, before the collapse of the World Trade Center, is decimated by a nuclear attack in *The Last War* (1961; original title *Sekai daisenso*, 1961)

Figure 6 The city collapses in *Tidal Wave* (1973; original title *Nippon chinbotsu*, 1973)

Figure 7 Airborne firefighters attempt to halt the rampaging fire that engulfs the failing metropolis in *Tidal Wave* (1973; original title *Nippon chinbotsu*, 1973)

Figure 8 Skyscrapers collapse from the intense heat in *Tidal Wave* (1973; original title *Nippon chinbotsu*, 1973)

Figure 9 The end of the world occurs through natural catastrophe in *When Worlds Collide* (1951)

Figure 10   Survivors carry on with the tasks of civilization in *The Bed Sitting Room* (1969)

Figure 11   The city is leveled by earthquake in *San Francisco* (1936)

Figure 12 The ruins of Manhattan in *Deluge* (1933)

Figure 13 Tragedy on a human scale in *The Day the Sky Exploded* (1961; *La Morte viene dallo spazio*, 1958)

Figure 14 The staging of Armageddon; synthetic destruction in *Hooper* (1978)

Figure 15 Transportation becomes superfluous in *The Last Days of Man on Earth* (1973; original title *The Final Programme*, 1973)

And while we're relaxing in our shelters, let's make sure we listen to the right music to keep up our spirits. If we don't make the correct choices, don't worry: corporate America is there to protect us from ourselves. Shortly after the events of September 11, Clear Channel Communications, the largest radio broadcasting conglomerate in the United States, with more than 1,000 stations, issued an e-mail list to its affiliates, advising them against playing certain songs on the radio because of inappropriate content. Included in the list were such titles as *Walk Like an Egyptian*, *Peace Train*, *Knockin' on Heaven's Door*, and *What a Wonderful World*, along with numerous other titles. As Douglas Wolk explains:

> The Clear Channel list proscribes whatever might serve as a reminder of reality: songs that allude to fire (*Disco Inferno*), flying (*Jet Airliner*), jumping (Van Halen's *Jump*, but not the Pointer Sisters' or Kriss Kross's), Tuesdays (*Ruby Tuesday*), New York (*On Broadway*), absence (*Black Is Black*), death (*Mack the Knife*), and life going on (*Ob-La-Di, Ob-La-Da*). Musical aggression is suspect; Alien Ant Farm's growly cover of *Smooth Criminal* is on the list, but not Michael Jackson's original. And left politics are out altogether, even in manifestations as blameless as the Youngbloods' *Get Together*. Hence the blanket dismissal of [Rage Against the Machine's entire catalogue] (they're loud, too), and the bizarre presence of John Lennon's *Imagine*.

Although Clear Channel predictably denied that such a ban was ever intended, blaming the entire affair on an "advisory" internal e-mail that accidentally made its way into the public sphere, the ban was real enough. Even though it was not a formal edict, it was clearly a reflection of corporate policy, and who wants to alienate his or her employer? Furthermore, most of the stations that Clear Channel owns use a 24-hour satellite music service, rather than spinning CDs "in house." Thus, these songs disappeared from Clear Channel's preferred national playlist for a time, another reminder, as if any were needed, of the dangers of hyperconglomerization.

And as the hypersurveillant state is monitoring what we listen to, it is also watching us at work or at play. We have grown sadly accustomed to security cameras in malls, shopping centers, banks, casinos, and convenience stores as one of the less desirable byproducts of the video age. Now, with the relatively new science of facial recognition technology, our faces can be scanned without our knowing it from a variety of angles and then compared to a database of "known terrorists" compiled by the US government. And where is the perfect place to install one of the first of these invasive devices? Why, the Statue of Liberty, naturally. As Sara Kugler reports, this is only the first step in a planned national rollout of the facial recognition devices:

> As visitors to the Statue of Liberty and Ellis Island board a ferry from Manhattan, a new surveillance system is taking their pictures and comparing them to a database of terror suspects compiled by the federal government.

> The system was installed just ahead of the Memorial Day weekend, days after the FBI said it had received uncorroborated information that terrorists had threatened New York and some of its landmarks, including the Statue of Liberty.

> "We're going to look at the facial recognition technology to see if it can be expanded for use in other parts of the city," Gov. George Pataki said on Saturday during a visit to the statue with his family.

> "People are still coming to New York City, to the Statue of Liberty, from around our country and around our world because they appreciate that this is a secure, safe and free city," he said.

> The facial recognition technology, provided by Visionics, of Jersey City, N.J., already is used in some airports and government buildings.

> Mustafa Koita, a manager for Visionics, said the system searches 1 million images per second. "It has not slowed any of the foot traffic and I think people feel a little safer, too," Koita said.

Several cameras at varying heights snapped tourists' photographs just before they walked through a security checkpoint to board a ferry to the statue and Ellis Island, both operated by the National Park Service. Koita said the cameras were positioned so it would be difficult for people to look away or hide their faces.

The system was received with enthusiasm by tourists waiting in line on Saturday.

"I think it's great. It's a good safety precaution that is definitely necessary," said Joe Scali, 57, of North Haven, Conn.

Surrounded in the ferry terminal by signs warning that facial recognition cameras were in use, Dave Miller, of Madison, Ala., accepted the increased security as part of post-Sept. 11 life in the United States.

"I've got nothing to hide, and neither should anyone else," said Miller, 49. "Life changed on Sept. 11, and we're going to have to give up some freedoms so that we can continue to have freedoms."

But the American Civil Liberties Union criticized the system, calling it "ineffective" and "an insult to the American people."

"To have such a system in place near the Statue of Liberty [...] is both ironic and disheartening," said Barry Steinhardt, director of the group's Technology and Liberty Program, in a statement on the group's Web site.

Aside from the observed irony of setting up such a hypersurveillance system at a location memorializing the concept of personal freedom and liberty, even more alarming is the apparent acquiescence of the public. "We're going to have to give up some freedoms so that we can continue to have freedoms." What on earth does this mean? Because the cameras are positioned so that it is "difficult for people to look away or hide their faces," we have in this new technology the nightmare of Jeremy Bentham and Michel Foucault's panopticon, in which everyone is under constant surveillance all the time, but with an added and even more sinister twist. Not only are we being photographed, but our faces are being compared to "1 million images a second" in the US database for facial characteristics, hair color, eyes, visible scars, height, skin color, and other identifiable external markers. One wonders exactly how many "faces" are in the monster database the FBI created for this system and precisely what profiling tools are used to create a possible match.

And what is the government doing with all the new information it gathers under this hypersurveillant regime? One is finally struck with the lack of choice an individual has in this matter. If one wishes to visit the Statue of Liberty, one is forced to submit to this invasive technological procedure. There is no appeal and no personal contact with the equipment, which impassively documents the thousands of visitors who pass by daily with the gaze of the machine that controls. A current television commercial shows several cars running a red light and getting an automatic ticket because of it, courtesy of a variation on this new technology, already in place in many cities throughout the United States. However, in the commercial, this technology is rendered anthropomorphic, almost "human," as it "falls in love" with a particular brand of car, repeatedly snapping the car's picture, even though it is not guilty of any traffic violation. At test screenings, the commercial was effective and got a laugh from its test group. We will grow to love these machines. We will "feel a little safer, too," because these facial recognition devices are watching over us, shuffling our faces through an ever-expanding database of enemies of the state. Where can we be alone? Where can we find privacy? Certainly not in the public sphere; how long before the privacy of our homes becomes compromised by such machinery as well?

In the meantime, administration officials are keeping up a steady drumbeat of terror, advising us, essentially, that the end is at hand. In an interview on CNBC, US Secretary of Defense Donald Rumsfeld was asked about his comments on the state of terrorism in the United States and also about comments Vice President Dick Cheney made. Alan Murray of CNBC opened his questions by noting that:

[Murray] Mr. Secretary [...], the Vice President was on TV on Sunday and said, "I think that the prospects of a future attack on the U.S. are almost a certainty. It could happen tomorrow, it could happen next week, it could happen next year, but they will keep trying and we have to be prepared." Is he talking about new information there, about imminent attacks?

[Rumsfeld] We get new information all the time. Some of it is valid and some of it proves not to be valid. There is no question but that the Vice President is exactly right. We have to know that there are hundreds and hundreds of these people trained in terrorist training camps. They had [a] massive fundraising activity base, very well trained, and they have been disbursed all across the world including the United States of America. It is only realistic to expect that there will be another attack, and we do have to be prepared. Although I would rephrase that slightly.

The only way to deal with terrorists is to go after them. You can't defend every place at every time. Even if you know there is going to be an attack, it's almost impossible. You simply have to go find them where they are and dry up their money and arrest them and capture or kill them. (Rumsfeld, "Interview with Alan Murray")

As the program progressed, Rumsfeld was asked, "What kind of conflict are we preparing for now?" He responded that, unlike the Cold War, with a readily identifiable enemy, the new war would be waged on many fronts, in a variety of "asymmetrical" ways:

What we can know is we have vulnerabilities. We know that. We know what we have strength in and what we have weaknesses in, and we know that the people who don't wish us well look at that and say to themselves there's no point in developing a big army, navy and air force trying to go up against the United States. So they look for asymmetrical ways they can go about it, and certainly about as asymmetrical as you can get is flying an American airliner into this building. But things like ballistic missiles, cruise missiles, cyber attacks, terrorist attacks, weapons of mass destruction, chemical, biological, nuclear, radiation weapons. All of those things have the advantage of an asymmetrical approach to it. So when we say capabilities based we can imagine the kinds of things people can do to us and the kinds of capabilities we need to deal with those potential threats. (Rumsfeld, "Interview with Alan Murray")

Quite a laundry list. And in other interviews, officials from George W. Bush on down have warned that the public must be on constant alert against the threat of new terrorist attacks from whatever source. The headlines tell the story; "US Officials Raise Spectre of Attack" (*Taipei Times*); "Rumsfeld Joins Grim Forecast on Terrorism" (*USA Today*); "Rumsfeld: Terrorists to Get Doomsday Bomb" (*Washington Times*); "Officials: Terrorists May Target Tall Apt. Bldgs.; FBI Chief: "We Will Not Be Able to Stop It," (*CNN.com*); "Rumsfeld: More Attacks Could Be Deadlier than Sept. 11th" (*Californian NC Times*); "Rumsfeld: Threat Warnings Are 'Just the Truth'" (*DefenseLink* web site); "'Be Vigilant, Heed Alerts,' Cheney Warns" (*DefenseLink* web site); and others too numerous to mention. On the other hand, any criticism of these dire predictions is met with furious dismissal, and here again, the surrounding news coverage gives some indication of the intensity of the debate. When word leaked out of the 1999 report that identified Osama bin Laden as a genuine terrorist threat, a report that was apparently lost in the shuffling of documents from one branch of the government to the other, a flurry of accusations followed. "1999 Report Warned of Suicide Hijack" by John Solomon of the Associated Press quoted the report *The Sociology and Psychology of Terrorism: Who Becomes a Terrorist and Why?* (Hudson), noting that the report directly stated that, "Suicide bomber(s) belonging to al-Qaida's Martyrdom Battalion could crash-land an aircraft packed with high explosives (C-4 and semtex) into the Pentagon, the headquarters of the Central Intelligence Agency (CIA), or the White House" [...] (Solomon), a warning that apparently went unheeded in Washington.

Soon, other critics jumped on the bandwagon, including US Rep. Cynthia McKinney (D–GA), who implied that the perceived intelligence failure was part of a deliberate government plot, a charge that most rejected (see Eilperin). Nevertheless, leading Democrats continued to press for an inquiry, most notably

US House Minority Leader Dick Gebhardt (D-MO), much to the administration's chagrin. Even some Republicans, such as US Senator Richard Shelby (R-AL), joined the chorus of criticism, noting that, "there was a lot of information. I believe and others believe that if it had been acted on properly, we may have had a different situation on Sept. 11" (Edozien and Morris). Gebhardt agreed: "Was there a failure of intelligence? Did the right officials not act on the intelligence in the right way? These are things we need to find out" (Edozien and Morris). To this cautious inquiry, Vice President Cheney reacted angrily, stating that:

> Democrats in Washington "need to be very cautious not to seek political advantage by making incendiary suggestions [...] that the White House had advance information that would have prevented the tragic attacks of 9/11," [and] labeled some of the criticism as "thoroughly irresponsible and totally unworthy of national leaders in time of war." (Edozien and Morris)

Solomon's article appeared on May 17, 2002. By May 21, Cheney was on the attack, using CNN's *Larry King Live* program to lash out at the administration's critics. Said Cheney:

> When members of Congress suggest that the president of the United States had foreknowledge of the attack on September 11, I think that's outrageous [...]. That's a gross outrageous political attack and it's totally uncalled for. The implication that somehow we had prior knowledge and didn't act on it, I think, is a despicable statement. (qtd. in Mohammed)

But according to Niall Ferguson, all of this political wrangling is beside the point. As he puts it, "ten years from now, historians will look back and see the events of Sept. 11 as mere ripples in a tidal wave of terrorism and political fragmentation," certainly the grimmest forecast of the lot. Ferguson sees the future as an intersection of several social "trends" that will inexorably alter the fabric of human existence, not only in the United States, but also around the world. Ferguson's first "trend" is, as he acknowledges, "obvious enough":

the spread of terrorism—that is to say the use of violence by nonstate organizations in the pursuit of extreme political goals—to the United States. This kind of terrorism has been around for quite a while. Hijacking planes is certainly not new: since the late 1960's, when the tactic first began to be used systematically by the Palestine Liberation Organization and its sympathizers, there have been some 500 hijackings. As for the tactic of flying planes directly at populous targets, what else were the 3,913 Japanese pilots doing who killed themselves and many more American servicemen flying kamikaze missions in 1944 and 1945?

All that was really new on Sept. 11 was that these tried-and-tested tactics were applied in combination and in the United States. Between 1995 and 2000, according to State Department figures, there were more than 2,100 international terrorist attacks. But just 15 of them occurred in North America, causing just seven casualties. It was the successful extension of international terrorism to the United States that was the novelty. (76, 78)

Coupled with the spread of terrorism to US soil is the current economic downturn, which Ferguson sees as being the result of "the nonglobal nature of globalization" (78); that is, the fact that "the overwhelming bulk of American, Canadian and Mexican trade now takes place within the North American Free Trade Area, just as most European trade takes place within Europe" (78). In other words, the United States is economically isolated from its European neighbors and allies, potential or actual. Ferguson then identifies a third trend, "the transition of American global power from informal to formal imperialism." As Ferguson puts it:

Since 1945, the United States has largely been content to exercise influence around the world indirectly: exercising economic leverage through multinational corporations and international agencies like the International Monetary Fund and political power through "friendly" indigenous regimes.

As Britain discovered in the 19th century, however, there are limits to what can be achieved by informal imperialism. Revolutions can overthrow the puppet rulers. New regimes can default on their debts, disrupt trade, go to war with their neighbors—even sponsor terrorism.

Slowly and rather unreflectively, the United States has been responding to crises of this sort by intervening directly in the internal affairs of far-away countries. True, it has tended to do so behind a veil of multilateralism, acting in the name of the United Nations or NATO. But the precedents set in Bosnia and Kosovo are crucial. What happened in the 1990's was that those territories became a new kind of colony: international protectorates underwritten by U.S. military and monetary might. (79)

As Ferguson states, when British Prime Minister Tony Blair and US President Bush joined forces against the Taliban regime in Afghanistan, they reverted to the kind of direct colonialism that Ferguson terms "pure Kipling" (79), alternating carpet bombing with food drops in an attempt to destabilize one regime and replace it with another. For the moment, the strategy seems superficially to have worked, and yet numerous internal factions exist within Afghanistan could easily send things awry. Moreover, in my travels to Europe in the post-September 11 era, I discovered that although much of Western Europe (France, the Netherlands, and Austria, especially) are simultaneously turning to the right, yet proclaiming their disdain for all things American, the British support our actions in the "War on Terror" and see us as the logical new ruler of the international empire. As one British tourist told me over drinks, "someone's got to do it—we've had our chance, and now it's up to you." Nor was this an isolated comment. Even as the policies of the Bush administration continue to create controversy elsewhere, the British seem united in their support of US policy, albeit with a touch of sadness and regret. After all, we used to be a British colony, along with much of the rest of the world, and "the sun never set" on the British Empire. But those days are gone; now, it seems, it's our turn.

At the conclusion of his essay, Ferguson identifies a fourth and final trend, which he dubs "the fragmentation of multicultural polity." As he explains:

Rather than anticipating a clash between monolithic civilizations, we should expect a continued process of political disintegration as religious and ethnic conflicts challenge the integrity of existing multicultural nation-states. Civil war has, after all, been the most frequent kind of war since 1945: something like two-thirds of all postwar conflicts have been within rather than between states. From Yugoslavia to Iraq to Afghanistan, what the United States keeps having to confront is not a united Islam but a succession of fractured polities, racked by internecine war. (The same could be said about Somalia, Sierra Leone and Rwanda.)

Why has economic globalization coincided with political fragment-ation in this contradictory fashion? One possible answer is that globalized market forces increase regional inequalities within traditional nation-states. Another is that the superficial homogenization of popular culture—through Hollywood, the pop-music industry and the Anglicization of technical communication—promotes an accentuation of parochial identities as a kind of a reaction. But the best answer may be that as more and more ethnically heterogeneous countries adopt (with American encouragement) the combination of economic openness and political democracy, their rationale simply falls away. Central government loses its legitimacy as the planner of the economy, and ethnic minorities vote for separatist parties. (79)

In this scenario, Ferguson dolefully argues, "terrorism will be a part of everyday life [...] and the divisions between ethnic and religious groups in the United States—indeed throughout the world—will be ever more pronounced" (79). As we move, then, toward the adoption of English as "the universal language" of business and cultural commerce, we increasingly marginalize those who are not a part of the global pop-culture and corporate trading machine— precisely the peoples who now, rather understandably, seek our destruction. In a global society based on sharing inequities, those without a voice will perpetually seek some means of enfranchisement, whether through diplomacy or terrorism. And as the channels of political and cultural communication become clogged with an onslaught of American movies, pop music, television programming, and hyperconglomerate mergers, the situation in Africa and the Middle East becomes even more desperate. Ferguson does not agree that a "supposedly inescapable 'clash' between a democratic West and an intolerant Islam" will occur because "the most striking features of modern Islam are its amazing heterogeneity and geographic dispersion" (79). In short, Ferguson sees the world as fragmenting into even smaller political units (64 independent countries in 1861 and 192 in 1995; 79), in which corporate interest supersede those of any political state. Islam has become a worldwide religion not confined to any one country or series of countries—or even one particular continent. The other factor to consider here is that the vast majority of the world's population—Jewish, Christian, Muslim, Buddhist—fervently believe in finding a peaceful solution to the current conflicts, whereas those on both the extreme left and right continue to fan the flames of conflict. Is Hollywood helping to bring these disparate factions together and mediate this dispute? Or is the world still one large marketplace for the majors, a territory to be sold with as much penetration as possible? The evidence seems to suggest the latter.

In the aftermath of September 11, Hollywood and the White House sought to find some common ideological ground to create new counterprogramming to further the war effort. As Jill Feiwell and Pamela McClintock of *Daily Variety* noted at a meeting between industry executives and members of the Bush administration at the White House on December 6, 2001, one of the first benefits of the new "war" for Hollywood was the possibility of improved relations with the Republican administration, which has often been sharply critical of the film industry. White House senior advisor Karl Rove set the tone for the meeting when, "[...] bearing a hint of political glory for an industry often maligned in Washington, Rove and other Bush administration officials thanked the entertainment biz for its aid and creative know-how" (Feiwell and McClintock 1).

Projects discussed included public service announcements, "movie trailers, USO tours and messages targeted at foreign audiences" (Feiwell and McClintock 1), as well as celebrity concerts and tours designed to spread the administration's message in the Middle East. This meeting followed a more substantive meeting at the Peninsula Hotel in Beverly Hills on November 11, 2001, which was chaired by Jack Valenti, president and CEO of the Motion Picture Association of America;

Sherry Lansing, president of Paramount Communications and chairman of Paramount Pictures' Motion Picture Group; and Rove. At this first meeting, they devised a plan to send DVDs of first-run films to overseas troops and to produce films to aid the war effort. However, both Rove and the Hollywood executives agreed "that blatantly propagandistic films, TV shows or songs are not the goal" (Hayes and McClintock 1, 17). Rove had clearly done his homework, and, in a brief address, outlined exactly the sort of programming the administration expected Hollywood to create. As *Daily Variety* noted:

> Rove invoked the industry's role in the patriotic ardor of World War II, alluding to early war pics such as Confessions of a Nazi Spy. He said any war-related material coming from Hollywood this time around will aim to express seven main themes:
>
> ☐ The war is against terrorism, not Islam;
> ☐ Industryites have an opportunity to issue Americans a call for service;
> ☐ Americans should support U.S. troops and their families;
> ☐ The Sept. 11 attack was a global attack requiring a global response;
> ☐ The war is a war against evil;
> ☐ Children and families need to be reassured;
> ☐ Propaganda will not be initiated. (Hayes and McClintock 17)

Yet in view of these requirements, how can one avoid the taint of "propaganda"? What emerges here is nothing less than a blueprint of the preferred shape of public opinion, which Hollywood is expected to adopt in the coming years. In a phantom conflict that will most likely last for decades, devoid of major "theater of war" conflict but rather comprised of a series of surprise terrorist attacks, creating this desired climate to last beyond the current administration, even if it remains in office until 2008, will be difficult. As Hayes and McClintock point out:

> [The] nexus between creative and corporate minds is at the heart of the Hollywood-Washington balancing act, an already delicate feat given one

participant's estimate that 90% of those in the room were registered Democrats. Several of those in the room indicated that it would take directors, actors, writers and producers—not solely CEOs and studio or network chiefs—to make Hollywood a factor in the war effort. (17)

As the war effort becomes more diffuse, and the warnings, alarms, and threats sap the energy of an already fatigued nation, how will Hollywood react?

One possibility is the creation of tales of September 11 heroism for an international audience, a concept that is already well on its way to successful implementation. As Michael Fleming reports:

> In one of three new deals for films based around the heroism surrounding Sept. 11, ABC has inked to use the Dennis Smith book *Report from Ground Zero* as the prime resource to tell the story from the vantage point of the first-response rescuers. Also, MGM closed a deal for Lawrence Wright to adapt his New Yorker article "The Counter-Terrorist" and ICM is shopping rights to a James Stewart article in the New Yorker, "The Real Heroes Are Dead," with a commitment from Susan Sarandon to star and Tim Robbins to write and direct the film.
>
> ABC is fast mobilizing on its project, a documentary that will be written and directed by Lloyd Kramer, who most recently wrote and directed *Oprah Winfrey Presents: Amy and Isabel.* Using Smith's exhaustive chronicle of the firemen, cops and emergency teams and managers who presided over the rescue and recovery mission, network prexy Susan Lyne and movies and minis exec Quinn Taylor are planning a film that will combine scripted drama with actual footage to create a documentary feel. ("Studios Chasing Tales")

No doubt we will see more of these films, even as the initial fervor surrounding September 11 fades. Unlike Pearl Harbor, which united the nation in one fighting force to defeat the Axis Powers, the attack on the World Trade Center, in which many more innocent victims died, has left the United States uncertain as to its future direction. Partisan politics from both sides seem to dominate the debate, even as the administration continually stresses the inevitability of future attacks and the need to form a cohesive social unit to combat these coming assaults. Yet the lack of a specific target, together with a certain malaise—one might even call it fatalism—has made the months since the World Trade Center disaster essentially a time of watchful writing. From the 1950s through the 1980s, invasion scenarios inevitably focused on a sweeping attack by a foreign power (usually the former Soviet Union) on US soil and our efforts as a nation to repel the invaders. But now, no convenient "other" exists to be identified. The battleground is as much an ideological front as it is a physical place of conflict. If, as everyone seems to suggest, further terrorist attacks are inevitable, how long will the citizens of the United States stand for it until they follow the example of Israel and declare war on the Palestinians? In *Mars Attacks!* (1996), perhaps the only film ever directly inspired by a series of bubble gum cards, the Martians land with protestations of peace and good will, only to reveal, after several abortive "peace" conferences, that their only aim is the annihilation of the human race. The President (Jack Nicholson) and his scientific advisor (Pierce Brosnan) at first counsel patience and understanding, but when diplomacy fails, force prevails. What will happen as the stakes are increased on each side with no middle ground in immediate view? The current conflict, a different sort of invasion for a new century, is a problem that resists an easy solution. The clash here is corporate, ideological, and faith based, and divisions exist within the opposing forces on both sides. What we will do to resolve this conflict is an open question. Even as we seek the readily identifiable antagonist who is the staple of the contemporary action film (and find him, to a degree, in the ephemeral figure of Osama bin Laden), the ground is shifting under us, promising new adversaries, new trouble spots, the potential for widening conflicts. The nuclear bomb has not been used as an offensive weapon since 1945, and even at that, the bombings of Hiroshima and Nagasaki are still hotly debated. Can we, as a society of imperfect humans, keep our collective finger off the nuclear trigger, no matter what our "cause" may be? The evidence suggests not, and it is this darkest of scenarios that we now face in the coming century.

CHAPTER THREE

THE LIMITS OF TIME

Time is running out. I can feel it. The romance of Armageddon is being replaced by the spectre of inevitable destruction, albeit on a smaller scale. Piece by piece, city by city, landmark by landmark, the delicate balance of post–World War II nuclear politics has given way to a new war, in which atomic bombs, capable of decimating an entire metropolis in just one blast, fit in suitcases. The global apocalypse of *Dr. Strangelove* now seems simultaneously remote and yet infinitely more tangible. The twenty-first century will be defined not by wars, but by terrorist incursions. In much the same way, film itself has become a twentieth-century artifact, rendered obsolete by the technical advances of twenty-first-century digital imaging. In 1960, Jean Cocteau declared, "I'm giving up making films since technological progress means anyone can do it" (in Virilio, *Vision Machine* 51). But the technology of the cinema has now abandoned us, leaving the viewer in a world composed of pixels and plot points via computer-generated imagery (CGI). Looking for substance in the legitimate theater? Guess again—Clear Channel has extended its reach past the airwaves and onto Broadway, working along the same lines as the Disney organization, which has similar plans for theatergoers. Disney's latest project is a Broadway version of *The Little Mermaid*, for which they've hired Matthew Bourne, who staged *Swan Lake* in 1996. Clearly, they have big plans for *The Little Mermaid*, and that's only the start of an aggressive merchandising campaign to embrace all of Disney's past properties, says critic Peter Marks. As always, Disney is interested in the "big idea," the way in which it can reach the maximum number of potential patrons while extending its marketing empire:

> "We all get in the room and look at the outline that we've put up on the board, and I say, 'Matt, let's go through it,'" said Thomas Schumacher, president of Disney Theatrical Productions. "It's how we say, 'Here's the

big idea.'" These days, Disney has a lot of big ideas. *Tarzan*, as conceived by the Tony Award–winning designer Bob Crowley. *When You Wish*, a compilation show based on dozens of songs from Disney movies. *Hoopz*, the story of the Harlem Globetrotters set to music, with book and lyrics by the Pulitzer Prize–winning playwright Suzan-Lori Parks. *Pinocchio* directed by Julie Taymor. *Mary Poppins* in a potential collaboration with Cameron Mackintosh. (20)

Although Disney's minions are thus occupied, Clear Channel has entered the Broadway arena through its purchase of SFX, an entertainment conglomerate that had itself swallowed up by Pace Theatrical Group and Livent, a production entity founded by Garth Drabinsky (Marks 20). Clear Channel currently has no fewer than eight shows on Broadway as investor or producer, including Mel Brooks's *The Producers*, of which Clear Channel owns 25% (Marks 20). Other projects include *Hairspray*, the musical based on John Waters's 1988 movie of the same name, and *Movin' Out*, a musical with songs by Billy Joel and choreography by Twyla Tharp (Marks 20). Clear Channel is also an investor in the musical version of *Thoroughly Modern Millie*, designed expressly for its Broadway afterlife, as cheap road-show companies tour the Midwest, presenting "an old-style song-and-dance" showcase for family values (Marks 20). Disney scored an enormous success with *The Lion King*, but had less luck with *Aida*, the Elton John version of the Verdi classic. "Any other producer would have closed it long ago" noted one highly regarded artistic director, speaking "on condition of anonymity" (Marks 20), but Disney is clearly unfazed by the criticism, as is Clear Channel. Both know that a Broadway launch is merely the prelude to the lucrative world of touring companies, as endless road-show units wring every last dollar out of each new property. In such an atmosphere, how can genuinely innovative work find an audience? The answer is simple: it cannot. As with motion picture production, the cost of mounting a Broadway play or musical has risen to the point that $100 matinee tickets are not uncommon, forcing producers to cut costs whenever possible. Thus, projects such as Christopher Plummer in *Barrymore* are more likely to reach the stage because they are essentially solo performances. The more experimental, challenging work has moved to off-off-Broadway, where numerous theater companies cling to life from production to production, remaining afloat financially by the slimmest of margins. For the most part, Broadway has become a wilderness of carefully calculated revivals, adaptations, and modestly produced, star-driven "limited runs," in which costs can be kept to a minimum. As always, finance drives all other concerns, with the mass audience serving as the ultimate arbiter of taste. And if one can find a presold commodity, such as *The Lion King* or *The Producers*, so much the better. Above all, risk must be avoided, or at the very least, minimized.

This extends to reviews as well. As hyperconglomerates continues to buy up new companies, the work of one "unit" is crossplugged in the pages of another "unit." Dissenting views are relentlessly marginalized. When Connie Chung of CNN suggested at the beginning of an interview with George Lucas that *Star Wars: Episode One—The Phantom Menace* (1999) was "to most, a disappointment," noting that "for all its special effects, critics complained about stereotyping, stale plot lines, even racism" (citing the controversial Jar Jar Binks character), Lucas retaliated by denying Chung and CNN access to the *Star Wars: Episode Two—Attack of the Clones* press junket the next day at Lucas's Skywalker ranch (Greppi). Industry insiders insisted that CNN's crew was actually "tossed off the ranch, but CNN says that's an exaggeration, that there was 'no physical removal' of anyone, that there was a 'conversation' and that as conversations like that go, it was fairly cordial" (Greppi). As for CNN's opinion of the affair, their "stance is that Mr. Lucas expected a one-hour love letter and a wet kiss in return for the access that CNN was allowed and didn't feel he got that" (Greppi). So much for freedom of critical discourse; with $140 million at stake (the approximate budget of *Attack of the Clones*), who has time for dissent?

When Jonathan Franzen's novel *The Corrections* was a surprise critical and commercial hit, talk-show host Oprah Winfrey wanted to get him on her program as part of the Oprah's Book Club segment. But the more Franzen became involved in the project, the more suspicious he became of the entire process of being, as he put it, "an Oprah author" (Franzen 74). When Franzen was first approached by Winfrey's staff, they told the author that *The Corrections* "is a difficult book for us" (Franzen 71), which is not surprising, considering that, in the words of critic Jonathan Yardley, Oprah's "average selection [for her book club] was a few steps up from a Harlequin penny dreadful" (20). Yardley argues that although some of Oprah's choices are noteworthy (such as Ernest Gaines's *A Lesson Before Dying*, Toni Morrison's *Sula*, and Isabel Allende's *Daughter of Fortune*), on the whole, "Oprah is big on whatever domestic distress happens to be Flavor of the Month—spousal abuse, incest, recovered memory—and she tended to choose titles in which such matters were addressed, one step behind the headlines" (20). No wonder that Franzen's book was "difficult" for Oprah's Book Club, and no wonder, too, that he was not in tune with Winfrey's method of publicizing his work. As Franzen admits, "one of the reasons I'm a writer is that I have uneasy relations with authority" (71), and Oprah's minions immediately rubbed Franzen the wrong way by insisting that the segment focus on his old Midwestern neighborhood rather than his current life in Manhattan. But Franzen understood how the medium of television worked: it "is propelled by images, the simpler and more vivid the better. If the producers wanted me to be Midwestern, I would try to be Midwestern" (71). But Franzen's "homecoming" is difficult, and he finds his old neighborhood changed beyond recognition, a place he can no longer relate to. Delivering stand-up homilies on his youth, strolling through the landscape of his childhood, Franzen realizes how the whole thing will "play on TV; as schmaltz" (74). Disgusted with the charade he is being forced to participate in, Franzen suddenly snaps.

"This is so fundamentally bogus!" he declares, to no one in particular, and is surprised when the cameraman "raises his face from his eyepiece and laughs and nods vigorously. 'You're right!' His voice is loud with merriment and something close to anger. 'You're right, it is totally bogus!'" (74). Needless to say, Oprah's producer is not especially pleased with this outburst, wrapping up the filming shortly thereafter, commenting, "I guess I'll find some way to make it work" (74). But worse is to come. At a book signing in Chicago the day after the shoot, Franzen makes the mistake of trying to please all the many customers standing in line, agreeing with those who say, "I like your book, and I think it's wonderful that Oprah picked it," and with those who solicitously murmur, "I like your book, and I'm so sorry that Oprah picked it" (Franzen 74). As Franzen states somewhat laconically, "I'll get in trouble for this" (75), and indeed he does. Winfrey uninvites him from her show with the accurate yet dismissive statement that Franzen "is seemingly uncomfortable and conflicted about being chosen" (Yardley 20), as indeed he is. What disturbed Franzen the most, apparently, was the Oprah sticker stamped on his book as "'a logo of corporate ownership'" (qtd. in Yardley 20), and in the resulting flap, he will be

> reviled from coast to coast by outraged populists. I'll be called a "motherfucker" by an anonymous source in New York, a "pompous prick" in *Newsweek*, an "ego-blinded snob" in the *Boston Globe*, and a "spoiled, whiny little brat" in *The Chicago Tribune*. (Franzen 75)

But this is not the end of the affair. Shortly after the Franzen/Winfrey incident, Winfrey decided to abandon the book club segment altogether, for reasons that still remain, at least to this writer, somewhat mysterious. In six years, Oprah had touted more than four dozen books, most of them rather bland commercial fare. *Publishers Weekly* noted that "between 1996 and 2000, Oprah selections enjoyed average sales of well over *a million* [copies] *each*, and that Warner Books alone, even at conservative estimates, raked in $50 million in Oprah dividends" (qtd. in Yardley 20). When one considers that a print run of 25,000 hardcover copies of an average "best seller" is quite respectable by ordinary standards (out of a possible 290 million readers in the United States alone), this is an astonishing figure (Yardley). No surprise, then, that Random House took out a full page ad in the *New York Times* thanking Oprah for her "unique and magnificent work over the past six years on behalf of books, authors and readers everywhere" (Yardley 20). It also didn't hurt that out of the 48 or so books that Oprah recommended, 20 were Random House books (Yardley 20). But the problem goes deeper than all of this—beyond the pique of one author, or the fact that, despite the appearance of Maya Angelou, Toni Morrison, and Isabel Allende, most of Oprah's choices were resolutely unchallenging pop books, designed to appeal (just like television) to the widest possible consumer base. The real issue is that the many readers in Oprah's Book Club read only the books that Oprah recommended, as Yardley comments:

> Oprah is the Queen of Self-Esteem, so no one should be surprised that her reading tastes incline toward self-improvement and pop psychology.

That's O.K.—you're O.K., too—and folks who like that sort of stuff are constitutionally entitled to read as much of it as they can stomach. Just please don't tell Oprah she's "unique and magnificent" because she's trying to pass it off as literature, and don't give her credit where credit hasn't been earned. She may have led people to read who might otherwise have found other forms of diversion and enrichment, but check some of her selections at Amazon.com and you'll see that people who buy Oprah books are mostly buying other Oprah books.

    All of which is to say that reading Angelou and Lamb and Quindlen does not necessarily lead to reading Edna O'Brien and Ian McEwan and Gabriel Garcia Marquez. Yes indeed, thank you, Oprah, for what you've done—in particular, thanks for enlarging the readership for black-American writers— but that wasn't exactly a Great Books discussion you were conducting, and it was about a country mile short of "unique and magnificent." (20)

Oprah's Book Club, then, is more a reflection of one person's taste and an indication of that public figure's commercial clout, than it is a dialogue about literature. The fact that it benefited certain large publishing houses does not really seem to me to be all that sinister; there are increasingly fewer publishers in the marketplace anyway, most of them hyperconglomerates that have survived by purchasing smaller, competing companies. The real problem is that by valorizing certain texts and marginalizing others, Oprah created a culture of false consensus centering on the production of literary texts. If Oprah liked a book and featured it on her show, her millions of loyal viewers followed her suggestion, and purchased the book, convinced that they were participating in a dialogue centering around the writer and her or his work. In fact, Oprah's strategy essentially "dumbed-down" the literary landscape in the United States even further, in a marketplace already dominated by the likes of Danielle Steele, Stephen King, Tom Clancy, and other commercial novelists. In early 2003, Winfrey announced plans to reactivate her book club, but this time concentrating only on "classics." What this portends remains to be seen.

    Oprah is also making noises about giving up her talk show and concentrating on her projects, one of which must undoubtedly be *O, The Oprah Magazine*, available at newsstands throughout the world. What is peculiar about *O* is that every cover features a picture of Oprah as a sort of perpetual celebrity, a cultural arbiter whose dominion cannot be denied. Talk-show host Rosie O'Donnell was hired to jack up the circulation of the ailing *McCall's* magazine, reincarnated as *Rosie*, but the project ended in commercial disaster and a flurry of law suits when O'Donnell demanded complete editorial control. *Rosie* has since ceased publication. Martha Stewart gazes serenely at the viewer each month from the cover of *Martha Stewart Living* magazine, but her image, too, has been tarnished by allegations of insider stock trading. Oprah's Book Club, just like Rosie O'Donnell's well-known affection for Broadway shows (which did a great deal to increase the box-office returns on musicals such as *Seussical*, which was otherwise dismissed by the critics) and Martha Stewart's fantasyland of domestic tranquility, offer the viewer a place to inhabit that transcends and replaces the realities of their own daily existence. Personal problems can be solved, books are showcased, casseroles prepared, and kitchens decorated, all to create a comfortable world of domesticity devoid of care or want. That this is beyond the economic reach of most viewers is beside the point, or perhaps it is the central consideration. If one cannot experience this life firsthand, at least one can live it on a daily basis, vicariously, through the agency of another.

Cosmopolitan also brands itself as the purveyor of a salable commodity to American women, that of the "fun, fearless female" (Carr 1). With the US market declining and production costs rising, *Cosmopolitan* is aggressively pushing its brand of female "empowerment" worldwide. Although 2.8 million women read *Cosmopolitan* in the United States (Carr 1), that is nothing compared to the possibilities afforded by the exploitation of the *Cosmopolitan* formula on an international scale. As David Carr comments:

With a formula almost as closely guarded as Coca-Cola's—there is a secret 50-page instruction manual—*Cosmopolitan*, Hearst's naughty girlfriend of a magazine, has increased its circulation to 8.2 million worldwide, even extending its brand to places where readers have to hide the magazine from their husbands. After adding nine editions in the past two years, *Cosmo* will soon publish in 50 countries, including the recently opened

Latvian edition and a Kazakhstan *Cosmo* that makes its debut in September. The magazine now flirts with newsstand shoppers on six continents and produces hundreds of millions of dollars in revenue for Hearst, suggesting that deep cleavage and thinner thighs have global legs.

"Things American are not viewed as negatively as we might read about," said George Green, president of Hearst Magazines International. "There's a huge appetite for these magazines out there." (1, 9)

Indeed. As Grazyna Olbrych, editor of the Polish version of *Cosmopolitan* puts it, "*Cosmo* is not about culture. When you are young, you want to have a young man who loves you and have great sex with him" (Carr 9). Despite national idiosyncrasies, *Cosmopolitan*'s message is flourishing around the world. The Chinese version cannot even mention sex because government censors forbid it; nevertheless, there is still plenty of room for makeup and wardrobe tips for the young Chinese female consumer (Carr 9). In Sweden, sex is not discussed for a different reason; everyone knows about it, thanks to a progressive and enlightened sex-education program, so the Swedish version of *Cosmopolitan* also concentrates on improving one's appearance (Carr 9). In France, readers are so bored with sex that the editor of the French version of *Cosmopolitan*, Anne Chabrol, "responded by running a contest asking, 'Does He Cheat On You?' with the winner being awarded the services of a private detective to find out for sure" (Carr 9). Singapore bans *Cosmopolitan* outright, but allows the publication of the rival Hearst publication *Harper's Bazaar* (Carr 9). In each case, the worldwide versions of *Cosmopolitan* flourish by presenting the same vision of unfettered sexuality and consumerist "freedom" tailored to meet the needs and desires of local consumers. Thus, American values are again exported throughout the world not for ideological reasons, but rather commercial considerations, which dictate that *Cosmopolitan* must increase its international presence if it hopes to hold on to its share of the marketplace. The new colonialism is driven by the incentive of economic gain, just as the physical colonization of countries in preceding centuries served the interests of Great Britain, the Netherlands, France, and Belgium by providing cheap goods and labor for ready export. In the 21st century, the colonialism of ideas and images has replaced the need for physical annexation; the market is there, so who needs to bother about the local government? By increasing the United States' imagistic hold on European and Third World countries, while at the same time seemingly "respecting" or paying obeisance to local cultural customs, the US megaconglomerate publishing and entertainment companies can literally conquer the world, replacing indigenous culture with their own copyrighted, brand-conscious regime.

As filmmaker Jean-Luc Godard remarked in the aftermath of September 11, "Progress is ambiguous, isn't it?" (qtd. in Osborne 53). He went on to note that "the Americans are everywhere," a theme he develops in his film *In Praise of Love* (2001; original title *Éloge de l'Amour*, 2001), which was screened at the New York Film Festival on October 14, 2001, but which has yet to find a US distributor. Godard's *In Praise of Love* is a typically idiosyncratic film from the director who initially stunned the world with *Breathless* (1961; original title *À bout de souffle*, 1960) and went on in the 1960s to create a series of deeply personal and disturbing films dealing with rampant commercialization, loss of human identity, the effects of megacorporate culture on society and the individual, and the evils of war and colonialist exploitation. In films such as *My Life to Live* (1962; original title *Vivre sa vie: Film en douze tableaux*, 1962), which documents several days in the life of a Parisian prostitute; *Alphaville, a Strange Adventure of Lemmy Caution* (1965; original title *Alphaville, une étrange aventure de Lemmy Caution*, 1965), a dystopian vision of a future civilization run by a giant computer; and *Weekend*, which depicts the total collapse of global society in a holocaust of murder, cannibalism, war, and rapacious selfishness, Godard painted a vision of the world as a hostile, cold, unforgiving zone of rampant consumerism and cultural nullity. Godard's early films, made on budgets of $100,000 each in black-and-white 35mm, still managed to recoup their modest cost through international theatrical distribution. By the time of *Weekend*, his budgets were slightly larger, and he had shifted to color to pacify his investors, but his vision was still his own. In the late 1960s, Godard retired from commercial filmmaking to form the Dziga Vertov group with Jean-Pierre Gorin, producing a series of violently political films in 16mm format on minuscule budgets, such as *British Sounds* (1969), *Wind from the East* (1969; original title *Le vent d'est*, 1969), and

Letter to Jane (1972), but eventually abandoned agitprop cinema as an artistic and personal dead end. Beginning with *Numéro Deux* (1975), Godard has staged something of a return to the commercial cinema with films such as his bizarre adaptation of *King Lear* (1987), *Hail Mary* (1985; original title *Je vous salue, Marie*, 1985), and *Germany Year 90 Nine Zero* (1991; original title *Allemagne année 90 neuf zéro*, 1991), this last film being a continuation of both the themes and characters of his earlier film *Alphaville*. In the 1990s, Godard increasingly turned to work in small format video as his preferred medium of expression, creating a series of videotapes entitled *Histoire(s) du cinéma* (1989-1994 and perhaps still ongoing), meditating on the history of the cinema, its effect on viewers, and the impact of the US cinema on global film production (see Dixon, *Godard*, for more on the filmmaker's long and distinguished career). In *In Praise of Love*, according to critic Lawrence Osborne, Godard delivers

> a loose, brooding rumination on globalist discontents, shot mostly in black and white. Although the film is nominally about the four stages of love—meeting, sexual passion, separation and rediscovery—it turns anxiously around larger themes: rampant commercialization, the preponderance of Hollywood and TV, the end of authenticity, the poor, the old, the disappearance of adulthood. (53)

As always, Godard is uneasy about the invasion of technology and false memory created by the media to replicate or explicate the past. As he argues, "I suppose that's a feeling that many people in the world have today—a kind of incoherent rage against all things technocratic. It comes from being powerless. Of course, that doesn't diminish the tragedy of what happened in New York" (53). In one of *In Praise of Love*'s most contentious subplots, "the representatives of Steven Spielberg try to buy the rights to the memories of a Jewish couple who were French Resistance fighters" (Osborne 53). Godard's dislike for Spielberg is well known and in itself perhaps explains why *In Praise of Love* is unlikely to receive widespread distribution in the United States, even on DVD or cable television, the new (and only) market for contemporary foreign films. But, as Osborne states, in the 1960s Godard's films had an air of insouciance and cheerfully nihilistic graveyard humor, as in *Alphaville*, where the central character, Lemmy Caution (Eddie Constantine), inserts a one franc coin in a vending machine, only to receive a plastic card with the word "merci" engraved on it. In his current work, such as *Oh, Woe Is Me* (1993; original title, *Hélas pour moi*, 1993), *For Ever Mozart* (1996), and *In Praise of Love*, Godard is an altogether different figure as he contemplates the ruins of civilization. It is no longer a matter for joking as in *Weekend*; the ruin of our shared international cultural heritage is an accomplished fact, and Godard mourns the passing of visual and artistic literacy with deep and unremitting intensity. As Godard comments, "I suppose old men always feel some sort of nostalgia for the past [and for] the loss of cultural memory. I wonder if Americans feel that loss too. I don't think so. But then I think you're just more nomadic and rootless by nature. For me, such a loss is catastrophic" (qtd. in Osborne 53). He complains that, "actors today just imitate other actors. They all want to be Gérard Depardieu or Julia Roberts" (Osborne 53). Godard's small-scale Swiss production company, Sonimage, which he operates with his "partner and collaborator Anne-Marie Miéville" (Osborne 53), gives him the kind of freedom he needs to make films that would never be welcomed by the commercial establishment precisely because his films seek to destabilize it. For Godard, "failure" is as important as the ephemerality of success because it gives one the freedom to act without the constraints of commercial film production. As he puts it, "I've known both success and failure equally, I'm glad to say. It's important to experience failure. Frankly, even being famous ultimately wasn't all it was cracked up to be" (qtd. in Osborne 53), which is why, unlike so many of his contemporaries, including the late François Truffaut, and the still active auteurs Eric Rohmer, Claude Chabrol, and Agnès Varda, Godard has withdrawn almost completely from the mainstream cinema marketplace. Whatever films he makes are his own entirely; their inherent lack of commercial appeal is of absolutely no concern. Fortunately for Godard, numerous patrons, both private and public, still admire his work to such a degree that they remain willing to finance his projects, even though they realize that the chances of recouping their investment is literally nonexistent. Godard could not work any other way. Having dispersed with narrative, the star system, and conventional editorial strategies, his contemporary films are an avalanche of images, texts, and scraps of music, combining to create an intensely personal vision that concedes nothing to the viewer. Godard's films are thus mysterious and resistant, precisely the opposite of what the dominant cinema aims for.

Simultaneously, a new group of feminist filmmakers is refiguring the French commercial cinema, even as a competing group of more calculating directors has pursued a new French-American hybrid, the "teen movie" of 21st century France, as is the case with Stéphane Kazandjian's *Sexy Boys* (2001). Produced on a budget of roughly $3 million, *Sexy Boys*, a sort of vulgar combination of *American Pie* (1999) and the teleseries *Friends*, has thus far been responsible for 500,000 theatrical admissions in France, not a bad showing in a country where US films traditionally dominate the box office. Although some critics and viewers are alarmed by the trend, claiming that it desecrates the illustrious past of French cinema, first-time director Kazandjian is unrepentant. As he told Kristin Hohenadel:

> I think there's a kind of "snobbisme" in France. [...] To make a film for an adolescent audience is considered vulgar, idiotic—because we are so much more intelligent than the Americans—and if we make a film for young people, it has to really raise the debate. All of the films I've seen in France about adolescents are made by 40-year-olds recalling adolescence as a troubled, tormented period. (21)

Citing *Porky's* (1981), *Ferris Bueller's Day Off* (1986), and *Clerks* (1994) as the major influences on *Sexy Boys*, Kazandjian first tried his hand in the United States, working as an intern on a Hollywood sitcom and writing two unproduced scripts for generic crime thrillers (Hohenadel 21). But nothing clicked, and so Kazandjian decided not only to return to France, but also to import the values of the Hollywood cinema with him. Predictably, the establishment French press savaged *Sexy Boys* on its initial release. *Le Monde* suggested that perhaps it should not mention the names of the actors out of "charity," while *Libération* noted that the film represented "a total Americanization of behaviors and settings" (Hohenadel 21). Despite near universal critical disdain, *Sexy Boys* became a substantial hit, something that was predicted by the film's sole favorable notice, by Lisa Nesselson, in *Weekly Variety*. Wrote Nesselson, "shot and edited with straightforward efficiency, [the] film has guts and energy as well as grossout ideas to spare" (qtd. in Hohenadel 21). And, of course, with an eye to the international market, *Sexy Boys* is shot in English, rather than French. This proves no barrier to contemporary Parisian youth. Indeed, Kazandjian is dismissive of the French cinema on a much larger scale, calling its supposed cultural superiority an illusion fostered by critics. Argues Kazandjian:

> There is a real French culture and a real American culture and between the two there is "*un melting pot*" with many references that everyone has in common. [...] Everyone is nourished by the things they grew up with, and my generation saw Spielberg in the same way that Scorsese saw Godard's *Breathless* and started making little films in black and white. I'm interested in this space between "*la culture trash*" and respectable culture. In France we really have this cult of the *auteur*, as if he's a kind of genius. But I don't really think there are more masterpieces in the French cinema than there are in the American cinema. (qtd. in Hohenadel 21)

Currently basking in the success of *Sexy Boys*, Kazandjian comments that "American films have a real energy that is missing in a lot of French films" (Hohenadel 21), and he is at work on a new, highly commercial project. *Bloody Mallory* (2002), "a sort of *Buffy* [*the Vampire Slayer* (1992)] *française*, an action comedy based on Roger Corman-style B movies," which will also be shot in English (Hohenadel 21). His favorite directors are the Coen brothers, Paul Thomas Anderson, and Steven Soderbergh, and after *Bloody Mallory*, he hopes to film a "trés Hollywoodienne" romantic comedy, combining elements of "Woody Allen and Billy Wilder" (Hohenadel 21).

In a sense, Stéphane Kazandjian, Luc Besson, and other current practitioners of what has been dubbed "*le cinéma du look*" are the logical consequence of a culture that has been systematically destroyed by US imports. American films do indeed move faster and have "more energy" than many of their Gallic counterparts; this is called introspection and character development. The new wave of "le teen movie" directors does not want to be considered auteurs, and they do not really want to make a personal statement, something that even Roger Corman aspired to in his early films such as *The Intruder* (1961), in which a young William Shatner plays a virulent racist out to inflame racial tensions in a sleepy Southern town. All that drives Kazandjian and his cohorts is commercial return through the importation of American cultural and social values to replace indigenous ones. Even the language is disposable; French-language films have such a limited market—let's shoot it in English! Surface slickness and calculated manipulation have replaced insight and an individual vision; the marketplace is the final arbiter of quality. Kazandjian is thus an example of the completely colonized individual, bereft of anything other than a phantasmal vision of Hollywood success. It's all very well to evoke the names of Billy Wilder and Woody Allen as mentors, until one remembers that both filmmakers often created resolutely noncommercial projects in which they expressed their own views of society without regard for the eventual box-office reception. Woody Allen may bemoan the fact that his newer films, particularly the brutally savage *Deconstructing Harry* (1997), itself a loose remake of Ingmar Bergman's *Wild Strawberries* (1959; original title *Smultronstället*, 1957), reap little return in their theatrical runs, but his films remain a reflection of his unique and increasingly bitter view of the human condition, right up through *Hollywood Ending* (2002). Allen, Wilder, the Coen brothers, Anderson, and Soderbergh are filmmakers possessing a unique and original vision that informed the creation of all their work; they possess a center. Borrowing from this and that, like so many condiments on a fast-food service bar, Besson and Kazandjian have nothing at the center. Cut off from their own heritage and inundated with hyperedited, presold, mass-marketed images from a monopolistic corporate construct that is effectively leveling alternative civilizations just as American and European loggers relentlessly level the Amazon rain forest, the "Franglais" filmmaker belongs to no true culture—except the discipline of all-consuming capitalism.

In contrast, the new French feminist filmmakers offer a vision that is far more intense and disturbing. Inspired by the early example of Agnès Varda, directors such as Brigitte Roüan, Catherine Breillat, Tonie Marshall, Agnès Jaoui, and Nicole Garcia have created a new cinema that reflects more accurately the passions and ambitions of their female protagonists with results that often shock mainstream audiences and critics. *Rape Me* (2001; original title *Baise-Moi*, 2000), directed by Virginie Despentes and Coralie Trinh Thi, tells the tale of two young women who go on a cross-country killing spree, much in the same vein as *Natural Born Killers* (1994) and the fatally compromised *Thelma & Louise* (1991). However, *Rape Me* depicts its protagonists as flawed yet impassioned heroines, fighting back against a male-dominated society that subjugates them through a regime of forced gender roles, domesticity, and rape. Unlike other films that have dealt with rape in the past, even Ida Lupino's groundbreaking *Outrage* (1950), rape in *Rape Me* is presented with graphic directness and no obfuscation. It is a brutal act motivated by power rather than sexual desire, and by depicting the rape of the two young women with documentary intensity; Despentes and Trinh Thi demonstrate the need for their full-scale rebellion. When *Natural Born Killers* was released, it received saturation booking throughout the world and although momentarily controversial for its often gratuitous violence, the R-rated film was eventually accepted as mainstream cinema to be discussed and dissected by critics and viewers alike. When *Rape Me* opened, it played in a few major US cities before disappearing to DVD, and the reviews were for the most part dismissive or directly hostile. Where director Oliver Stone's *Natural Born Killers* presented Woody Harrelson and Juliette Lewis as an updated, often parodic 1990s version of *Bonnie and Clyde* (1967), complete with Rodney Dangerfield and Robert Downey Jr. for comic relief, *Rape Me* is unadorned and straightforward, offering two porn actresses, Raffadla Anderson and Karen Bach, in the leading roles. Based on Virginie Despentes's novel of the same name (*Baise-Moi*), which was a *success du scandale* when first printed in France, *Rape Me* is shot on digital video rather than film, which gives the completed work a bare bones, stripped-down quality, a look favored by many New Wave feminist directors. In contrast, Oliver Stone switches camera stocks from color to black and white, intercuts video with film, projects slides onto the bodies of his protagonists, even artificially scratches and cuts the film, all to keep the visuals moving at a hyperedited pace, to disguise the fact that the film is, at its center, essentially empty. The other factor to consider is that *Rape Me*, while staged to conform to a fictive narrative, has a greater command on our attention because of the raw verisimilitude of its sexual discourse; in contrast, everything in *Natural Born Killers* is synthetic. Everything in Stone's film is told from the point of view of the male viewer; *Rape Me* sides completely with its feminist protagonists, operating entirely on their level, without artifice or adornment.

Other films from French New Wave feminist directors include Catherine Breillat's *Fat Girl* (2001; original title *À ma soeur!*, 2001), a harrowing tale of a 13-year-old girl's coming of age as her 15-year-old sister embarks on a series of sexual relationships. With explicit sexual scenes and a brutal narrative structure, *Fat Girl* has already been banned in Ontario, Canada, and severely restricted to adult audiences only throughout the rest of the world. Breillat's earlier film *Romance* (1999) is similarly graphic, exploring the life of a young woman who engages in a series of romantic trysts, one involving sadomasochist bondage, when her putative boyfriend fails to satisfy her emotional and physical needs. In Brigitte Roüan's *After Sex* (1997; original title *Post coitum animal triste*, 1997), a woman in her 40s, played by Roüan herself, loses everything she has when an extramarital affair ends badly. Agnès Jaoui's *The Taste of Others* (2001; original title *Le goût des autres*, 1999) is a rather elegant and restrained romantic comedy; Danièle Thompson's *Season's Beatings* (1999; original title *La Bûche*, 1999) is a domestic comedy drama set during the Christmas holiday season; Nicole Garcia's *Place Vendôme* (1998) is a stylish thriller starring Catherine Deneuve; and Tonie Marshall's *Venus Beauty Institute* (2000; original title *Vénus beauté [institut]*, 1999) is a sort of *Grand Hotel* (1932) drama centering on the lives and loves of a group of women who operate a Parisian fashion shop.

Taken together, these films comprise a feminine revolution in the cinema. As Agnès Varda commented, "I was a lone woman director in the French New Wave[;] now there are 50 women making feature films. The evolution has been earth-shattering" (James, "Femmes Directors" A4). Catherine Breillat agrees, noting that her films deal precisely with that subject matter that other directors have avoided in the past. Says Breillat, "I am passionate about looking at things that are taboo. I film what other people hide" (James, "Femmes Directors" A4). In addition, this new wave of feminist cinema has provided work for many actors who otherwise would have remained idle. Agnès Jaoui flatly states that, "for every two roles for women, there are 12 for men. I got fed up waiting for acting parts

[and] started writing between jobs" (James, "Femme Directors" A4). Working with her partner and co-scenarist Jean-Pierre Bacri, Jaoui now finds herself in demand as a director with the immense commercial and critical success of *The Taste of Others*, which won four Césars (the French equivalent of the Academy Award). This is all the more remarkable because of the fact that *The Taste of Others* was Jaoui's debut as a director (James, "Femme Directors" A4).

But while their films reflect more of the woman's point of view, most of the members of the New Wave of French feminist cinema do not think of themselves as provocateurs—with the exceptions of Roüan and Breillat. Rather, they seek to open their films to the entire spectrum of human experience. Says Danièle Thompson, "Although I support some specific women's issues, I wouldn't call myself a 'feminist,' because being a woman isn't an obstacle to success. The attitude to women in the French film industry is extremely open" (James, "Femme Directors" A4). Agnès Jaoui agrees, saying that, "I don't think my films have a 'woman's point of view,' I wouldn't want that and, anyway, I write them with a man. But if I can insert a good female role into the plot, well of course I do" (James, "Femme Directors" A4).

Thus, what is really happening here is a leveling of the playing field, a respite from the days of the first New Wave when Chabrol, Godard, Truffaut, Resnais, Rohmer, and other young men from the Cahiers du Cinéma school dominated cinema practice. In France, at least, the cinema has become reasonably democratic, and despite the influx of the new teen movies, the country seems able to incorporate the past of cinema into the present, creating works that are simultaneously commercial and thoughtful. This will not continue if US global cinematic dominance finally prevails. A US studio would never even produce any of the films mentioned here because American audiences have become numbed by a succession of violent spectacles and imbecilic comedies to the point where originality is suspect, almost outside the realm of US viewers' limited experience. Creating scenarios for contemporary mainstream films is much like writing for television in the 1950s: avoid controversy at all costs. In 1953 Rod Serling observed that, "because TV is a mass medium, you have to be governed by mass medium taboos. Easy on sex. Easy on violence. Nix on religion. Gently does it on the controversial themes" (qtd. in Friend 46). Mainstream films have the appearance of genuine engagement, yet in fact they are carefully contrived to reach, but not challenge, their target audiences. Although community standards have changed considerably in the United States since the 1950s, I argue that we are now living in one of the most deeply repressive and conservative eras since Joseph McCarthy first entered the public consciousness. What we have learned in the intervening years is the symbolic value of token tolerance; the gesture that suggests unity and social consensus. The "news" is now more stage managed than it was in the Eisenhower era; even the most cursory viewing of the BBC World Service news versus the three nightly US network news broadcasts (ABC, CBS, and NBC) reveals a complete myopia when it comes to world affairs, particularly when reports of famine or disaster do not directly affect US interests. This is not to suggest that the BBC, or Agence France-Presse, or Reuters, or any other news organization is free from chauvinist bias. But for sheer insularity, the mainstream US news outlets mimic the mainstream film, television, and cable outlets. Everything is homogenized; everything is the same. Dissenting voices are filtered out. American audiences want their "news," as well as their entertainment, predigested to avoid surprises and to be centered solely on their own personal and financial interests.

In an era when fading action superstar Arnold Schwarzenegger can command $30 million up front for *Terminator 3: Rise of the Machines* (2003), what we have been trained to expect is the expected. As Dave Kehr declares:

> If movies become a medium in which anything that can be imagined can be presented in photo-realist terms, the consequences will probably be a shrinking of the sense of fantasy and escape, because nothing will seem extraordinary anymore. As shocking as they were, even the images of the attack on the World Trade Center seemed weirdly familiar, accustomed as we are to seeing New York blasted by aliens (*Independence Day*) and flattened by tidal waves (*Armageddon*). ("Cyberstar" 1)

This is even more true when one considers that movies in Hollywood are no longer made by individuals, but rather committees, focus groups, and ancillary advertising interests so that the concept of a film "directed by" anyone in the dominant cinema is so hopelessly mediated by commercial manipulation that it is altogether meaningless. *Battlefield Earth: A Saga of the Year 3000* (2000), the John Travolta/L. Ron Hubbard vehicle that zoomed through theaters on its way to pay-cable limbo, had its roots in a financial deal that was advantageous to the film's producer, Franchise Pictures, if not ultimately to the film's star, Travolta, who actually invested $5 million of his personal fortune to finance the film. Travolta had been trying to get the project off the ground for 15 years, but even with a string of box-office hits, no one would touch it. Travolta is well known as a member of the Church of Scientology, and *Battlefield Earth* was written by Hubbard, the group's founder and author of the controversial book *Dianetics*. Although no studio specifically mentioned this connection as a stumbling block, the project went from MGM to Fox to Warner Brothers without any firm offers, despite Travolta's star status. One studio executive who passed on *Battlefield Earth* noted that, "It was risky. On any film there are 10 variables that can kill you. On this film there was an 11th: Scientology. It just wasn't something anyone really wanted to get involved with" (Hirschberg 49).

But Elie Samaha, the head of Franchise Pictures, had a formula that ultimately made the film possible. As Hirschberg describes it, the process works in five easy steps:

> 1. Find a script that nobody in Hollywood wants. Nobody, that is, except one eager movie star. 2. Buy the script for cheap—and skip the rewrites. 3. Save a lot of money by shooting in Canada. 4. Pay your star a fraction of his usual rate. (It is his pet project, after all.) 5. Rake in the profits. (46)

As long as Samaha followed these rules, he was ready to bankroll *Battlefield Earth*.

Nevertheless, *Battlefield Earth* was massacred by the critics and became a running joke on American late-night television variety shows. Samaha has used this same five-step process to create several more aesthetically successful projects, such as *The Big Kahuna* (2000) starring Kevin Spacey; *The Pledge* (2001), a "sleeper" detective thriller starring Jack Nicholson and directed by Sean Penn; *Get Carter* (2000), a remake of the 1971 Michael Caine/Mike Hodges film, starring

Sylvester Stallone; and *The Whole Nine Yards* (2000), a Bruce Willis comedy that breaks the mold of his usual high-octane action persona (Hirschberg 48). Some of these projects made more money than others, and *The Whole Nine Yards* was a modest hit. Most important, however, none of the films lost money because Samaha keeps his overhead down through draconian cost consciousness.

With *Battlefield Earth*, Samaha cut the film's original budget from $90 million to $65 million, and then raised 70% of the budget by selling overseas rights to the film, territory by territory (Hirschberg 49). Selling the film was easy: Samaha simply ignored the Scientology connection. "I would yell at everyone, 'This is a science-fiction film starring John Travolta!' again and again," he told Lynn Hirschberg (49), and in the end even got Intertainment AG, a German company notoriously suspicious of projects with possible controversy attached, to commit to a major stake in the production. In many ways, although the projects Samaha produces are frankly commercial affairs, the company is one of the last bastions for individual creative input. Unlike Miramax Films and other "boutique" production companies, Samaha is interested only in the packaging and merchandising of a project. Once a star has signed on and the budget is set, Samaha cedes all creative decisions "to on-set personnel" (Hirschberg 49). This approach, of course, can have its pitfalls because "no one [other than the film's stars, writers, and/or directors] seems to care whether or not the film has any artistic merit" (Hirschberg 49). It doesn't matter; the film is presold, and in all probability will at least break even. And by leaving his stars and directors alone, Samaha affords them that rarest of all luxuries in an increasingly micromanaged industry: creative freedom.

In contrast, films such as *Artificial Intelligence: A.I.* (2001), the Steven Spielberg film that the director "inherited" from Stanley Kubrick, are good examples of committee-made movies. As Lloyd Kaufman, the head of Troma Pictures, producers of intentionally awful films such as *Surf Nazis Must Die* (1987), *Tromeo and Juliet* (1996), and *Teenage Catgirls in Heat* (1997), observes, *A.I.* represents a kind of "emotional pornography [...] a soulless prefab blockbuster that wasn't so much written or directed as assembled by a committee intent on creating a product impervious to criticism of any type" (qtd. in Lidz and Rushin 30). Yet films such as *A.I., Patch Adams* (1998), *Grand Canyon* (1991), *Pay It Forward*

(2000), and numerous others garner awards and critical acclaim because they insist on their importance, cloaking their emptiness in period costumes or myriad computer-generated special effects. They fill the screen with scenery and guest stars (*Around the World in Eighty Days*, 1956), they present us with sympathetic Nazis in period drag (*The English Patient*, 1996), they suffocate us with period splendor and the purloined pedigree of their source texts (*Howards End*, 1992). But as Kaufman ruefully exclaims, "pointing out the flaws in *A.I.* is like saying you hate love or children or teddy bears" (Lidz and Rushin 30). These are films designed to deflect all criticism, films that announce their scope and ambition through the use of sweeping music cues, supposedly daring themes, and meticulous (if uninspired) technical execution. These films are deliberately flawless, without a doubt. They are also devoid of humanity, insight, or anything approaching a personal vision. Troma's films, like AIP's films of the 1950s, are honest exploitational "trash," and they acquire resonance as they age, becoming authentic totems of their era and cultural origins.

In contrast, the paint-by-numbers movies of the majors sell quickly and then burn out, becoming texts without a function. The more bloated the spectacle, the more divorced it is from the culture that created it and the less it has to offer us as scholars and historians. *The Mouthpiece* (1932) tells the story of an overzealous prosecutor, Vincent Day (Warren William), who fights to get a conviction in a murder case and is resoundingly successful. However, just as the defendant is being executed, another man confesses to the crime—the real killer. Plagued by grief and self-doubt, Day quits his government job and becomes the defense council for a string of gangsters, pimps, bootleggers, and triggermen. This narrative, told in unadorned long takes with minimal settings, tells us more about the Depression era than any conventional historical document ever will. The palpable air of desperation that surrounds Day's activities, his attempts to drown his guilt in bootleg liquor, his unsatisfying dalliances—all are presented to the viewer in near documentary fashion without the support of extradiegetic music. *The Mouthpiece* is a raw slice of Depression era life as observed by an omniscient camera that grinds on mercilessly, as in the documentaries of Frederick Wiseman or in the cold, clinical films of Andy Warhol.

King Kong overwhelmes us with spectacle; *Gone with the Wind* (1939) takes a popular novel and turns it into an equally popular commercial success; *The Wizard of Oz* (1939) has a claim on our memory because of the enduring icons of Dorothy's red slippers, the yellow brick road, and the wicked witch of the West. Yet all are escapist fantasies, although they perpetually appear on "most beloved" film lists year after year and tell us little about the social and political forces that led to their creation. The Great Depression was at its height when *King Kong* was produced; who would have known it from the film itself, which whisked willing audiences to Skull Island to witness Kong battle for survival against an unending procession of natural enemies? *Gone with the Wind* and *The Wizard of Oz* were made on the eve of World War II; where are the traces of the coming conflict apparent in these fictive narratives? All three films are primarily escapist entertainments. All are films with multiple directors, numerous camera operators, and sprawling schedules that taxed the studio system to the limit, making each an expensive gamble for their producers. Yet in *She Had to Say Yes* (1933), in which stenographer Loretta Young has to chose between date rapist Lyle Talbot or Regis Toomey as a suitable husband, or *Skyscraper Souls* (1932), in which Warren William portrays the corrupt builder of a huge skyscraper, ruthless in his transactions in commerce and personal relationships, there is more to be seen and experienced about the human condition than in any of the conventional canonical classics.

In the same fashion, *Citizen Ruth* (1996) and *Election* (1999), both by director Alexander Payne, are the most authentic exemplars of life in the Great Plains, just as Sinclair Lewis's novels *Babbitt*, *Main Street*, and *Elmer Gantry* crystallized the narrow-mindedness of Midwestern culture for all time. In *Citizen Ruth*, Laura Dern plays a glue-sniffing mother-to-be who haunts the alleyways of Omaha, Nebraska, and gets caught up in a brutally satirical battle between pro-choice and pro-life forces; in *Election*, Reese Witherspoon portrays the class perfectionist who will use any means to get ahead in high school, much to the chagrin of her teacher, Matthew Broderick. *Citizen Ruth* and *Election* were marginal hits, allowing Payne to continue working the contemporary cinematic marketplace. But with *About Schmidt* (2002), Payne has crossed over into much more conventional territory, essentially draping the film around star

Jack Nicholson as the film's central attraction, settling for easy laughs rather than the searing penetration of the his first two works. In *About Schmidt*, Nicholson plays an insurance actuary whose wife has died, leaving him adrift in a landscape of meaningless family obligations, even as he converges daily on the emptiness of his existence. Yet the film is little more than a running joke, hollow at the center, something like Harold Ramis' *Analyze That* (2002). Payne is, at length, giving in to the demands of the contemporary commercial cinema marketplace. As with so many other promision talents, it's sad to see finances win out over individual vision and creative autonomy. Reese Witherspoon, so perfectly cast in *Election*, disappointed many when she essentially reprised her role in *Legally Blonde* (2001), a poorly scripted legal comedy that nevertheless handily outperformed *Election* at the box office. She wants to be a star; can one really blame her? Time is short, and the list of stars who can "open" a film is shorter still. Better to get what you can now and appeal to the largest possible audience.

This sense of instant disposability and planned obsolescence dominates the discourse of all of popular culture, from the cinema, to video games, to cell phones and other props of the twenty-first-century teen fantasy zone. Films, pop music, and consumer goods are driven primarily by teen audiences. *Friends* is being kept on the air for a ninth, and hopefully final, season at an astronomical cost of $150 million for 24 half-hour shows, a rough cost of $6.5 million per episode (Adalian 1). Cutting out commercials, main titles, bumpers, and promos, the running time of each episode will be slightly more than 20 minutes. The stars of the show—Lisa Kudrow, David Schwimmer, Courteney Cox Arquette, Matt LeBlanc, Matthew Perry, and Jennifer Aniston—will all receive substantial pay raises, making *Friends* the "most expensive half-hour program in TV history" (Adalian 1), but worth it if it can hold on to teen audiences. Celebrities, not only in the United States, but also around the world, constitute the new instant royalty with purses to match their ephemeral status. Russell Crowe earned $15 million for his work in 2001; Tracey Ullman took home $7.25 million from a variety of projects. Gérard Depardieu's 2001 pay packet is estimated at $11.6 million, with Daniel Auteuil ($3.3 million), Juliette Binoche ($2.2 million), and Catherine Deneuve ($1.7 million) also comfortably in the seven-figure bracket. Jackie Chan earns $15 million a picture, whereas his frequent costar Michelle Yeoh is not far behind with $13 million for her 2001 salary.

In India, Aamir Khan averages $4.1 million per year in salary, making roughly $700,000 per film. In the United States the star salaries are the most inflated, led by Tom Cruise, who banked $70 million for his work in 2001. Jim Carrey, Chris Tucker, Mel Gibson, Tom Hanks, Harrison Ford, Bruce Willis, Julia Roberts, and Cameron Diaz all charge roughly $20 million per film; Nicolas Cage, Robert De Niro, Jodie Foster, Gwyneth Paltrow, Helen Hunt, and Will Smith are not far behind. Compare these figures to what the stars of the 1940s received during their peak earning years. In 1930, Humphrey Bogart earned roughly $39,000 a year, or $418,725 in today's currency. In 1941, Spencer Tracy took home $233,460, or $2.75 million today (all salary figures, Granier-Deferre 17). And what sort of projects do these stars produce for contemporary audiences? According to Robert Altman:

> Things certainly have to change. "Hollywood" has become an archaic term, even though the center of the business is there. It's actually only the toy factory; the art galleries are elsewhere. All the Hollywood money is being spent to make films for kids between the ages of 11 and 14—everything. What kills me is that the actors, directors and producers responsible for such junk stand up with great pride, as if they've done something artistic, when all they've done is to get the attention of preteens. Everyone else seems to be shut out. No one even draws attention to more sophisticated films other than film festivals and certain small groups in America. People call what I make "art films," as if it were something shameful. Can you imagine that? (qtd. in Spitz 42–43)

But a certain perverse logic is inherent in the derogatory label "art film," as veteran screenwriter Larry Gross points out. Art films, of course, are synonymous with "indie" films, narratives designed to appeal to a niche audience and nothing more. With salaries as high as they now are, why should anyone take a chance on a film that is not designed to be profitable? As Gross argues, indie films are not profitable. The studios are still unsure of what they should make, but they now have a self-evident indicator of what they shouldn't make. Indie films consistently perform too poorly at the box-office to make anyone at the studios anything but terrified or contemptuous of following their lead. And there is little that is intelligent or interesting in the aspirations of studio directors that does not in some dangerous way overlap with observable characteristics of indie films.

Indie films supply a road map of what to avoid, what mistakes not to make. Everything unconventional in technique and possibly marginal in content, anything not made with a palpable design on every demographic, now exists in a visible and intelligible framework that defines what it makes absolutely no sense to try. [...] The idiosyncratic story, the story with the less-than-sympathetic hero, the film connected to too specific a region or group, gets damned with more than just, "I don't see how we can sell it." An alarm bell goes off in the executive's head. Ding: "That sounds like an indie. That's not the business we're in." That's the other business, the one with the people who aren't concerned with and hence don't make money—the loser's business.

No one in Hollywood ever holds it against you when you make a good film. What people hold against you is not being serious about putting profits first. And the problem with indie films is that they created a tangible way of identifying that heresy, that sin. (13)

In such a landscape, how can anything even faintly original or subversive get made without a star who is willing to accept a massive salary cut, a producer who is willing to gamble on a risky project, and most important, a distributor who will find a way to get the film into theaters so that it can at least return its investment? And furthermore, if your film is not a mainstream project, what chance do you have of getting it reviewed in the press? *Daily Variety*, the show business newspaper that used to review every feature film (and often shot film) that was being theatrically released, has cut back sharply on its press coverage of "noncommercial" films in the past few years. And without a positive review in *Daily Variety*, a small film's commercial chances are severely limited. As veteran *Daily Variety* film critic David Rooney admits:

> Yeah, more and more now there is the push now to limit commercially marginal films to a couple of paragraphs. [...] There's a certain responsibility also in shaping a film's commercial potential and its commercial prospects, because for better or worse (and I'm not saying this is accurate and I'm not saying it's fair) but a lot of people use *Variety* as their guideline. A lot of buyers will say, "Well, maybe it's worth checking it out" (or maybe it's not) based on a *Variety* review. So there is a real responsibility and there's certain amount of pressure involved with that too, especially when there is so little time to think about it at Cannes. (qtd. in Simon 23-24)

And what, precisely, defines a "commercially marginal" film? It is a film with no distribution behind it. Think of all the alternative voices that are being silenced—and that would have been silenced—if there were not at one time a level playing field on which all films competed solely for theatrical exploitation. Films such as *Men Must Fight* (1933), a pacifist film that predicts with eerie accuracy the outbreak of war in 1940, was a small-scale project for MGM in the 1930s, but the constant need for theatrical programming ensured that it would find an audience, either at the top or the bottom of a double bill. Watching *Men Must Fight* is an eerie experience because the film details the effects of a massive air attack on New York City, complete with the collapse of the Brooklyn Bridge and the destruction of the then newly erected Empire State Building. Men are seen as unreasoning aggressors by reason of their gender alone; in the film's final moments, an elderly matriarch speculates that the world would be much better if governed by women with men serving as "ornaments." At 72 minutes, the film is densely packed with incident and characterization, and the capable cast, including Diana Wynyard, Lewis Stone, May Robson, and a very youthful Robert Young, give depth and reality to their respective characters. At the film's conclusion, we are left to wonder whether war, in a male-dominated society, is indeed inevitable. When the final attack comes, it is not a gloriously "thrilling" spectacle, but rather a menacing series of depressing images graphically illustrating the doom of civilization. The film leaves it to the viewer to draw the final conclusions; would such a film be possible today?

Robert L. Lippert, a cost-conscious producer who was active from 1946 until 1965, churned out a remarkable series of low-budget films in a wide variety of genres, including *The Murder Game* (1965), *The Earth Dies Screaming* (1964), *Night Train to Paris* (1964), *Witchcraft* (1964), *Lost Continent* (1951), *The Steel Helmet* (1951), *The Baron of Arizona* (1950), *Arson, Inc.* (1949), and *I Shot Jesse James* (1949), for a total of 58 films during his long career. Along the way, Lippert gave opportunities to gifted filmmakers such as Terence Fisher, Samuel Fuller, Don Sharp, and many others who learned their trade on Lippert's six-day feature films. Unlike contemporary television series, which conform to a rigid format and a continuing set of characters, or music videos, which traffic in recycled imagery from 1960s experimental films intercut with conventional pop iconography, small-budget films offered freedom to their directors, actors, and scenarists as long as they stayed on time and under budget. Producer Val Lewton's remarkable series of 1940s fantasy films, such as *I Walked with a Zombie* (1943), were designed by RKO Pictures to conform to strict budget and scheduling requirements with a heavily presold and sensationalistic title attached. But once Lewton accepted the assignment, RKO pretty much left him alone because the cost of his films was comparatively minuscule. We recognize *The Seventh Victim* (1943), *Cat People* (1942), and *The Body Snatcher* (1945) as classics of the macabre and a significant departure from the Universal "monster rally" films of the same era, such as *Frankenstein Meets the Wolf Man* (1943), *House of Frankenstein* (1944), and *House of Dracula* (1945). But their genesis was made possible only by the fact they were low-budget, no-risk investments for their producer and distributors, as well as by the fact that the major studios all owned their own chains of theaters, which were perpetually hungry for new product. *Deluge* (1933) is another apocalyptic film in which New York is destroyed by a giant tidal wave; again, it is a modestly budgeted film, considered no more than a sound commercial investment at the time. Nevertheless, as with *Men Must Fight*, the film raises a number of serious issues regarding mankind's delicate balance with the forces of nature, and for most of the film, dramatic exposition takes precedence over special effects. How different is the strategy of *Invasion U.S.A.* (1985), which bears no relationship to the 1952 film of the same name? *Invasion U.S.A.* is merely an excuse for action star Chuck Norris to load up on weaponry and wage a one-man war against invading foreign forces. The thoughtfulness of films such as *Atomic Attack* (1950), in which a family living on the outskirts of Manhattan are forced to flee when an A bomb wipes out the city, is entirely absent from contemporary apocalypse dramas. All that matters is destruction, with a continual wave of fresh victims as scenery.

Nor is this absence of characterization confined to the contemporary cinema alone. Video games, which have rapidly become a hotter rental commodity throughout the world than conventional DVDs of noninteractive films, are notorious for their reliance on violence and weaponry at the expense of any human element. *Doom III*, created by id Software, is the latest version of the popular single-player "point-and-shoot" video game that first appeared in 1993. It exemplifies this new trend toward creating an "adrenaline-crazed shooting experience that celebrates violence, blood and gore" (Markoff E5). Indeed, *Doom III* "virtually erase[s] the line between video game and animated Hollywood movie [... using] ear-bending Dolby 5.1 sound" (Markoff E5) and state-of-the-art special effects to make the brutally dystopian world of *Doom III* come to life. As Markoff reports:

> The newest *Doom* is set on Mars in 2145. In the beginning the camera pans in to the vast Union Aerospace Corporation, where a scientist sitting inside at a computer terminal is nervously entering commands.
>
> Moments later an explosion unleashes some kind of transformed human monster. What follows is designed to scare the daylights out of the game player. (E5)

The game, which John Carmack designed, uses new graphic rendering techniques that give the look and feel of the game a greater tactile presence. All that is missing is a narrative—or character motivation. But for Carmack, *Doom III* is "all about the realism of the graphics" (Markoff E5), not the story. The technical sophistication of *Doom III* intrigues Carmack, rather than its content, which is essentially a kill-or-be-killed race through an endless series of skilfully rendered labyrinthine tunnels:

> "We've been able to do things that for years have basically been water-cooler talk among programmers," Mr. Carmack said of the newest *Doom*. [...] In *Doom III*, "the world just works," he said. "I like the elegance." Of course one person's elegance might be another's painfully detailed hyperviolence. Asked about a violent scene played out in an industrial bathroom with gleaming stainless steel urinals in which a doglike monster eats the entrails of one of *Doom*'s omnipresent zombies, id's chief executive, Todd Hollenshead, maintained that the game was really not about violence. "The demo raises eyebrows," he said. "But we're going for a scary game over violence." Then, seemingly as an afterthought, he added, "It's not a game for small kids." (Markoff E5)

Nor is *Return to Castle Wolfenstein*, which allows players to relive (or experience at secondhand for the first time) the violent battles of World War II. Players can choose to be Allied soldiers or members of the Axis forces; unlike *Doom III* and its predecessors, *Return to Castle Wolfenstein* is a game for multiple players (Kay 1). *Day of Defeat*, another video game, traffics more openly in its embrace of Nazi iconography, showing "battlefields decorated with swastikas and Nazi posters [which] attracts many players with an enthusiasm for neo-Nazi role playing [as it] recreates specific World War II battles" (Kay 1). id Software produces these games, too, and id CEO Todd Hollenshead is quick to point out that, as far as he is concerned, they merely reflect the current social and political environment.

> The trend you're seeing with new games is, to some extent, a reflection of what's going in the culture. [...] For instance, you've now got games with terrorists and counterterrorists. And World War II games such as *Return to Castle Wolfenstein* and *Day of Defeat* reflect what you see in popular movies. (Kay 1)

Perhaps, but as Kay describes it, the chat rooms associated with *Day of Defeat* bristle with neo-Nazi sentiments, as Axis players with "noms de guerre like Mein Kampf, Hitler Youth and Zyklon B" discuss their strategy for future campaigns (1). Although this disturbs many observers, the game players themselves insist that the entire game is played in the spirit of innocent fun and that no one really gets hurt. Besides, it is great preparation for the real thing. As Matthew Lane, age 17, a *Day of Defeat* player from North Carolina enthuses:

> There's nothing like traveling back more than half a century to put yourself in the boots of a World War II soldier storming the beaches at Normandy. [...] As kids, many of us have dreamt what our grandfathers and fathers suffered through, and fought for, more than 50 years ago. *Day of Defeat* just brings these things to reality. (Kay 7)

This is something the US Army has certainly noticed as it discovers that new recruits are more interested in video games than in actual mock combat. To this end, the Army has created a series of specially modified games based on actual commercial video games to introduce would-be soldiers to the excitement and intensity of actual combat. As Alex Pham comments:

> One of the video games is a sanitized version of *Unreal Tournament*, a classic first-person shooting game known for its graphic, nonstop killing. Another is a take on *The Sims*, a popular game said to mimic life itself. But instead of dismembering mutants or pursuing romance, players can work on their organizational skills, free hostages and rise to the rank of first sergeant. The games are part of the *Army of One* marketing campaign, which stresses professionalism and the importance of the individual, themes that marketers say resonate with youths. (14)

The Army spent $5 million to develop these games, which have the deceptively generic names of *Soldiers*, *Operations*, and the like (Pham 14). In *Soldiers*, potential recruits are taken through the initial phases of life in the military, whereas *Operations* deals with elements of actual combat. As Pham comments, "the games show mostly action, leaving out the boring parts. [... P]layers going through sniper training in the more action-oriented *Operations* game do not have to camp out for hours waiting for terrorists to show up" (14). It is also great training for the experience of actual "video combat," in which soldiers involved in real military campaigns—such as the war in Afghanistan in early 2002—are forced to fight with video drones looking over their shoulders, sending a continual video feedback to headquarters, so that their commanding officers can critique their behavior under fire (Ricks 1). Not surprisingly, the soldiers themselves take a dim view of this invasion of privacy, complaining that their superiors display a tendency to treat them as mere pawns in an all-too-real video "game." The video surveillance system, known as Predator, is so much of a distraction to the soldiers that even some of the commanders find it less than useful. Colonel Kevin Wilkerson, a 10th Mountain Division brigade commander, commented that, "tactically, I don't think it affected what I did on the ground. To be honest with you, I didn't watch it a lot [because] Predator can be mesmerizing—like watching TV" (qtd. in Ricks 4). And like television, you keep watching in the hope that something exciting will happen—or else you turn it off.

Teens have a notoriously short attention span, and you have to grab them with something that piques their interest immediately or you've lost them as consumers. This is the guiding principle behind the creation of movie trailers, both classical and contemporary. Show the audience what you've got, but give them only a taste of it to whet their appetite for the entire experience. And with teenagers comprising the bulk of the modern cinema audience, the viewers you want to reach most are the 13–18 set, who spend on average $104 per week (in the United States), almost all of it on leisure items that strike their momentary fancy (Lee E6). Working with Teenage Research Unlimited, a long-established company that tracks teen spending and socializing habits, merchandisers have "boiled down teenage experience into a Venn diagram with three circles: entertainment, relationships and fashion" (Lee E6). But at the same time, contemporary teens want individuality without effort and prefer preprogrammed games and electronic devices that make most of the decisions for them. In creating software for the new generation, it's important not to put "too much pressure on kids to be artists. They don't want to be artists. They don't want to be completely unique," as one business executive flatly states (Lee E6). Furthermore, as Michael Wood, a vice president at Teenage Research Unlimited discovered, "While adults adopt new technologies for convenience, teenagers adopt new technologies largely for socializing," such as instant messaging (Lee E6). But the potential for social engagement has been drastically reduced also through the use of newly emerging technologies. We've routinely come to expect that, when we pick up the phone and dial a number, we will no longer hear a human voice on the other end. Even Jane Barbe, whose voice is used throughout the United States on numerous telephone systems to read prompts and deliver instructions, laments the current depersonalized state of affairs, noting that:

> It's a shame that we've come to this, that our lives are so busy that we can't even speak to a real person. So I try not to be a computerized voice, [but] to make it feel like you're really having a conversation with a person, rather than a recording. (qtd. in Leland 3)

But it is a recording, and it has come to this, and yet we are forced to continue on. The current US administration seems intent on upping the ante with each new pronouncement, even as tension spots in India and Pakistan, the Middle East, Africa, and Northern Ireland continue to simmer, even after decades of conflict. In a speech at the US Military Academy at West Point (USMA) on June 1, 2002, George W. Bush declared that "preemptive" military strikes may be necessary to "confront the worst threats before they emerge," thereby creating a scenario in which attack becomes defense. Said Bush to a crowd of some 25,000 in USMA's Michie Stadium, including 958 members of the class of 2002:

> The war on terror will not be won on the defensive. [...] We must take the battle to the enemy, disrupt its plans, and confront the worst threats before they emerge. [...] This government and the American people are on watch. We are ready, because we know the terrorists have more money and more men and more plans.

The gravest danger to freedom lies at the perilous crossroads of radicalism and technology. When the spread of chemical and biological and nuclear weapons, along with ballistic missile technology, when that occurs, even weak states and small groups could attain a catastrophic power to strike at great nations. (qtd. in Lindlaw)

This policy of perpetual alarmism, it seems to me, creates a self-fulfilling prophecy, just as violent action thrillers and video games inspire those who become addicted to them to take the "games" to the next step: real weapons, real victims. Not everyone who plays *Doom III* will become a mass murderer, but even a casual glance at the social landscape of contemporary America reveals that it has become a nation marked by outbursts of senseless violence, as Michael Moore so brilliantly documented in his film *Bowling for Columbine* (2002). The culture of guns, of death, of "kill or be killed" must inevitably lead to violence; is that not its message?

THE COPENHAGEN DEFENSE

In the play *Copenhagen*, the Nazi scientist Werner Heisenberg meets with Niels Bohr to discuss the creation of the atomic bomb, and whether Germany or the Allied Powers will use it. For decades, historians have argued that Heisenberg deliberately sabotaged the Nazi's research, knowing the catastrophe it would inevitably bring. However, new information has come to light that suggests that Heisenberg had no qualms about building the atomic bomb for Hitler. In a letter that Bohr wrote Heisenberg, but never sent, which is now archived in the Niels Bohr Archive (NBA) in Copenhagen, Bohr makes it clear that Heisenberg meant to go on with his work. As Finn Aaserud, NBA director states, "essentially, the letter shows that [Heisenberg] told Bohr that it was possible that the war would be won with atomic weapons, indicating that he was involved in such work" (qtd. in Glanz 4). Richard Rhodes, author of *The Making of the Atomic Bomb*, concurs with this revised view of Heisenberg's activities. Rhodes feels that Heisenberg "simply failed despite his best efforts" (Glanz 4), and only his limitations as a physicist held him back from the final breakthrough. Says Rhodes:

> This letter confirms what I think was always pretty clear in the record, and that is that Heisenberg was not making some deal with Bohr. He was trying to find out what Bohr knew. He was trying to do a little espionage. (qtd. in Glanz 4)

Bohr abruptly terminated the meeting and completely broke relations with Heisenberg, although the two men had been friends for years. Gerald Holton, emeritus professor of physics at Harvard University, agrees with Rhodes's analysis based on his own examination of the unsent letter. Glanz reports that Dr. Holton stated:

"Dr. Aaserud's report about some of its content is quite coherent with what we know" from other sources, including statements by a son of Mr. Bohr, the physicist Aage Bohr. Mr. Holton said, "It is significant that Dr. Aaserud does not mention that any moral scruples or intention to sabotage the bomb project were reasons for Heisenberg's visit to Bohr." [...] Mr. Holton also shed new light on why Mr. Bohr suddenly cut off the meeting and why it destroyed what had been Mr. Bohr's lifelong friendship with Mr. Heisenberg. Though some have attributed Mr. Bohr's reaction to anger, another explanation is more likely, Mr. Holton said.

"The first thing that would come to mind is not anger but deep fright," he said of Mr. Bohr's reaction to learning of a Nazi bomb program. "He understood what that would mean for civilization." (4)

But now the stakes are significantly higher. Every nation that wants nuclear capability can purchase it, either through legitimate channels or on the black market. In a world where one person can wipe out an entire metropolis with a nuclear device no larger than a suitcase, everyone is at risk. International boundaries vanish. Territories are zones of commerce. The entire world has become a potential battleground, a vivid and unsettling demonstration of what physicists have dubbed "the mediocrity principle," which states that no one place in the universe is more important than any other. We all live in a nuclear nation, no matter what our nationality. Our beliefs, our values, our memories, and our careers fade into insignificance, even as we contemplate our own mortality and the inherent transience of all our works. As the tagline for *The Texas Chainsaw Massacre* (1974) rhetorically asked, "Who will survive, and what will be left of them?" What remnants of our shared civilization will survive a nuclear holocaust, and what sort of new existence will we be faced with?

In 1969 the music festival at Woodstock, New York, was a relatively peaceful, if undisciplined, affair in which hundreds of thousands of people gathered to celebrate three days of "peace, love and music." The event was a financial disaster, but a cultural milestone. Banners proclaiming "We Proved It at Woodstock" perpetuated the myth that somehow society had been fundamentally altered and that the fabric of American consciousness would never be the same. But the reality was something far more disturbing: the concept of Woodstock had become a commodity to be marketed and repackaged at will. When the festival was "revived" in 1994, it was a paean to corporate sponsorship, rather than to countercultural social values. As Caryn James reports, "Häagen Dazs paid $1 million to be the official Woodstock ice cream, Vermont Water $1 million to become the official water, and Pepsi $5 million as a major sponsor" ("Woodstock" B1). More significant, the artists who performed at the 1994 concert were openly contemptuous of the original model. Trent Reznor of Nine Inch Nails described Woodstock 1969 "an ancient, hippie-oriented thing," and Henry Rollins declared, "I'm staying at the Marriott" ("Woodstock" B5) rather than pitching a tent in an open field. By Woodstock 1999, punctuated by rapes, random violence, and looting, society clearly had changed, and the concept of a music festival with it. Violent times demand violent music, and Woodstock 1999 did not disappoint in this regard.

But had Woodstock ever existed? Was the spirit of anarchy and freedom that typified the 1960s merely an impressive and persuasive illusion? Or has technology, and our reliance on it, substantially altered our lives? If one looks at our shared cinematic past, we can see that we have always been playing with disaster, fascinated by destruction. The 2,823 victims of the September 11 disaster, and the 16 acres of damage at the World Trade Center and the Pentagon are merely the fulfillment of a dream of annihilation that has fascinated us for centuries. It is only in the latter part of the 19th century, the 20th century, and now the 21st century, that we can give these phantasmal visions faces and sounds a sense of concrete actuality. The regime of CGI effects has made the illusion even more seamless. Where once matte lines and other technical imperfections created "limit zones" of visual reality that distanced us from the spectacle we witnessed, now CGI makes a tidal wave, an atomic blast, a hurricane, or a meteor impact seem as real as late afternoon sunlight spilling through a back porch window. There is no separation anymore, no zone of the real and the not real. The cinema of the 21st century makes our most violent dreams of self-destruction simultaneously mundane and yet instantly attainable.

While we entertain ourselves with staged "celebrity boxing" matches, such as the much-touted Tonya Harding/Paula Jones bout on Fox television, the clock of the *Bulletin of Atomic Scientists* keeps ticking, now set (in 2002) at seven minutes to midnight (*Bulletin of the Atomic Scientists*). We can amuse ourselves, momentarily, by enumerating the various natural and/or man-made scenarios of apocalyptic destruction, such as:

an asteroid impact, a gamma ray burst, collapse of the vacuum, rogue black holes, giant solar flares, reversal of the earth's magnetic field, volcanic eruptions, global epidemics, global warming, ecosystem collapse, biotech disaster, environmental toxins, global war, a war on humans by a race of self-procreating robots, mass insanity, alien invasion, divine intervention (the Rapture), or perhaps the fact that someone wakes up and realizes that all of human recorded history is merely a dream. (See Powell for more on these variant theories.)

But all of these hypothetical end games are something to do to pass the time. Of all the scenarios previously listed, global nuclear war is the only one that has any genuine credibility. Smaller scale visions of the apocalypse, such as that offered in *San Francisco* (1936) or *The Day the Sky Exploded*, offer an exit point for the viewer. In *San Francisco*, the earthquake is containable, confined to one area and one reel of the film's running time. In *The Day the Sky Exploded*, a missile explodes in the upper atmosphere, bringing down a rain of cosmic debris on the earth's inhabitants, but once again the threat is transient. In *Hooper* (1978), two stunt men earn their living creating realistic scenes of death and destruction for the cinema, climaxing in a final sequence involving a "rocket car" that nearly kills them both. But nothing is really at risk; what has been staged can be deconstructed, and the "chaos" is both staged and formulaic. In *The Last Days of Man on Earth* (1973; original title *The Final Programme*, 1973), the backdrop of destruction serves merely as a setting for a romance between the film's two protagonists, who wander about a landscape littered with heaps of rusting automobiles in no particular hurry to escape their putative fate.

In *The Bed Sitting Room* (1969), the banalities of class struggle continue even after the world and most of its inhabitants have been vaporized in a final, massive conflict. Yet amidst the ruins, civilization retains a pernicious hold on the film's characters, who perform Beckettian slapstick routines as they struggle toward a vision of normalcy in a world that no longer cares about their existence. *When Worlds Collide* (1951) presents a genuine vision of Armageddon, as a stray planet crashes into Earth. But the scenes of Earth's demise are balanced by the escape of a handful of survivors in a custom-made rocket, which takes them to a new, Edenic planet. Significantly, the images of flooding and disaster that punctuate the final reel of the film are conspicuously devoid of people. We are not one of the dead, but rather one of the survivors, and the new paradise is ours to share with the privileged few who have cheated catastrophe. This is the secret hope that lies behind all scenarios of apocalyptic destruction: because we have witnessed them, we have survived, and the simulacrum of Armageddon has somehow replaced the reality of the event itself. There is always a way out. There has to be. Otherwise, how could these documents have survived to give us a warning?

> The H-Bomb! The H-Bomb! The H-Bomb! Flash of brightness. A tremendous roar. [...] And I, the complacent American, thinking that on one would ever dare attack an American city. And I told my friends that nuclear war would never happen [...] but it did. I always thought I was a good American—patriotic and civic minded. But I was wrong. I failed myself and my country. (Conelrad, "Complacent")

This first-person confession comes from a 1961 record album entitled *The Complacent Americans*, in which an unprepared "good American" is vaporized by a hydrogen bomb attack. Now, speaking from beyond the grave, he laments his lack of vigilance, his lack of cooperation with civil defense authorities, his inability and unwillingness to fit into the milieu of Cold War American paranoia:

> I can see people alive in the fallout shelters. Had I learned the rules as set forth by the Office of Civil Defense, I would be alive and in that shelter now. How simple it looked—those who knew what to do and where to go are still amongst the living. I had my opportunity, but I was the Complacent American. (Conelrad, "Complacent")

Could he have done anything differently? Could he have survived? In a sense, as with the films just discussed, because he can relate his experience even after death, he has survived if only to create this aural artifact. But does *The Complacent Americans* promote civil defense awareness, or does the hysteria and fear surrounding the possibility of an atomic invasion promote *The Complacent Americans* as a product to be purchased? Is the threat genuine? Is the record itself genuine? When *Invasion U.S.A.* first appeared in theaters in 1952, the promotional suggestions for theater managers included staging air raid drills, civil defense parades, even displaying actual nuclear weapons in the theater lobby, all in the cause of selling the picture to the public. Among other ideas to sell *Invasion U.S.A.* to potential patrons, theater owners were urged to:

> Work out, if possible, a "siren" opening of your film—a test "alert" for civilian defense workers. This practice drill, called in conjunction with *Invasion U.S.A.*, should be an invaluable promotion idea.
>
> Distribute posters, for use in all public buildings throughout your city, boosting civilian defense and your showing of *Invasion U.S.A.* Sample poster copy: "Learn What Will Happen If the Bombs Start Falling! Join the Civilian Defense Corps. [...] See Columbia's *Invasion U.S.A.* State Theatre Friday."
>
> Arrange a special exhibit of new techniques of warfare that are off the secret list, but are not too generally known. Display photos and, if possible, weapons themselves. (*Invasion U.S.A.* pressbook)

Above all other considerations, *Invasion U.S.A.* was an exploitation film, as producer Albert Zugsmith made abundantly clear in a 1973 interview. After beginning his career in the eastern United States as a newspaperman, Zugsmith sold his interests and moved to Los Angeles, hoping to break into the film industry. Always an able self-promoter, Zugsmith struck a deal with arch anti-Communist crusader Howard Hughes, who was then running RKO Pictures into the ground through inept management. Hughes was hungry for product, so Zugsmith came to him with an offer to make three very low-budget pictures at prices which Howard Hughes was reputed to have said: "It can't be done." They were $100,000 each. Under strictly union conditions, IATSE conditions, and on the old RKO-Pathé lot, now called the Culver City Studios, which were the old Selznick studios. So we made them with our own money, but Hughes reimbursed us, up to $100,000—no more than that!—on each picture. (McCarthy and Flynn, "Zugsmith" 412)

Right from the start, Zugsmith was interested in films that dealt with the Apocalypse because he knew that spectacles of mass destruction always performed reliably at the box office. Not that he was under any illusions that he was creating something of value; no, what Zugsmith wanted to do was make money, and the end of the world was as promising a prospect as one could imagine. After all, Zugsmith was financing the films with his own money, which amounted to an interest-free loan to Hughes and RKO, and he had to be certain to recoup his investment. Zugsmith recalled that:

We made these three pictures for RKO and, of course, we were forced to use people we didn't want to take as actors, so the pictures weren't that great. The first one was a look into the future, which we called *3000 A.D.* RKO, possibly on Mr. Hughes's orders, changed the title to *Captive Women* [1952]. It was a look at what would happen to places like New York after the atomic bomb fell, and so forth. Something like *Beneath the Planet of the Apes* [1971]. So I was determined then to make a picture of my own and I made *Invasion U.S.A.* [1952], which was my first big sleeper. I made that for $127,000 cash and about $60,000 deferred. [...] And while it's far from perfect, for $127,000, for a film shot in seven days, I feel it's a good job. Of course, full of heartaches and headaches, but worth it. And I suppose the public responded, because the net profits on the film were close to $1,000,000. (McCarthy and Flynn, "Zugsmith" 413)

The trailer for the film certainly helped with taglines such as, "SEE! New York Disappear! SEE! Seattle Blasted! SEE! San Francisco in Flames!" as nominal stars

Gerald Mohr and Peggie Castle stroll through the wreckage of Manhattan, and Mohr observes sanguinely that, "War or no war, people have to eat and drink [...] and make love." As the film's pressbook noted, "*Invasion U.S.A.*, in which cities vanish before your eyes, will inspire awareness of civilian defense in everyone" (*Invasion U.S.A.* pressbook). Or perhaps it will just inspire them to sit at home, draw the blinds, and prepare for the worst.

Economies in the film are everywhere. William Schallert, perhaps best known for his role as Patty Duke's father on *The Patty Duke Show* in the 1960s, worked only one day on the film (April 7, 1952) and was paid $75 for his efforts (Conelrad, "*Invasion U.S.A.*"). Amazingly, for a film with such a spectacular exploitation campaign, the production is, for the most part, confined to three or four cheap sets (a bar, an apartment, a television station, and a munitions plant office), interspersed with miles of stock footage of the Allied offense during World War II, which was obtained without cost from the US National Archives and Records Administration. The *New York Times*, for one, was not deceived, noting in their review of May 1, 1953, that:

> *Invasion U.S.A.*, the Columbia release opened yesterday at the Globe, is an atomic-war picture showing the invasion and subjugation of the United States by an unnamed, but obviously Soviet, army. It is almost wholly composed of stock combat newsreel footage taken during World War II. But its clever editing makes it a war of the future, complete with atom-seared American cities, drowned American children (when Boulder Dam is atomized), and gut-shot senators on Capitol Hill. And, as a *pièce de résistance*, a stately and desirable American girl commits suicide to avoid being revoltingly pawed by a fat, brutish, whiskey-swilling soldier whose accent places his origin just north of Minsk. It is a message picture. All the actors in it, especially the leads, Gerald Mohr, Peggie Castle, Dan O'Hierlihy [sic], and Robert Bice are dismal in their roles. (qtd. in Conelrad, "*Invasion U.S.A.*")

But no matter. The film seduced its patrons into theaters with a promise of the ultimate conflict and then delivered precisely what $127,000 and seven days would allow: a shoddy spectacle that, in the end, turned out to be the result of a hypnotic trance created by Mr. Ohman (Dan O'Herlihy)—just another nuclear nightmare. Although *Invasion U.S.A.* has attained a certain cult status as an authentic artifact of Cold War hysteria, it is not one of a kind, and it speaks to our current political climate, just as *The Sum of All Fears* caters to contemporary paranoia. There is no end to the list of atomic apocalypse movies, but the genre is far from being moribund or confined to the concerns of a single title. Films such as *Survival Under Atomic Attack, Genbaku Shi: Killed by the Atomic Bomb* (1994), *America's Atomic Bomb Tests* (1998), *America's Atomic Bomb Tests: At Ground Zero* (1997), *America's Atomic Bomb Tests: Operation Hardtack* (1997), *Enola Gay: The Men, the Mission, the Atomic Bomb* (1980), *Trinity and Beyond* (1995), *My Mother-in-Law Is an Atomic Bomb* (1952; original title *Hamati kombola zorria*, 1952), *R.C.A.F. Nuclear Defence: H Hour Now* (1959), *The Atomic City* (1952), *Atomic Journeys* (1999), *Atomic Juggernaut* (1971), *The Atomic Kid* (1954), *Atomic Lady* (1963), *Atomic Power* (1946), *Atomic Rulers of the World* (1964), *Atomic Samurai* (1993), *The Atomic Submarine* (1959), *The Fiend with the Atomic Brain* (1972; original title *Blood of Ghastly Horror*, 1972), *Canadian Mounties vs. Atomic Invaders* (1953), *Class of Nuke 'Em High* (1986), *How We Stole the Atomic Bomb* (1967; original title *Come rubammo la bomba atomica*, 1967), *Atomic Rocketship* (1936; original title *Flash Gordon*, 1936), *Invasion by the Atomic Zombies* (1980; original title *La Invasión de los Zombies atómicos*, 1980), *Atomic Monster* (1953; original title *Man Made Monster*, 1941), *Atomic Cyborg* (1986; original title *Mani di pietra*, 1986), *The Atomic Brain* (1964; original title *Monstrosity*, 1964), *Atomic Agent* (1959; original title *Nathalie, agent secret*, 1959), *Atomic Reporter* (1991; original title *Revenge of the Radioactive Reporter*, 1991), *Atomic Secret* (1967; original title *Tecnica per un massacro*, 1967), *The Atomic Man* (1956; original title *Timeslip*, 1956), and numerous other titles offer reassurance, if that is the right word, that the thought of imminent destruction is never far from our cinematic consciousness. Numerous Web sites, such as Conelrad (which specializes in nuclear disaster scenarios) and It's A Mad, Mad, Mad Max World (which deals with all sorts of apocalyptic visions, be they natural, nuclear, or supernatural), proliferate on the World Wide Web. If anything, the current appetite for corporeal and spiritual destruction is nothing more than a manifestation of manic information overload. We now have access to everything, but the sheer quantity of information overwhelms us. From the Nazi cinema's obsession with death, evident in necrophilic spectacles such as *S.A.—Mann Brand* (1933), *Hitler Youth Quex* (1933; original title *Hitlerjunge Quex: Ein Film vom Opfergeist der deutschen Jugend*, 1933), and *Blutendes Deutschland* (1932), which glorified mob violence, self-sacrifice for Hitler, and virulent racism, to after-the-fall ruminations on the lingering effects of the Third Reich such as *Hitler: The Last Ten Days* (1973), *The Night Porter* (1974; original title *Il portiere di notte*, 1974), and *The Damned* (1969; original title, *La caduta degli dei*, 1969), all is available to us. The more contemporary films distance us from the Nazi regime, aestheticizing it as a phenomenon to be observed, dissected, and understood, as if such a thing were possible. No matter what the makers of these later films intend, they serve only to keep the memory of Nazism alive, a potentially "cool" lifestyle (as we have seen in the use of Nazi imagery in video games) that loiters about, waiting to seduce those who wish to toy with the themes of destruction. In contrast, Alain Resnais' masterful short film, the 28-minute *Night and Fog* (1955; original title *Nuit et brouillard*, 1955), positions the existence of memory as an unreliable guide to comprehension of the past, intercutting captured Nazi atrocity footage with scenes of the death camps 10 years after their reign of human destruction. In *Hitler Youth Quex*, the story of a blond Hitler youth who is killed by Communist thugs and thus becomes a martyr to the Nazi party, the dead youth becomes the symbol of a new, "racially pure" Germany, his figure superimposed on the swastika flags and Baldur von Schirach's marching song booming across the soundtrack:

> For Hitler we march through night and through dread
> With the flag of youth for freedom and bread [...]
> Yes, the flag means more than being dead! (Phillips 50)

This is the same cult of death we pursue now, as the ultimate decadent recreation.

Yet all of it remains remote, carefully contained within a box of homicidal and genocidal dreams. In the middle of *Jason X*, two of the film's characters play a video game in which they create an alternate universe and then proceed to hack each other to pieces with graphic verisimilitude. When Jason unexpectedly enters their game world, they both shout, "Game over," at which point everything in their synthetic playground vanishes, except for Jason himself. As Jason lumbers toward his two victims, the players cry, "Pause, pause!" expecting Jason to freeze in his tracks. But Jason, of course, is not part of the game; he is, within the construct of the film's narrative, real. And thus both players meet "actual" death, as Jason wordlessly dispatches one and then the other. Yet all of this moves us not at all because we know that *we* are "playing" a game, that we can hit the pause button at any time, or exit the theater without fear of reprisal. It is as if the events we witness in *Jason X* were produced in another world. As Paolo Cherchi Usai movingly writes:

> We know little or nothing about the moving images produced in remote parts of the world and lost soon after their first exhibition. What kind of images can be seen in Baku? What is available to a viewer in Taveuni? What do they make of our images? Their relative distance leaves us with the same lack of involvement we feel at the news of the passing away of a person we have never heard of before. (97)

I once knew a man named Andrew Meyer, who created a series of lyrically beautiful films in New York in the 1960s, when a number of us were involved in what was euphemistically called the "Underground Cinema." Working at first in standard 8mm, Meyer made the silent *Shades and Drumbeats* (1964), which chronicled the life of a group of his friends living on the Lower East Side of Manhattan. This first film was met with considerable critical acclaim, even receiving a number of public screenings (impossible in the current marketplace for such a personal project) and moved Meyer to create the 8mm film *Annunciation* (1964) and then the 16mm short *Match Girl* (1966), based on the Hans Christian Andersen story. As with most experimental films, *Match Girl* grew organically as Meyer sought to shape the storyline to his own personal world. At the time of the film's release, Meyer commented:

I started out knowing I was going to do a film based on Hans Christian Andersen's tale of the poor little match girl, which had been filmed by Renoir in 1927. However, this got mixed up in my mind with a poor little rich girl story about a successful but lonely fashion model who idealizes herself as a story-book character. Out of this confusion comes one of the themes of the film: that what is most illusive can also be most real. Thus, when the girl hallucinates, she is watching Hitchcock's *Vertigo*, a film which revolves around similar ideas. Besides the character of the girl, interpreted by model Vivian Kurz, there is a sort of Prince Charming, played by poet Gerard Malanga, also trying to maintain a certain image of himself. Andy Warhol appears as a witch or overlord of the pop milieu in which the action takes place. The grandmother in the story is replaced by Marilyn Monroe as a sort of fairy godmother to the girl. (*New American Cinema Group* 108)

The finished film, running slightly less than one-half hour and photographed in sumptuous color, won prizes at the 1966 Ann Arbor Film Festival and the Festival of Two Worlds in Spoleto, Italy, also in 1966, and Meyer's career seemed truly launched. His next project, the ineffably romantic *An Early Clue to the New Direction* (1967), won First Prize at the 1967 Ann Arbor Film Festival, and moved *Village Voice* critic James Stoller to declare the film "unexpected, glorious, and indescribably moving [...] I can't forget it" (qtd. in New American Cinema Group 108). Set in Boston, the film starred Prescott Townsend, a well-known Boston avant-garde figure, caught in a relationship triangle with Joy Bang and René Ricard, who both compete for his affections. Nearly plotless, the film drifts through a world of lazy afternoons spent bicycling down the streets of nearby Cambridge, having tea in Prescott's suitably bohemian apartment, and tangentially considering what the future might bring. With the success of this second 16mm film, Meyer pooled all of his money and produced *The Sky Pirate* (1970), a 16mm feature film starring Joy Bang, which was indifferently received. Meyer's meager resources were not adequate to the task he had set for himself and so, after due consideration, he left New York for Hollywood.

By 1972, Meyer had become part of Roger Corman's New World Pictures and was given a chance to direct *Night of the Cobra Woman* (1972), a low-budget horror film shot in the Philippines, which was an unsatisfying experience for all concerned, both critically and commercially. Thus, in 1973, it was pretty much a do-or-die proposition when Corman handed Meyer a print of the Japanese disaster movie *Tidal Wave* (1973; original title *Nippon chinbotsu*, 1973), and told him that he had two days with the Canadian actor Lorne Greene (best known for his work on the teleseries *Bonanza* and *Battlestar Galactica*) to revamp the film into a US version. Meyer slashed the original film's 140-minute running time to 70 minutes and then shot 20 minutes of linking footage featuring Greene as Ambassador Warren Richards, with a cameo by future director Joe Dante. As Meyer told me, the material with Lorne Greene was shot hurriedly with little time for rehearsal. The one concession to visual luxury that Meyer's linking footage possessed was that it was shot in Panavision to match the existing Japanese material. For most of his screen time, Greene reads speeches at the viewer, essentially saying, "just look at these scenes of terrible destruction," as earthquakes, volcanoes, and hurricanes threaten to sink Japan into the Pacific Ocean. By the film's end, of course, cataclysmic disaster is averted, but not before scene after scene of violence and destruction is unspooled before the eyes of the spectator. Intercutting and shortening the Japanese version to suitable length for commercial US distribution, Meyer edited out all of the exposition sequences, keeping only the scenes of violent destruction. Confined to a single set for his two days of shooting, Lorne Greene could do little more than gesture at the audience, reciting meaningless dialogue to fill up time and—not incidentally—lend the prestige of his name to the film's credits. The film was a moderate success for New World, but no more than that. *Tidal Wave* was Andrew Meyer's last film. He died in Los Angeles on March 8, 1987.

When Meyer was working in New York in the company of other experimental filmmakers such as Warren Sonbert, Gerard Malanga, and Andy Warhol, we would run into each other occasionally at parties, discuss plans for future projects, exchange gossip, and go our separate ways. The last time I saw Meyer was at a screening of the Soviet/US coproduction *The Blue Bird* (1976), a lackluster children's fantasy film with an all-star cast including Elizabeth Taylor,

Jane Fonda, Ava Gardner, Cicely Tyson, and Robert Morley. Meyer invited me to the film's premiere screening at the Academy of Motion Picture Arts and Sciences to welcome me to Los Angeles; I was spending the summer there working for an experimental television group called TVTV, headed by Michael Shamberg. It was not a pleasant evening. Despite George Cukor's direction, *The Blue Bird* was a failure, and everyone in the auditorium knew it. Even at a modest 99 minutes, the film seemed interminable. As the first cinematic joint venture between Russia and the United States, it was hardly an auspicious beginning. The affair was black tie, and I felt somewhat out of place in a jacket and tie, whereas Meyer had clearly taken the occasion more seriously, renting a tux and greeting industry figures in the lobby before and after the film. It was all so cold, so joyless, and so calculated, that I knew then that I could never possibly live or work in Los Angeles. There was money to be made, true, but there were too many compromises. Meyer had strayed from his original vision to become just another commercial moviemaker, and his heart was not in it, even as part of him yearned for mainstream success.

What happens to us when part of ourselves dies? What happens to us when the world dies? At what point is annihilation so total that there is no possibility of repairs, no hope of rehabilitation, no possible way to recover what has been lost? When we view images in the darkness that prefigure our own end, we are trying to visualize our perfect death, to choreograph the end of time to our own personal advantage. When we cease to exist, the world ceases to exist because we can no longer apprehend it. And it is this moment that we fear and anticipate above all others because it represents the complete disintegration of the self. The visions of the apocalypse discussed in this book, and the strategies we may use to forestall them, are but a part of the stakes of cinematic representationalism. As we enter the era of holographic computer games in which we can die and die again, painlessly and in a variety of aesthetically pleasing ways, we must ask ourselves: what are we afraid of? The answer is simple. When we dream of the certainty and inevitability of the apocalypse, we are afraid of life itself.

WORKS CITED AND CONSULTED

Adalian, Josef. "Staying *Friends*: NBC Pays $150 Million for Final Year." *Daily Variety* 12 Feb. 2002: 1, 18.

Adbusters Media Foundation. "Organized Crime." Broadside. 2002.

Adee, Peter. "View from the Top." *Daily Variety* 25 Apr. 2002: A4.

Adrian, Werner. *Speed: Cinema of Motion*. London: Lorrimer, 1975.

Ajami, Fouad. "What the Muslim World Is Watching." *New York Times Magazine* 18 Nov. 2001: 48-53, 76, 78.

Al-Manar Television. Web site. 25 May 2002 <http://www.manartv.com/html/about.html>.

"Al-Qaida Got Ideas from *Godzilla* Movie." *Omaha World Herald* 27 May 2002: 3A.

Alton, John. *Painting with Light*. Berkeley: U of California P, 1995.

"And in This Corner." Editorial. *New York Times* 8 Mar. 2002: A22.

"Angel or Devil? Viewers See Images in Smoke." 13 July 2002 <http://www.clickon detroit.com/sh/news/stories/nat-news-96283920010917-120936.html>.

Associated Press. "High Court Hears Copyright Case." *Wired Online* 19 Feb. 2002. 13 July 2002 <http://www.wired.com/news/politics/0,1283,50521,00.html>.

Associated Press. "Rumsfeld Joins Grim Forecast on Terrorism." *U.S.A. Today* 21 May 2002. 23 May 2002 <http://www.usatoday.com/news/attack/2002/05/21/rumsfeld-attacks-warning.htm>.

Associated Press. "U.S. Officials Raise Specter of Attack." *Taipei Times Online* 23 May 2002. 23 May 2002 <http://www.taipeitimes.com/news/2002/05/23/story/0000137223>.

"Atom Bomb Loosed on Nagasaki." *New York Times Online* 9 Aug. 1945. 23 May 2000 <http://www.nytimes.com/learning/general/onthisday/big/0809.html>.

Auletta, Ken. "Battle Stations: How Long Will the Networks Stick with the News?" *New Yorker* 10 Dec. 2001: 60-67.

Bach, Deborah. "The Sexploiter Was Rather Proper." *New York Times* 29 May 2002, sec. 2: 37.

"The Bad Fads Museum: Fallout Shelters." 23 May 2000 <http://www.badfads.com/pages/activities/bomb.html>.

Craig Baldwin. Web site. 16 May 2000 <http://www.hi-beam.net/mkr/cb/cb-bio.html>.

Barson, Michael, and Steven Heller. *Red Scared! The Commie Menace in Propaganda and Popular Culture*. San Francisco: Chronicle, 2001.

Baard, Erik. "The Guilt-Free Soldier: New Science Raises the Spectre of a World Without Regret." *Village Voice* 22-28 Jan. 2003: 33-5.

Bart, Peter. "H'W'D War Summit: White House Summons Biz Chieftains." *Daily Variety* 7 Nov. 2001: 1, 39.

Battaglio, Stephen. "Black Comedy that Looks Frighteningly Prophetic." *New York Times* 3 Feb. 2002, sec. 2: 25, 31.

Becker, Julian. *Hitler's Children: The Story of the Baader–Meinhof Terrorist Gang.* Philadelphia: Lippincott, 1977.

Belson, Ken. "Japan Holds Back on Films by Cell Phone." *International Herald Tribune* 23 Apr. 2002: 13.

Benjamin, Mark. "Rumsfeld: Terrorists to Get Doomsday Bomb." *Washington Times* 21 May 2002. 23 May 2000 <http://www.washtimes.com/upi-breaking/21052002-061915-1682r.htm>.

Bergman, Andrew. *We're in the Money: Depression America and Its Films.* New York: Harper and Row, 1971.

Berkowitz, B. J., et al. *Superviolence: The Threat of Mass Destruction Weapons.* Santa Barbara, CA: ADCON, 1972.

Binns, Stewart, and Adrian Wood. *The Second World War in Colour.* London: Pavilion, 1999.

Blomquist, Brian. "Top Aides Rally Round the Prez." *NYPost.com.* 13 July 2002 <http://pqarchiver.nypost.com/nypost/>.

Bodansky, Yossef. *Bin Laden: The Man Who Declared War on America.* Rocklin, GA: Prima, 1999.

Brackett, D. W. *Holy Terror: Armageddon in Tokyo.* New York: Weatherhill, 1996.

Brockman, Alfred. *The Movie Book: The 1930s.* New York: Crescent, 1987.

Brottman, Mikita, ed. *Car Crash Culture.* New York: Palgrave, 2001.

Brown, Patricia Leigh. "Megachurches as Minitowns." *New York Times* 9 May 2002: D1, D6.

Bulletin of Atomic Scientists. Web site. 4 Apr. 2000 <http://www.thebulletin.org/clock_print.html>.

Burns, Robert. "Rumsfeld: More Attacks Could Be Deadlier than Sept. 11." *North County Times* 1 Feb. 2002. 23 May 2000 <http://www.nctimes.com/news/2002/20020201/52535.html>.

Busch, Anita M., and Beth Laski. "Total Recall." *Premiere* Dec. 2001: 46, 48, 50–1.

"Bush Gives the Go-Ahead for Cyber Attack Strategy." *The Hindu Online* 7 Feb. 2003 <http://www.hinduonnet.com/thehindu/stories/2003020801891400.htm>.

Calabresi, Massimo, and Romesh Ratnesar. "Can We Stop the Next Attack?" *Time.com* 3 Mar. 2002. 13 July 2002 <http://www.time.com/time/nation/printout/0,8816,214064,00.html>.

Canemaker, John. *Tex Avery: The MGM Years, 1942–1955.* North Dighton, MA: JG Press, 1998.

Carr, David. "For *Cosmo,* It's Sex and the World." *International Herald Tribune* 27 May 2000: 1, 9.

Carter, Ashton B., John M. Deutch, and Philip D. Zelikow. *Catastrophic Terrorism: Elements of a National Policy.* 25 May 2002 <http://www.ksg.harvard.edu/visions/publication/terrorism.htm>.

Cha, Ariana Eunjung. "Bye-Bye Borderless Web: Countries Are Raising Electronic Fences." *International Herald Tribune* 5–6 Jan. 2002: 1, 4.

Cheshire, Godfrey. "The Not-So-New Wave: Iran's High-Water Mark." *Village Voice* 24 Apr. 2001: 142.

Chomsky, Noam. *9-11*. New York: Seven Stories P, 2001.

___. *Media Control: The Spectacular Achievements of Propaganda*. New York: Seven Stories P, 1997.

Chow, Rey. "A Phantom Discipline." *PMLA* 116.5 (Oct. 2001): 1386-1395.

Cohen, David. "Studios Raise Synergy Bars." *Daily Variety* 25 Apr. 2002: A6.

Cohen, Scott Lyle. "Talking to Mom Sharon, the Wizard of Ozz." *Interview* June 2002: 62.

___. "Talking to Ozzy, the Big Daddy." *Interview* June 2002: 69.

Combs, Cindy C. *Terrorism in the Twenty-First Century*. Upper Saddle River, NJ: Prentice Hall, 1997.

Conelrad. "All Things Atomic." 25 May 2002 <http://www.conelrad.com/>.

Conelrad. "The Complacent Americans." 2 June 2000 <http://www.conelrad.com/media/atomicmusic/complacent.html>.

Conelrad. "*Invasion U.S.A.:* Ephemera and Reviews." 13 July 2002 <http://www.conelrad.com/features/invasionusa/ephemera.html>.

Conelrad. *Invasion U.S.A.* Pressbook. 2 June 2002 <http://www.conelrad.com/pressbooks/militarydefense.html> and <http://www.conelrad.com/pressbooks/civiliandefense.html>.

"Copyright Forever?" Editorial. *Washington Post* 5 Mar. 2002: A18.

Curtis, Bryan. "4,000 Jews, 1 Lie: Tracking an Internet Hoax." *Slate* 5 Oct. 2001. 12 June 2000 <http://slate.msn.com/?id=116813>.

Doa, James. "American Officials Disclose 2-Year Plan to Rebuild Iraq." *New York Times Online* 12 Feb. 2003 <http://www.nytimes.com/2003/02/12/international/middleeast/12POST.html?ex=1045717200&en=bf633853a659c79f&ei=5062&partner=GOOGLE>.

Davies, Joseph. *Mission to Moscow*. New York: Garden City Publishing, 1941, 1943.

Di Orio, Carl. "Digital Gurus Can't Send in 'The Clones.'" *Daily Variety* 14 Feb 2002: 1, 32.

___. "*Spider*'s in Outer Space." *Daily Variety* 6 May 2002: 1, 14.

Dixon, Wheeler Winston. "Twenty-five Reasons Why It's All Over." *The End of Cinema as We Know It*. Ed. Jon Lewis. New York: New York UP, 2001: 356-366.

___. *Collected Interviews: Voices from 20th Century Cinema*. Carbondale: Southern Illinois UP, 2001.

___. *The Films of Jean-Luc Godard*. Albany: State U of New York P, 1997.

Donner, Frank J. *The Un-Americans*. New York: Ballantine, 1961.

Dumpert, Hazel-Dawn. "Her Name Is Nina Foch." *LA Weekly* 4-10 Sept. 1998. 18 May 2002 <http://www.laweekly.com/ink/98/41/film-dumpert.shtml>.

Duncan, Paul. *Film Noir: Films of Trust and Betrayal*. Herts, UK: Pocket Essentials, 2000.

Dunlap, David W. "From 88 Searchlights, an Ethereal Tribute." *New York Times* 4 May 2002: A23.

Dupont, Joan. "Allen Comes to Town in 'A Gesture of Reciprocity.'" *International Herald Tribune* 15 May 2002: 17.

___. "The Dark Side of a French Filmmaker." *International Herald Tribune* 21 May 2002: 18.

Eaton, Mick. *Anthropology-Reality-Cinema: The Films of Jean Rouch*. London: BFI, 1979.

Eberhart, David. "Fallout Shelters Fall Short in U.S. *NewsMax.com* 15 Feb. 2002. 23 May 2002

<http://www.newsmax.com/archives/articles/2002/2/14/202328.shtml>.

Edelstein, David. "An Actor So Prolific It's Downright Scary." *Sunday New York Times* 12 May 2002, Special Summer Movies sec.: 3, 17.

Edozien, Frankie, and Vincent Morris. "Cheney: Dems' 9/11 Criticism Is 'Irresponsible.'" *NYPost.com.* 13 July 2002 <http://pqarchiver.nypost.com/nypost/>.

Edwards, Anne. *Early Reagan: The Rise of An American Hero.* London: Hodder and Stoughton, 1988.

Eilperin, Juliet. "Democrat Implies Sept. 11 Administration Plot." *Washington Post* 12 Apr. 2002. 13 July 2002 <http://www.washingtonpost.com/ac2/wp-dyn/A34565-2002Apr11?language=printer>.

Eisenberg, Anne. "What's that Sign Say? Point, Shoot, Translate." *International Herald Tribune* 18 Mar. 2002: 12.

El Deeb, Sarah. "Taliban: U.S. Doomed in Afghanistan." *Guardian Unlimited* 17 May 2002. 13 July 2002 <http://www.guardian.co.uk/worldlatest/story/0,1280,-1742184,00.html>.

Eldred v. Ashcroft. Openlaw. 15 May 2002 <http://eon.law.harvard.edu/openlaw/eldredv ashcroft/>.

Eliot, Marc. *Walt Disney: Hollywood's Dark Prince.* New York: Birch Lane, 1993.

Elley, Derek, and Andrea R. Vaucher. "Croisset Crowd Craves Its Faves." *Daily Variety* 25 Apr. 2002: 1, 38, 39.

Elliott, Paul. *Brotherhoods of Fear: A History of Violent Organizations.* London: Blandford, 1998.

Ellis, Robert. "Ida Lupino Brings New Hope to Hollywood." *Negro Digest* Aug. 1950: 47–49.

Epstein, Dan. *Twentieth-Century Pop Culture.* London: Carlton, 1999.

Fallout Bomb Shelter. "Fallout, Bomb, Hurricane and Tornado Shelters; It's Your Life...Get the Best Shelter Available." 23 May 2002 <http://www.falloutbombshelter.com/>.

Federal Bureau of Investigation Memo on *That Darn Cat.* Smoking Gun Archives. 15 May 2002 <http://www.thesmokinggun.com/archive/darncat2.html>.

Feiwell, Jill. "Family Films Tap 'Alpha' Girl Power." *Daily Variety* 25 Apr. 2002: A4.

Feiwell, Jill, and Pamela McClintock. "White House Sez H'W'D True Blue." *Daily Variety* 7 Dec. 2001: 2, 52.

Ferguson, Niall. "2011: Ten Years from Now, Historians Will Look Back and See the Events of Sept. 11 as Mere Ripples in a Tidal Wave of Terrorism and Political Fragmentation." *New York Times Magazine* 2 Dec. 2001: 76–79.

Fleming, Michael. "Studios Chasing Tales of Sept. 11 Heroism." *Daily Variety* 12 Feb. 2002: 19.

___. "*T3* Rights Sale to Morph $30 Mil for Arnold." *Daily Variety* 4 Dec. 2001: 32.

Frank, Michael. "A Mélange of Writings that Defy Time's Toll." *International Herald Tribune* 4–5 May 2002: 9.

Franzen, Jonathan. "Meet Me in St. Louis: A Writer's Televised Homecoming." *New Yorker* 24–31 Dec. 2001: 70-5.

Friedrich, Otto. *City of Nets: A Portrait of Hollywood in the 1940s.* Berkeley: U of California P, 1986.

Friend, Tad. "You Can't Say That." *New Yorker* 19 Nov. 2001: 44-9.

Fuller, Graham. "Shots in the Dark: There's always Been Violence in Movies. But Now, It's All Out War." *Interview* Mar. 2002: 122.

Gallagher, David F. "In France, Scents Waft over the Web." *New York Times* 4 Mar. 2002: C4.

Geerhart, Bill. "Atomic Honeymooners: Well-Sheltered Love May Last a Lifetime." Conelrad. 2 June 2002 <http://www.conelrad.com/atomic_honeymooners.html>.

Gentry, Curt. *J. Edgar Hoover: The Man and His Secrets.* New York: Norton, 1991.

Givens, Bill. *Son of Film Flubs.* Secaucus, NJ: Citadel, 1991.

Glanz, James. "Nazi Scientist Voiced No Qualms on an Atom Bomb for Hitler." *International Herald Tribune* Jan. 8, 2002: 4.

Goldman, Eric. *The Crucial Decade, and After: America, 1945-1960.* New York: Vintage, 1956, 1960.

Goldsmith, Jill. "You've Got Nailed: AOL Posts $54 Bil Loss as Internet Revs Drop." *Daily Variety* Apr. 25, 2002: 1, 41.

Goldstein, Adam M. "The Method to His Madness." *Moviemaker* 37.7 (Jan.-Feb. 2000): 64-7.

Goode, Erica. "With Video Games, Researchers Link Guns to Stereotypes." *New York Times* 10 Dec. 2002: D1, 6.

Goodman, Walter. *The Committee: The Extraordinary Career of the House Committee on Un-American Activities.* Baltimore, MD: Penguin, 1969.

Gorman, Steve. "TV Execs to Help White House in War Effort." Reuters 18 Oct. 2001. 13 July 2002 <http://www.brycezabel.com/mediapage/yahoo101801a.htm>.

"Grabbing the Auds 2001; Ad Spenders by Film." *Daily Variety* 25 Apr. 2002: A4.

Granier-Deferre, Karine. "Big Names, Big Money." *International Herald Tribune* 15 May 2002: 17.

Greenhouse, Linda. "20-Year Extension of Existing Copyrights is Upheld." *New York Times* 16 Jan. 2003: A22.

Greppi, Michele. "The Insider: CNN's Ticket Out of Lucas Land." *Electronic Media Online.* 27 May 2002 <http://www.emonline.com/insider/052002insider.html>.

Gross, Larry. "Hollywood Journal." *Film Comment* 37.5 (Sept.-Oct. 2001): 13

Grossberg, Josh. "Movie Studios React to Attack" *E! Online* 12 Sept. 2001. 13 July 2002 <http://www.eonline.com/News/Items/0,1,8811,00.html>.

Gurr, Ted Robert. *Why Men Rebel.* Princeton, NJ: Princeton UP, 1970.

Hacker, Frederick J. *Crusaders, Criminals, Crazies: Terror and Terrorism in Our Time.* New York: Norton, 1996.

Hake, Sabine. *Popular Cinema of the Third Reich.* Austin: U of Texas P, 2001.

Haran, Tim. "Biggest Bang for the Buck: Some Master's Degrees Boost Pay More than Others." *CBS Marketwatch Online* 23 Apr. 2002. 13 May 2002 <http://netscape5.mar ketwatch.com/news/story.asp?guid=%7BC06AE0BB%2D9C10%2D4763%2D888B%2DBC 56C76356CB%7D&siteid=netscape&dist=special>.

Harris, Dana, and Claude Brodesser. "Biz Rues the Blues: Terrorism, Recession Take Toll on

Industry." *Daily Variety* Nov. 8, 2001: 1, 30.

Harrison, Martin. *David Bailey: Birth of the Cool: 1957-1969.* New York: Viking, 1999.

Hatty, Michele. "Fighting to Heal War's Wounds." *U.S.A. Weekend* 1-3 Mar. 2002: 12.

Hauptman, Jodi. *Joseph Cornell: Stargazing in the Cinema.* New Haven: Yale UP, 1999.

Hayes, Dade, and Pamela McClintock. "War Chores for H'W'D: White House, Moguls Agree to Step Up Showbiz Efforts." *Daily Variety* 12 Nov. 2001: 1, 17.

Herman, Arthur. *Joseph McCarthy: Reexamining the Life and Legacy of America's Most Hated Senator.* New York: Free Press, 2000.

Herman, Edward S., and Noam Chomsky. *Manufacturing Consent: The Political Economy of the Mass Media.* New York: Pantheon, 1988.

Hessler, Peter. "Straight to Video: How the Attacks Are Playing in the Provinces." *New Yorker* 15 Oct. 2001: 83-87.

Higham, Charles, and Roy Moseley. *Cary Grant: The Lonely Heart.* San Diego: Harcourt Brace Jovanovich, 1989.

Hingley, Ronald. *Russia: A Concise History.* Rev. ed. London: Thames and Hudson, 1991.

Hirschberg, Lynn. "The Samaha Formula for Hollywood Success." *New York Times Magazine* 14 May 2000: 46-51.

Hispanic Broadcasting Corporation. Advertisement. *Daily Variety* 25 Apr. 2002: A5.

Hoberman, Jim. "All as It Had Been." *Village Voice* 11 Dec. 2001: 109-10.

——. "Operation Infinite Justice." *Village Voice* 2 Apr. 2002: 43.

Hoge, James F., Jr., and Gideon Rose. *How Did This Happen?: Terrorism and the New War.* New York: Public Affairs, 2001.

Hohenadel, Kristin. "For the Youth of France, '*Un Teen Movie*' of Their Own." *New York Times* 3 Feb. 2002, sec. 2: 1, 21.

Holland, Gina. "Court Upholds Copyright Extension: Justices' Decision Will Mean Billions of Dollars to Publishers, Moviemakers and Song Writers." *Lincoln Journal Star* 16 Jan. 2003: 5A.

Holson, Laura M., and Rick Lyman. "Hollywood's Internet Efforts Provoke Scrutiny." *International Herald Tribune* 3 Jan. 2002: 13.

Holson, Laura M., with Bill Carter. "Disney's Chief Seems Cool on a Hot Seat." *New York Times* 15 Feb. 2002: C5.

Hoover, J. Edgar. *Masters of Deceit: The Story of Communism and How to Fight It.* New York: Holt, 1958.

Horton, Robert. "Distributor Wanted: *La ville est tranquille.*" *Film Comment* Mar.-Apr. 2001: 18-19.

Houseman, John. "Lost Fortnight: A Memoir." *The Blue Dahlia: A Screenplay by Raymond Chandler.* Ed. Matthew R. Bruccoli. New York: Popular Library, 1976. 7-23.

Hudson, Rex A., with Marilyn Majeska, Andrea M. Savada, and Helen C. Metz. *The Sociology and Psychology of Terrorism: Who becomes a Terrorist and Why?* Federal Research Division, Library of Congress. 17 May 2002 <http://www.loc.gov/rr/frd/Sociology-Psychology%20of%20Terrorism.htm>.

Isaacs, Jeremy, and Taylor Downing. *Cold War: An Illustrated History.* New York: Little,

Brown, 1998.

Information Times. Web site. 25 May 2002 <http://www.informationtimes.com/>.

"It's A Mad, Mad, Mad Max World." 23 May 2002 <http://www.geocities.com:80/Athens/Oracle/9941/madmax1.html>.

James, Allison. "For France's Femme Directors, Bold Is Beautiful." *Daily Variety* 14 Nov. 2001: A4.

James, Allison, and Andy Stern. "U.S. Pix Rule Europe." *Daily Variety* 14 Nov. 2001: 12.

James, Caryn. "That Lovable Sitcom Dad Who Likes to Nibble Bats." *New York Times* 5 Mar. 2002: B7.

____. "Woodstock Just Isn't What It Used to Be." *New York Times* 16 Aug. 2001: B1, B5.

JamMovies. "Spirit to Bring Back Older Animation." 26 June 2002 <http://www.canoe.ca/JamMoviesArtistsK/katzenberg.html>.

Jones, Jonathan. "Candid Camera." *Guardian Unlimited* 21 Aug. 2001. 18 Apr. 2000 <http://www.guardian.co.uk/warhol/story/0, 11478, 637635, 00.html>.

Juergensmeyer, Mark. *Terror in the Mind of God: The Global Rise of Religious Violence.* Berkeley: U of California P, 2000.

Kahn, Jenette, ed. *9-11: The World's Finest Comic Book Writers and Artists Tell Stories to Remember.* New York: DC Comics, 2002.

Kanfer, Stefan. *A Journal of the Plague Years.* New York: Atheneum, 1973.

Kay, Jonathan. "Swastikas Invade Video Combat Games: Once Taboo Themes Attract Players Who Express Neo-Nazi Sentiments." *International Herald Tribune* 9 Jan. 2002: 1, 7.

Keane, Stephen. *Disaster Movies: The Cinema of Catastrophe.* London: Wallflower Press, 2001.

Kearney, Cresson H. "Permanent Family Fallout Shelters for Dual Use." *Nuclear War Survival Skills.* 23 May 2002 <http://www.oism.org/nwss/s73p928.htm>.

____. "The Dangers from Nuclear Weapons: Myths and Facts." *Nuclear War Survival Skills.* 23 May 2002 <http://www.oism.org/nwss/s73p912.htm>.

Kehr, Dave. "Aiming for More and Getting It." *New York Times* 10 May 2002: B6.

____. "When a Cyberstar Is Born." *New York Times* 18 Nov. 2001, sec. 2: 1, 26.

Kifner, John. "Alms and Arms: Tactics in a Holy War." *New York Times* 15 Mar. 1996: A1, A8.

King, John. "Bush Briefed on Hijacking Threat before Sept. 11." CNN 16 May 2002. 13 July 2002 <http://www.cnn.com/2002/US/05/15/bush.sept.11/>.

King, Tom. "Meryl Streep Makes History, Tracks." *Wall Street Journal* 14 Feb. 2003: W4.

Kisselhoff, Jeff. *The Box: An Oral History of Television.* New York: Penguin, 1995.

Kissell, Rick. "Plotline Predicament: TNN, MTV Cautions with Violence in Sensitive Times." *Daily Variety* 27 Nov. 2001: A1-A2.

Knight, Jerry. "AOL Merger Doesn't Add Up." *International Herald Tribune* 2 Apr. 2002, 13.

Knowlton, Brian. "A Rising Anti-American Tide: War With Iraq Would Even Alienate Friends, Survey Finds." *International Herald Tribune* 5 Dec. 2002: 1, 8.

Kozaryn, Linda D. "Rumfeld: Threat Warnings Are 'Just the Truth.'" DefenseLink 23 May 2002. 13 July 2002 <http://www.defenselink.mil/news/May2002/n05232002_200205231.html>.

——. "'Be Vigilant, Heed Alerts,' Cheney Warns." DefenseLink 23 May 2002. 13 July 2002 <http://www.defenselink.mil/news/May2002/n05232002_200205231.html>.

Kuczynski, Alex. "In Hollywood, Everyone Wants to Be Ozzy." *New York Times* 19 May 2002, sec. 9: 1, 4.

Kugler, Sara. "Face Scans Set Up at Lady Liberty." *Anniston Star* 26 May 2002. 13 July 2002 <http://www.annistonstar.com/news/2002/as-nation-0526-0-2e26a0742.htm>.

Lardner, James. "Hollywood versus High-Tech." *Business 2.0* May 2002: 41–48.

Lathem, Niles. "Fed Report Warned of Al Qaeda Kamikaze Threat." *NYPost.com.* 18 May 2002 <http://www.nypost.com/cgi–bin/printfriendly.pl>.

Lee, Jennifer. "Youth Will Be Served, Wirelessly." *New York Times* 30 May 2002: E1, E6.

Leland, John. "The Telephone Lady Ad-Libs." *New York Times* 3 Mar. 2002, sec. 9: 3.

Lemann, Nicholas. "Dept. of Simulation: Crash Practice." *New Yorker* 17 Dec. 2001: 36–7.

Lewis, Mark. *The Movie Book: The 1940s.* New York: Crescent, 1988.

Lewis, Paul. "Michael Todd, Jr., 62, a Creator of Smell-o-Vision Movies." *New York Times* 8 May 2002: A27.

Lidz, Franz, and Steve Rushin. "How to Tell a Bad Movie from a *Truly* Bad Movie." *New York Times* 5 Aug. 2001, sec. 2: 1, 30.

Lillington, Karlin. "Why Copyright Laws Hurt Culture." *Wired Online* 27 Nov. 2001. 13 July 2002 <http://www.wired.com/news/culture/0,1284,48625,00.html>.

Lindlaw, Scott. "Bush Pledges Pre-Emptive Strikes." *Star Telegram* 1 June 2002. 13 July 2002 <http://www.dfw.com/mld/dfw/news/3380767.htm>.

Linn, Allison. "After Terrorist Attacks, Ad Agencies, Film Companies Seek New Ways to Show NYC." *Lincoln Journal Star* 26 Mar. 2002: 4A.

Louderback, Jim. "Once More, with Feeling." *U.S.A. Weekend* 22–24 Feb. 2002: 10.

Lupino, Ida. "Me, Mother Directress." *Action* May–June 1967: 14–15.

Lyman, Rick. "Summer of the Spinoff: Hollywood Banks on Sequels and Prequels." *New York Times* 17 Apr. 2002: B1, 10.

——. "Even Blockbusters Find Fame Fleeting in a Multiplex Age." *New York Times* 13 Aug. 2001: A1, A12.

Lyons, Eugene. *The Red Decade: The Stalinist Penetration of America.* New York: Bobbs–Merrill, 1941.

MacFarquhar, Larissa. "Oakdale Days." *New Yorker* 15 Apr. 2002: 64–71.

——. "The Producer." *New Yorker* 15 Oct. 2001: 176–87.

Mackey, Robert. "Paint It Forward." *New York Times Sunday Magazine* 12 May 2002: 20.

Mark, Roy. "DoJ: We Want to Read Your E-Mail." *dc.internet.com* 12 Feb. 2003 <http://dc.internet.com/news/article.php/1582401>.

Markoff, John. "From Shadows to Gore, A Hyperrealistic Doom." *New York Times* 30 May 2002: E5.

Marks, Peter. "The Giants in Suits Descend." *International Herald Tribune* 22 May 2002: 20.

Marty, Martin E. "The Sin of Pride." *Newsweek* 10 March 2003: 32-3.

McCarthy, Todd, and Charles Flynn. "The Economic Imperative: Why Was the B Movie Necessary?" *Kings of the Bs: Working within the Hollywood System.* New York: Dutton, 1975. 13-43.

___. "An Interview with Albert Zugsmith, Sept. 3, 1973, Los Angeles, California." *Kings of the Bs: Working within the Hollywood System.* New York: Dutton, 1975. 411-24.

McCoid, Sheridan. *Hollywood Lovers.* London: Orion, 1997.

McCullagh, Declan. "Perspective: Ashcroft's Worrisome Spy Planes." *c/netnews.com* 12 Feb. 2003: <http://news.com.com/2010-1071-983921.htm.html>.

McGillivray, David. *Doing Rude Things: The History of the British Sex Film, 1957-1981.* London: Sun Tavern Fields, 1992.

McIntyre, Gina. "Fear Factory." *Hollywood Reporter Weekly* 30 Oct.-5 Nov. 2001: 12-13.

McNeil, Alex. *Total Television: A Comprehensive Guide to Programming from 1948 to the Present.* 4th ed. New York: Penguin, 1997.

Mead, Russell Walter. "Apocalypse Now - or Soon." *Washington Post National Weekly Edition* 10-16 Feb. 2003: 22, 23.

Michelson, Annette, ed. *Andy Warhol.* Cambridge: MIT P, 2001.

Miller, Frank, John J. Muth, et al. *9-11: Artists Respond.* Milwaukie, OR: Dark Horse, 2002.

Miller, Judith. "Sheik's Son and Bin Laden Spoke of Plots, Officials Say." *New York Times Online.* 13 July 2002 <http://www.nytimes.com/2002/05/18/politics/18SHEI.html>.

Miller, Toby, Nitin Govil, John McMurria, and Richard Maxwell. *Global Hollywood.* London: BFI, 2001.

Millman, Joyce. "*The X-Files* Finds the Truth: Its Time Is Past." *New York Times* 19 May 2002, sec. 2: 34, 41.

Mitchell, Elvis. "Kelly and Jack Osbourne: Ozzy Gave Birth to Heavy Metal. But His Other Offspring Gave MTV Its Biggest Hit Ever—and New Life to His Career." *Interview* June 2002: 59, 62-3.

Mohammed, Arshad. "Cheney Fears Leaks from Any New Sept. 11 Inquiry." *Reuters.* 13 July 2002 <http://www.reuters.com/news_article.jhtml;jessionid=JYUHAXWU3AMOKCRBAEZSFFAKEEATIIWD?type=politicsnews&StoryID=996981?>.

Moore, Michael. *Stupid White Men.* New York: HarperCollins, 2001.

Muller, Eddie. *Dark City Dames: The Wicked Women of Film Noir.* New York: Regan Books/HarperCollins, 2001.

New American Cinema Group. *Filmmaker's Cooperative Catalogue No. 4.* New York: New American Cinema, 1967.

Newton, Christopher. "Bush Defends Hijack Warning Reaction." *Guardian Unlimited* 17 May 2002. 13 July 2002 <http://www.guardian.co.uk/uslatest/story/0,1282,-1742043,00.html>.

Nourmand, Tony, and Graham Marsh, eds. *Film Posters of the 50s: The Essential Movies of the Decade.* London: Aurum P, 2002.

___. *Film Posters of the 60s: The Essential Movies of the Decade.* London: Aurum P, 1997.

"Officials: Terrorists May Target Tall Apt. Bldgs.; FBI Chief: "We Will Not Be Able to

Stop It." CNN 20 May 2002. 13 July 2002 <http://www.cnn.com/2002/US/05/20/gen.war.on.terror/>.

Offman, Craig. "ABC Plans 9/11 Anni." *Daily Variety* 1 May 2002: 4.

Olaf, Erwin, and Jonathan Turner. *Violence and Passion.* Amsterdam: Reflex, 2002.

Oltmans, Willem. *Global Terrorist.* Amsterdam: Papieren Tijger, 2002.

1112 Networks. "The Last Page of the Internet." 4 Apr. 2002 <http://www.1112.net/lastpage.html>.

Opposing Copyright Extension. "Help Protect Your Rights to the Great Works in the Public Domain." 15 May 2002 <http://www.law.asu.edu/HomePages/Karjala/OpposingCopyrightExtension/>.

Osborne, Lawrence. "An Enfant Terrible at 70." *New York Times Magazine* 30 Sept. 2001: 52-3.

Ottaway, Robert, ed. *Picturegoer Film Annual 1959-1960.* London: Odhams P, 1961.

Pareles, Jon. "Spit Out by the Star-Making Machinery." *New York Times* 3 Feb. 2002, sec. 2: 28.

"Past Statements: Remarks by the Bush Administration on Warning Signs before the Sept 11 Attacks." *Washington Post* 18 May 2002 <http://www.washingtonpost.com/wp-srv/national/daily/graphics/past_statements_051702.html>.

"Patriot Act: The Sequel." Editorial. *Washington Post* 12 Feb. 2003 <http://www.washingtonpost.com/wp-dyn/articles/A59690-2003Feb11.html>.

"Patriot Act II Draft Legislation." 12 Feb. 2003 <http://www.dailyrotten.com/source-docs/patriot2draft.html>.

"Pentagon to Prepare Nuclear Weapons, Report Says." *Yahoo! News from Reuters* 9 Mar. 2002. 10 Mar. 2002 <http://story.news.yahoo.com/news?tmpl=story&u=/nm/20020309ts_nm/bush_nuclear_dc_2aprinter=1>.

Pham, Alex. "A New Way to Play War: U.S. Army Lures Youths With Video Games." *International Herald Tribune* 23 May 2002: 14.

Phillips, Baxter. *Swastika: Cinema of Oppression.* London: Lorrimer, 1976.

——. *Cut: The Unseen Cinema.* London: Lorrimer, 1975.

Porton, Richard. *Film and the Anarchist Imagination.* London: Verso, 1999.

Powell, Corey S. "20 Ways the World Could End." *Discover* Oct. 2000. 4 Apr. 2002 <http://www.discover.com/oct_00/featworld.html>.

Pratt, Jane. *Beyond Beauty: Girls Speak Out on Looks, Style, and Stereotypes.* New York: Clarkson Potter, 1997.

Prelinger, Rick. Web site. *Internet Archive Movie Collection.* 15 May 2002 <http://www.archive.org/movies>; and <http://www.archive.org/movies/list_C-E.html>.

Quesada, Joe, ed. *Heroes: The World's Greatest Super Hero Characters Honor the World's Greatest Heroes.* New York: Marvel Comics, 2001.

"Regional Coding Enhancement." DVD Talk. 27 Feb. 2002 <http://www.dvdtalk.com/rce.html>.

Rhodes, Richard. *Making of the Atomic Bomb.* New York: Simon and Schuster, 1986.

Rich, Frank. "The Weight of an Anchor." *New York Times Magazine* 19 May 2002: 34-9,

65-6, 82, 85.

Richtel, Matt. "Comcast Says It Will Stop Storing Data on Customers." *New York Times* 14 Feb. 2002: C5.

Rickitt, Richard. *Special Effects: The History and the Technique.* London: Virgin, 2000.

Ricks, Thomas E. "Keeping Eye on Combat." *International Herald Tribune* 27 Mar. 2002: 1, 4.

Ridgeway, James. "Mondo Washington: You Talkin' to Me?" *Village Voice* 29 Jan. - Feb. 4: 36.

Robertson, Patrick. *Film Facts.* New York: Billboard Books, 2001.

Roderick, Klye, ed. *Married in the Movies.* San Francisco: HarperCollins, 1994.

Roquemore, Joseph. *History Goes to the Movies.* New York: Doubleday, 1999.

Rosenbaum, Jonathan. *Movie Wars.* London: Wallflower, 2002.

Ross, Jonathan. *The Incredibly Strange Film Book: An Alternative History of the Cinema.* London: Simon and Schuster, 1995.

Rothman, Wilson. "Mission Control for the Living Room." *New York Times* 9 May 2002: E1, E4.

Rumsfeld, Donald. Interview with Alan Murray, CNBC. DefenseLink 20 May 2002. Transcript. 13 July 2002 <http://www.defenselink.mil/news/May2002/t05222002_t0520cnb.html>.

____. Interview with Jim Lehrer, *NewsHour with Jim Lehrer,* PBS. DefenseLink 22 May 2002. Transcript. 13 July 2002 <http://www.defenselink.mil/news/May2002/t05232002_t0522sd.html>.

Rutenberg, Jim. "War or No, News on Cable Already Provides the Drama: Bitter Competition Drives Exuberant Iraq Coverage." *New York Times* 15 Jan. 2003: C1, 4.

Ruoff, Jeffery. *An American Family: A Televised Life.* Minneapolis: U of Minnesota P, 2002.

Saether, Linda, and Peter Dykstra. "Asteroid on Possible Collision Course, in 900 Years." CNN 10 June 2002 <http://www.cnn.com/2002/TECH/space/04/04/lost.asteroid/index.html>.

Salamon, Julie. "Grabbing Viewers 'tween 8 and 14." *New York Times* 15 Feb. 2002: B1, B32.

Sanders, Don, and Susan Sanders. *Drive-in Movie Memories.* Middleton, NH: Carriage House, 2000.

Sayre, Nora. *Running Time: Films of the Cold War.* New York: Dial P, 1979.

Schwarts, Evan I. "Televisionary." *Wired* 10.4 (Apr. 2002): 68, 70, 73-4.

Scott, A. O. "Kicking Up Cosmic Dust." *New York Times* 10 May 2002: B1, 20.

Shearer, Harry. "Tone-Deaf Corporations in Search of the Perfect Pitch." *New York Times* 12 May 2002, sec. 4: 7.

Shenon, Philip. "F.B.I. Knew for Years about Terror Pilot Training." *New York Times* 18 May 2002 <http://www.nytimes.com/2002/05/18/politics/18FLIB.html>.

Shipman, David. *Caught in the Act: Sex and Eroticism in the Movies.* London: Elm Tree, 1985.

Simon, Alissa. "Covering Cannes: Interview with *Variety* Critic David Rooney." *Facets Features* (Fall 2001): 23-25.

Slansky, Paul. "Nixon on Tape: The Quiz." *New Yorker* 15 Apr. 2002: 43.

Solomon, John. "1999 Report Warned of Suicide Hijack." *First Coast News* 17 May 2002.

13 July 2002 <http://www.firstcoastnews.com/news/2002-05-17/usw_report.asp>.

Sound the Alarm Ministry. "Fallout Shelter." 23 May 2002 <http://www.alarmministry.com/shelter.htm>.

Speed, F. Maurice, ed. *Film Review 1962–1963*. London: Macdonald, 1964.

Spitz, Bob. "Director's Cut: 76 Films and Counting for Robert Altman." *Sky* Jan. 2002: 39–43.

Staples, William. "Little Cameras Everywhere." Spec. advertising supplement to *New Yorker* 3 June 2000: 26.

Stark, Lisa. "JetBlue Eyes: Airline to be First to Install Cameras on Planes." *ABCNews.com* 30 Mar. 2002. 13 July 2002 <http://abcnews.go.com/sections/wnt/DailyNews/jetblue_cameras020330.html>.

Stern, Jessica. *The Ultimate Terrorists*. Cambridge, MA: Harvard UP, 1999.

Stirland, Sarah Lai. "Other People's Property: Academics Square Off against Hollywood on Internet Content." *Village Voice* 23 Apr. 2002: 43.

Strauss, Neil. "Mixing a 'Mash-up' with Bootleg Music: New Technology Breeds a New Genre." *International Herald Tribune* 10 May 2002: 12.

Summers, Anthony. *Official and Confidential: The Secret Life of J. Edgar Hoover*. New York: Putnam's, 1993.

"Survive a Nuclear Attack." 23 May 2002 <http://www.surviveanuclearattack.com/>.

Talbot, Margaret. "Girls Just Want to Be Mean." *New York Times Magazine* 24 Feb. 2002: 24–6, 27–9, 40, 58, 64–5.

Tanenhaus, Sam. *Whittaker Chambers*. New York: Random House, 1997.

"Terrorist Attacks on the U.S.—Internet Rumors Hoaxes Folklore." 23 May 2002 <http://urbanlegends.about.com/library/bixterror2.htm>.

Theoharis, Athan G., and John Stuart Cox. *The Boss: J. Edgar Hoover and the Great American Inquisition*. Philadelphia: Temple UP, 1988.

Thomas, Owen. "The Meteoric Rise of the DVD." *Business 2.0* May 2002: 34.

Tommasini, Anthony. "The Devil Made Him Do It." *New York Times* 30 Sept. 2001, sec. 2: 28.

Towers, Harry Alan, and Leslie Mitchell. *The March of the Movies*. London: Sampson Low, 1947.

Turner, Megan. "Superhero Invasion." *New York Post* 7 May 2002: 37.

Two Tigers Radiological. "Tools for Nuclear Emergencies." 25 May 2002 <http://www.twotigersonline.com/products.html>.

"TV Execs to Help White House in War Effort." *Tops Stories at Netscape*. Reuters 19 Oct. 2001. 19 Oct. 2001 <http://dailynews.netscape.com/mynsnews/print.tmpl?&talbe=n&cat=50900&id=200110190825000251426&cp=>.

Urban Legends and Folklore. "Rumor Watch: Terrorist Attack on U.S." Urban Legends and Folklore 20 Sept. 2001. 13 July 2002 <http://urbanlegends.about.com/library/weekly/aa09110a.htm>.

Urban Legends and Folklore. "Rumor Watch: Terrorist Attacks on U.S. Part 3: Did Nostradamus Predict the Tragedy?" Urban Legends and Folklore. 23 May 2002 <http:

//urbanlegends.about.com/library/weekly/aa091101b.htm>.

Urban Legends and Folklore. "The Tourist Guy—'Last Photo' from Atop the World Trade Center—Netlore Archive." 23 May 2002 <http://urbanlegends.about.com/library/biphoto-wtc.htm>.

Usai, Paolo Cherchi. *The Death of Cinema: History, Cultural Memory and the Digital Dark Age.* London: BFI, 2001.

Van Natta, Don, Jr. "Democrats Raise Questions over Remarks in Warnings." *New York Times Online.* 18 May 2002 <http://www.nytimes.com/2002/05/18/politics/18THRE.html>.

Vaucher, Andrea R., and Lisa Klaussman. "Viv U chief keeps cool amid le fracas français." *Daily Variety* 25 Apr. 2002: 1, 41.

Vaughn, Robert. *Only Victims: A Study of Show Business Blacklisting.* New York: Putnam's, 1972.

Virilio, Paul. *The Aesthetics of Disappearance.* Trans. Philip Beitchman. New York: Semiotext(e), 1991.

———. *A Landscape of Events.* Trans. Julie Rose. Cambridge, MA: MIT P, 2000.

———. *Strategy of Deception.* Trans. Chris Turner. London: Verso, 2000.

———. *The Vision Machine.* Trans. Julie Rose. Bloomington: Indiana UP, 1994.

———. *War and Cinema: The Logistics of Perception.* Trans. Patrick Camiller. London: Verso, 1989.

Wakin, Daniel J. "National I.D. Cards: One Size Fits All." *New York Times* 7 Oct. 2001, sec. 4: 3.

Wax, Emily. "In Times of Terror, Teens Talk the Talk: Boys Are 'Firefighter Cute,' Messy Bedrooms Are 'Ground Zero,'" *International Herald Tribune* 20 Mar. 2002: 1, 5.

Waxman, Sharon. "Hollywood Exhales as Sales Hit Record Respite Sept. 11." *International Herald Tribune* 5-6 Jan. 2002: 11.

Weber, Jonathan. "The Ever-Expanding, Profit-Maximizing, Cultural-Imperialist, Wonderful World of Disney: The Serious Business of Selling All-American Fun." *Wired* Feb. 2002: 69-79.

Weisberg, Jacob, ed. *George W. Bushisma: The Slate Book of the Accidental Wit and Wisdom of Our 43rd President.* New York: Fireside, 2001.

Weldon, Michael. *The Psychotronic Encyclopedia of Film.* New York: Ballantine, 1983.

Wesslau, Fredrik. "Movie Profit: A Storyboard for Investors." *International Herald Tribune* 11-12 May 2002: 15-16.

White, E. B. *Here Is New York.* New York: Harper, 1949.

Wiedeman, Julius. *Digital Beauties: 2D and 3D Computer Generated Digital Models, Virtual Idols and Characters.* Köln: Taschen, 2001.

Wilmington, Michael. "Oscars Watershed Night for African-Americans." *Lincoln Journal Star* 26 Mar. 2002: 6A.

Wilson, Ivy Crane, ed. *Hollywood Album.* London: Sampson Low, Marston, 1948.

Witcombe, Rick Trader. *Savage Cinema.* London: Lorrimer, 1975.

Wojick, Daniel. *The End of the World as We Know It: Faith, Fatalism and Apocalypse in America.* New York: New York UP, 1997.

Wolcott, James. "Original Sin." *Vanity Fair* Apr. 2001: 194, 196, 198, 201-2, 204.

Wolk, Douglas. "And the Banned Played On." *Village Voice* 26 Sept.-2 Oct. 2001. 25 May 2002 <http://www.villagevoice.com/issues/0139/wolk.php>.

Wollenberg, H. H. *Fifty Years of German Film.* London: Falcon, 1948.

Woodward, Richard B. "Tied to TV to the Very Last." *International Herald Tribune* 18 Apr. 2002: 20.

Worth, Robert F. "Truth, Right, and the American Way: A Nation Defines Itself by Its Evil Enemies." *New York Times* 24 Feb. 2002, sec. 4: 1, 7.

Wykes, Alan. *H. G. Wells in the Cinema.* London: Jupiter, 1977.

Yardley, Jonathan. "The Book World Goes over the Top." *International Herald Tribune* 19 Apr. 2002: 20.

Zalewski, Daniel. "Once, in the Jungle." *New York Times Magazine* 25 Mar. 2001: 54-7.

Zedd, Nick. *Totem of the Depraved.* Los Angeles: 2.13.61 Publications, 1996.

Zielbauer, Paul. "Idol Available. Teens Please Apply." *New York Times* 14 Feb. 2002: C18.

Zimmerman, Patricia R. *Reel Families: A Social History of Amateur Film.* Bloomington: Indiana UP, 1995.

INDEX

Aaserud, Finn 130, 131
About a Boy (2002) 17
À bout de souffle (1960) 105, 109
About Schmidt (2002) 118-19
Abraham, Mark 13
A.C. Nielsen Corporation 29
Academy of Motion Picture Arts and Sciences 67
Action in the North Atlantic (1943) 64
Act of Violence (1948) 65
Adalian, Josef 119
Adbusters Media Foundation 11
Adee, Peter 32
advertising, global reach of 35-6; newsprint 33; television 32
Affleck, Casey 45
After Sex (1997) 112
Agency, The (television) 72
Aida (musical) 98
Air Force (1943) 64
Air Force One (1997) 72
Ajami, Fouad 68-70
Albright, Hardie 71
alienation 9
Al Jazeera 69-70
Allegmagne annèe 90 neuf zèro (1990) 106
Allen, Tim 72
Allen, Woody 4, 31, 110
Allende, Isabel 100-1
All Quiet on the Western Front (1930) 75
Al-Manar network 78-79
Almereyda, Michael 45
Alphaville, a Strange Adventure of Lemmy Caution (1965) 105-7
Altman, Robert 72-3, 120
À ma soeur! (2001) 112
American Beauty, The (1961) 23
American Civil Liberties Union 85
American Family, An (television) 55
American Family: The Final Episode (television) 56
American Film Institute 24
American International Pictures 25-7, 42, 117
American Pie (1999) 108
America Online 54
America's Atomic Bomb Tests (1998) 138
America's Disaster: The Pearl Harbor of the Twenty-First Century (2001) 73
Analyze That (2002) 119
Andersen, Hans Christian 140-1
Anderson, Paul Thomas 31, 109-10
Anderson, Raffadla 111
Angelou, Maya 101
Aniston, Jennifer 119
Annunciation (1964) 140
anti-semitism 64
AOL Time Warner 15, 30, 36

apocalypse 2-4
Apocalypse Now (1979) 60, 75
Apocalypse Now Redux (2001) 74
Arkoff, Samuel 25
Armageddon (1998) 6
Arnaz, Desi 66
Arnelo Affair, The (1947) 8-9
Arness, James 67
Around the World in Eighty Days (1956) 117
Arquette, Courteney Cox 119
Arrivano i titani (1961) 21
Arson, Inc. (1949) 123
Artificial Intelligence: A.I. (2001) 116
Assayas, Olivier 31
Atomic Agent (1959) 138
Atomic Attack (1950) 124
Atomic Brain, The (1964) 138
Atomic City, The (1952) 138
Atomic Cyborg (1986) 138
Atomic Journeys (1999) 138
Atomic Juggernaut (1971) 138
Atomic Kid, The (1954) 138
Atomic Lady (1963) 138
Atomic Man, The (1956) 138
Atomic Monster (1953) 138
Atomic Power (1946) 138
Atomic Reporter (1991) 138
Atomic Rocketship (1936) 138
Atomic Rulers of the World (1964) 138
Atomic Samurai (1993) 138
Atomic Secret (1967) 138
Atomic Submarine, The (1959) 138
Atomic War Bride (1960) 77
Austin Powers: International Man of Mystery (1997) 13
Austin Powers: The Spy Who Shagged Me (1999) 13
Austin Powers in Goldmember (2002) 5
Auteuil, Daniel 119
Avalon, Frankie 42

Bach, Karen 111
Bachelor Daddy (1941) 64
Backdraft (1991) 19
Bacri, Jean-Pierre 113
Baise-Moi (2000) 111
Baker, Roy Ward 23-4
Baldwin, Craig 49-50
Bambi (1942) 32
Bang, Joy 141
Barlow, John Perry 47
Baron of Arizona, The (1950) 123
Barrymore (play) 98
Bartel, Paul 45
Bartok, Dennis 23
Bataan (1943) 64
Batman 5, 12

Batman, The (serial) (1943) 76
Battaglio, Stephen 70
Battlefield Earth: A Saga of the Year 3000 (2000)
    115–16
Battle of San Pietro, The (1945) 61
Bava, Mario 23
BBC World Service 114
Bed Sitting Room, The (1969) 133
Behind Enemy Lines (2002) 74–5
Behind Locked Doors (1948) 65
Belson, Ken 54
Bendix, William 65
Beneath the Planet of the Apes (1971) 136
Benigni, Roberto 13
Bergman, Ingmar 22, 110
Berkeley, Martin 67
Besson, Luc 109–10
Best Years of Our Lives, The (1946) 61
Bewitched (1945) 65
Bice, Robert 137
Big Brother (television) 51
Big Clock, The (1948) 65
Big Daddy (1999) 18
Big Deal on Madonna Street (1958) 21
Big Jim McLain (1952) 67
Big Kahuna, The (2000) 115
Big Parade, The (1925) 75
Big Red One, The (1980) 75
Big Sleep, The (1946) 46
Big Trouble (2002) 72
Billy Jack (1971) 34
Binoche, Juliette 119
Black Hawk Down (2001) 8, 74–6
blacklist 66–7
Black Sunday (1961) 21
Blair, Tony 91
Blondie series 5
Blood of Ghastly Horror (1972) 138
Bloody Mallory (2002) 109
Blue Bird, The (1976) 142–3
Blue Dahlia, The (1946) 65
Blutendes Deutschland (1932) 139
Body Snatcher, The (1945) 123
Boetticher, Budd 40
Bogart, Humphrey 120
Bohr, Aage 131
Bohr, Niels 130
Bonnie and Clyde (1967) 111
Born Losers, The (1967) 34
Boston Blackie series 5
Boudu Saved from Drowning (1932) 41
Bound (1996) 8
Bourne, Matthew 97
Bourne Identity, The (2002) 18
Bowling for Columbine (2002) 129
Brave One, The (1956) 66
Breillat, Catherine 31, 110, 112
Brett, Jeremy 45
Bridges, Lloyd 67
British Sounds (1969) 105
Brockman, Alfred 63
Broderick, Matthew 118
Bromberg, J. Edward 67
Brooke, Hillary 22
Brooks, Mel 98
Brosnan, Pierce 96

Brown, Patricia 36
Bruckheimer, Jerry 13, 72–3
Buñuel, Luis 31
Burnett, Frances Hodgson 44–5
Busch, Anita 71, 74
Bush, George W. 91, 128

Cage, Nicolas 74, 120
Cahiers du Cinéma 113
Caine, Michael 76, 115
Campus on the March (1942) 38
Canadian Mounties vs. Atomic Invaders (1953) 138
Cannes Film Festival 31–2
Capitalism (1948) 38
Captive Women (1952) 136
Care of the Hair and Nails (1951) 38
Carmack, John 124–5
Carnovsky, Morris 67
Carr, David 103–4
Carrey, Jim 120
Carry On Nurse (1958) 21
Casablanca (1942) 46
Castle, Peggy 137
Cat People (1942) 123
Century's Great Catastrophe, The (2001) 73
Chabrol, Anne 104
Chabrol, Claude 11, 107, 113
Chamberlain, Richard 18
Chan, Charlie 71
Chan, Jackie 18, 72, 120
Chandler, Raymond 65
Chaplin, Charlie 64
Charlie Chan in Rio (1941) 64
Charlie's Angels (2000) 52
Charlotte Gray (2002) 74
Cheney, Dick 86, 89
Chikyu Boeigun (1957) 49
Chrichton, Charles 23
Chung, Connie 99
Cinema, digitization of 24; effects of terror attack on
    59; end of 1; hypocrisy in 62–3; juvenilization
    of 32
CinemaScope 42
Citizen Kane (1941) 46
Citizen Ruth (1996) 118
Clancy, Tom 74, 102
Class of Nuke 'Em High (1986) 138
class struggle 133–4
clear channel communications 82, 97–8
Clerks (1994) 108
Clio Awards 28
Cobb, Lee J. 67
Coburn, James 32
Cocteau, Jean 97
Coen brothers 12, 109–10
Cohen, David 34
Cohen, Scott Lyle 55, 57–8
Collateral Damage (2002) 8, 72
colonialism 90–1; and economic gain 104–5; ideas/
    images of 105
Columbia Pictures 52
Come rubammo la bomba atomica (1967) 138
competitive media reporting 29
Complacent Americans, The (record album) 134–5
computer generated imagery 97, 132
Conan series 12

Conelrad 134, 137–8
Confessions of a Nazi Spy (1939) 63
conflict, ethnic 92; religious 92
conformity 15
Conner, Bruce 49
Conspirator (1949) 67
Constantine, Eddie 107
Conway, Tom 22
Copenhagen (play) 130
Coppola, Francis Ford 75
copyrights 43–8
Core, The (2003) 6
Corey, Wendell 40
Corman, Roger 12, 22, 110, 142
Cornell, Joseph 49–50
Coronet Instructional Films 38, 40
Corrections, The (book) 99
Corvette K-225 (1943) 64
Cosmopolitan (magazine) 103–4
Cries and Whispers (1972) 22
Crossroads (1976) 49–50
Crowe, Russell 75, 119
Crowley, Bob 98
Cruise, Tom 18, 120
Cukor, George 143
culture, brand-conscious 105; capitalist 15; corporate
    36; destruction of 109; homogenization of 92;
    planned obsolesence of 119; popular 119;
    replacement of indigenous 105; social 2
Culver City Studios 136
Curtis, Bryan 78–80

Dakota Kid, The (1951) 14
Damaga (1992) 20
Damnation Alley (1977) 16
Damned, The (1969) 139
Damon, Matt 18
Dangerfield, Rodney 111
Daniel, Sean 12
Dante, Joe 142
Daredevil (2003) 5
Dark Blue World (2002) 75
Darklight Digital Film Festival 47
Da Silva, Howard 67
Dassin, Jules 67
Date With Your Family, A (1950) 38
Dating Dos and Don'ts (1949) 39
Day of Defeat (video game) 125–6
Day the Earth Caught Fire, The (1961) 6, 23
Day the Sky Exploded, The (1961) 21, 133
D-Day Minus One (1945) 38
Dearden, Basil 9
Deconstructing Harry (1997) 110
Deep Impact (1998) 71
Deer Hunter, The (1978) 60
Deluge (1933) 123
Deneuve, Catherine 112, 119
De Niro, Robert 120
Denis, Claire 31
Depardieu, Gérard 107, 119
Der ewige Jude (1940) 64
Dern, Laura 118
De Sica, Vittorio 61
Design for Dreaming (1956) 39
Despentes, Virginie 111
Deuces Wild (2002) 8

Dhéry, Robert 23
Diaz, Cameron 120
Dickinson, Thorold 22
Die Hard (1988) 71
Die Hard 2 (1990) 72
Die Hard with a Vengeance (1995) 72
Die Mörder sind unter uns (1946) 61
Diesel, Vin 4
Dinner Party (1945) 39
Di Orio, Carl 11
Disney, Roy 40
Disney, Walt 50–1
Disney Theatrical Productions 97–8
dissent 60
distribution, aggressive 41; digital 27, 31; electronic
    25; foreign films 20; limiting 41; need for 122;
    niche markets 33
Dive Bomber (1941) 64
Dixon, Wheeler Winston 24
Dmytryk, Edward 67
*Dr. Strangelove, or, How I Learned to Stop Worrying and
    Love the Bomb* (1964) 6
Donlevy, Brian 22
Don't Talk to Strangers (1950) 39
Doom III (video game) 124–5
Double Date (1941) 64
Dowling, Doris 65
Down Argentine Way (1940) 64
Downey, Robert Jr. 14, 111
Down to Earth (album) 57
Doyle, Sir Arthur Conan 45
Drabinsky, Garth 98
DreamWorks 12, 31, 72
Dropout, The (1962) 39
Drug Abuse: The Chemical Tomb (1969) 39
Drug Addiction (1951) 39
Duck and Cover (1948) 77
Dunst, Kirsten 5
DVD format 20, 23–4, 51; obsolescence of 54; region
    coding, 51–3
Dynamic American City, The (1956) 39

Early Clue to the New Direction, An (1967) 141
Early Settlers of New England (1940) 39–40
Earth Dies Screaming, The (1964) 16, 123
Earth vs. the Spider (1958) 18
East of Borneo (1931) 50
Easy Rider (1969) 34
economic, crises 90; gain 104; globalization 92;
    openness 92
Edelstein, David 10
Edison Newsreels 40
Edozien, Frankie 89
Edwards, James 60
Eight Legged Freaks (2002) 18
Eilperin, Juliet 88
Eisenberg, Anne 55
Élage de l'Amour (2001) 105
Eldard, Ron 76
Election (1999) 118
Electronic Frontier Foundation 47
Eliot, Mark 51
Elley, Derek 31
Endfield, Cy 75
English Children: Life in the City (1949) 40
English Patient, The (1996) 117

Enola Gay: The Men, the Mission, the Atomic Bomb
   (1980) 138
Enright, Ray 62
Ercole al centro della terra (1961) 21
Escape (1940) 40
Eternal Jew, The (1940) 64
Executive Decision (1996) 72
Exercise and Health (1949) 40
Exodus (1960) 66
Exorcist series 12

Fail-Safe (1964) 6
fallout shelters 81-2
Fantastic Four (2003) 5
Fatale (1992) 20
Fat Girl (2001) 112
Father Knows Best (television) 5
Faulkner, William 5
Federal Bureau of Investigation 50; surveillance issues
   86
Feiwell, Jill 33, 93
Ferguson, Niall 89-91, 93
Ferrer, José 8
Ferris Bueller's Day Off (1986) 108
Fiend with the Atomic Brain, The (1972) 138
Films, action 22; action comedies 18; actor salaries
   119-20; agitprop 106; apocalyptic 3, 96, 123-5,
   133-43; art 120; atomic apocalypse 137-8;
   availability of 40-1; budgets 14, 105, 108, 116;
   capitalist consumption and 108-10; cartoons 18;
   classic 41; classroom 49; commercially marginal
   122; commercial manipulation of 114-21;
   commercial shelf life 40; committee-made, 114-20;
   copyrights and 41; destruction of 3; digital 9-11,
   111; documentary 7-8; dubbed 21-2; educational
   78; experimental 123, 140; exploitation 26, 60,
   135; family 74; fantasy 123, 142; feature 1;
   feminist 31, 110-13; foreign 20-2, 27, 52, 105-14;
   gangster 46; hero tales 95; holocaust, 6-8, 96,
   133-43; horror 142; indie 120-1; industrial 38,
   49; instant classics 21; instructional 38, 50; low-
   budget 123, 142; mainstream 113; militaristic 64;
   monster 7; musical 46; neo-noir 8-9, 66; noir 8,
   65-6; pacifist 122; political 105; post-apocalypse
   8; post-noir 8; promotional 38; propaganda 64,
   69, 76, 94; ratings 32; Red Scare 66-7, 71, 77;
   remakes 12-13, 24; restoration of 41; scenario
   creation 113; sequels 2, 5, 13; series 5; source
   24; sponsored 38, 40; subtitled 21-2; summer 18,
   25, 27; teen 28, 108, 113; terrorist 71-2; trailers
   127; training 77; war 60-5, 74-6, 95-6
Final Fantasy: The Spirits Within (2001) 36
Fisher, Terence 123
Five Graves to Cairo (1943) 65
Flash Gordon (1936) 138
Fleming, Michael 95
Flight Simulator (video game) 70
Flying Serpent, The (1946) 49
Flynn, Charles 14, 136
Following (1998) 18
Fonda, Jane 143
Ford, Harrison 120
Ford, John 14
Ford, Philip 14
Foreman, Carl 67
For Ever Mozart (1996) 107

Fortuyn, Pim 60
40 Days and 40 Nights (2002) 8
Foster, Jodie 120
Franier-Deferre, Karine 120
Frank, Michael 17
Frankenstein Meets the Wolf Man (1943) 123
Franzen, Jonathan 99-101
Fremaux, Thierry 31
Friday the 13th (1980) 4
Friedrich, Otto, 5
Friend, Tad 113
Friends (television) 108, 119
Fuller, Graham 75
Fuller, Samuel 75, 123
Full Monty, The (1997) 19

Gabor, Zsa Zsa 67
Gaines, Ernest 100
Gance, Abel, 9
Gangs of New York (2002) 31
Garcia, Nicole 112
Gardner, Ava 143
Gebhardt, Dick 89
Genbaku Shi: Killed by the Atomic Bomb (1994) 138
General Agreement on Tariffs and Trades (GATT) 41
Germany Year 90 Nine Zero (1991) 106
Get Carter (2000) 115
Ghost of Dragstrip Hollow (1959) 26
Ghosts of Mars (2001) 52
Gibson, Mel 18, 61-2, 120
Gifford, Frances 8-9
Gill, Mark 74
Gilliat, Sidney 45
Girl in the Kremlin, The (1957) 67
Girls Intelligence Agency 33
Gitai, Amos 31
Giulietta degli spiriti (1965) 21
Giv'a 24 Eina Ona (1955) 22
Givens, Bill 34
Glanz, James 130
Gleaners & I, The (2000) 18-19
globalization 90; economic 92
Godard, Jean-Luc 105-9, 113
Godzilla (1998) 73
Godzilla, King of the Monsters! (1956) 7
Godzilla series 21
Goebbels, Joseph 63
Gojira (1954) 7
Goldsmith, Jill 30
Gone With the Wind (1939) 118
Gooding, Cuba Jr. 32
Gordon, Gordon 50
Gorin, Jean-Pierre 105
Graham, Billy 15
Graham, Heather 14
Grand Canyon (1991) 116
Grand Hotel (1932) 112
Grant, Cary 6
Grant, Hugh 17
Graves, Peter 71
Great Dictator, The (1940) 64
Great Gilbert and Sullivan, The (1953) 45
Green, George 104
Greene, Lorne 142
Greenhouse, Linda 44
Greppi, Michele 99

Groppe, Laura 33
Gross, Larry 120
Guédiguian, Robert 31
Guest, Val 23
Gung Ho! (1943) 62

Hagen, Jean 42
Hail Mary (1985) 106
Hairspray (musical) 98
Haldeman, Bob 15
Hamati kombola zorria (1952) 138
Hamlet (2000) 45
Hammer Films 22
Hammett, Dashiell 67
Hanks, Tom 73, 120
Harding, Tonya 132
Harper's Bazaar (magazine) 104
Harrelson, Woody 111
Harry Potter series 12, 32
Hartley, Ted 13
Hart's War (2002) 75
Hatty, Michele 60-1
Hauptman, Jodi 50
Hawke, Ethan 45
Hayes, Dade 94
Hayes, Helen 67
Hearts and Minds (1974) 60
Heisenberg, Werner 130
Hèlas pour moi (1993) 107
Hellman, Lillian 67
Helm, Matt 12
Hercules in the Haunted World (1964) 21
Hessler, Peter 73-4
Hewitt, Jennifer Love 18
Hideous Sun Demon, The (1959) 49
Higham, Charles 6
High and Low (1963) 21
Hill 24 Doesnt't Answer (1955) 22
Hillyer, Lambert 76
Hirschberg, Lynn 115-16
Histoire(s) du cinèma (1989-1994) 106
Hitler: The Last Ten Days (1973) 139
Hitler: Dead or Alive (1942) 64
Hitler Gang, The (1944) 64
Hitlerjunge Quex: Ein Film vom Opfergeist der deutschen Jugend (1933) 139
Hitler's Children (1942) 64
Hitler's Madman (1943) 64
Hoberman, Jim 71-3
Hodges, Mike 115
Hodiak, John 8
Hohenadel, Kristin 108-9
Holland, Agnieszka 44
Hollenshead, Todd 125
Hollow Man, The (2000) 52
Hollywood Ending (2002) 4, 31, 110
Holton, Gerald 130-1
Home of the Brave (1949) 60
Honeymoon for Three (1941) 64
Hooper (1978) 133
Hopper, Dennis 34
Horowitz, Mark 29
Houseman, John 65
House of Dracula (1945) 123
House of Frankenstein (1944) 123
House Un-American Activities Committee 66-7

Howard, Adina 48
Howard, Ron 19
Howards End (1992) 117
How We Stole the Atomic Bomb (1967) 138
Hubbard, L. Ron 115
Huggins, Roy 67
Hughes, Howard 66, 135-6
Hulk, The (2003) 4
Hunt, Helen 120
Huston, John 60-1
hyperconglomerization 2, 83, 93, 99, 102; media 34-5, 47, 83; in religion 36-7

Ice Age (2002) 8
id Software 124-5
Il Mulino delle donne di pietra (1960) 41
Il portiere di notte (1974) 139
images, control by 1
I Married a Communist (1949) 66
immortality 5
imperialism 90-1
Independence Day (1996) 71-2
Information Times (website) 78-9
In Praise of Love (2001) 105-7
Insomnia (2002) 18
International Alliance of Theatrical Stage Employees 23
Internet 17, 48, 78-80, 138; expansion 30; lack of corporate control 54; piracy 25, 27; spam 54
Intertainment AG 116
Intruder, The (1961) 110
Invasion by the Atomic Zombies (1980) 138
Invasion U.S.A. (1952) 67, 135-7
Invasion U.S.A. (1985) 124
Invisible Ghost, The (1941) 64
I Shot Jesse James (1949) 123
Island Records 48
I soliti ignoti (1958) 21
I Walked with a Zombie (1943) 123
I Wanted Wings (1941) 64
I Was a Teenage Frankenstein (1957) 26
I Was a Teenage Werewolf (1957) 26

Jackman, Hugh 5
Jackson, Peter 10
Jagger, Dean 67
James, Allison 112-13
James, Caryn 132
Jaoui, Agnès 110, 112-13
Jason X (2001) 4, 139-40
Jaws (1975) 26
Jenny Jones (television) 51
Jerry Springer (television) 51
Je vous salue, Marie (1985) 106
Jewison, Norman 24
Joel, Billy 98
John, Elton 98
Johnson, Ben 14
Jones, Paula 132
Journey to the Seventh Planet (1962) 49
Juliet of the Spirits (1965) 21

Kaijû daisenso (1965) 7
Kane, Bob 76
Katzenberg, Jeffrey 32
Kaufman, Lloyd 116-17
Kay, Jonathan 125-6

Kazan, Elia 67
Kazandjian, Stéphane 108-10
Kearny, Cresson 80, 82
Kehr, Dave 11, 114
Kerouac, Jack 6
Khan, Aamir 120
Kiarostami, Abbas 31
Killer is Loose, The (1956) 40
King, Stephen 102
King Kong (1933) 71, 118
King Lear (1987) 106
Kinnaman, David 36
Klaussmann, Lisa 30
Knack, The, and How to Get It (1965) 21
Koita, Mustafa 84
KPMG 35
Kramer, Lloyd 95
Kubrick, Stanley 116
Kudrow, Lisa 119
Kugler, Sara 84
Kurosawa, Akira 12
Kurz, Vivian 141
Kwaidan (1964) 21

L.A. Confidential (1997) 8
La belle Américaine (1961) 23
La Bûche (1999) 112
La caduta degli dei (1969) 139
Ladd, Alan 65
La Dolce Vita (1960) 21
Lady and the Duke, The (2001) 13
Ladybug, Ladybug (1963) 16
La Femme Infidèl (1969) 12
La Invasión de los Zombies atómicos (1980) 138
La maschera del demonio (1960) 21
La Morte viene dallo spazio (1958) 21
Lane, Diane 11
Lang, Fritz 2
L'Anglaise et le duc (2001) 13
Lansing, Sherry 94
Lara Croft: Tomb Raider (2001) 26
Laski, Beth 71, 74
Last Day, The (1975) 7
Last Days of Man on Earth, The (1973) 133
Last War, The (1961) 6-8
Late Great Planet Earth, The (1979) 16
Laughton, Charles 65
Lavender Hill Mob, The (1951) 23
Lebanese Broadcasting Corporation International 69-70
LeBlanc, Matt 119
Lee, Ang 4
Lee, Christopher 5, 10
Lee, Jennifer 127-8
Legally Blonde (2001) 119
Le goût des autres (1999) 112
Leigh, Janet 71
Leigh, Mike 31, 45
Leland, John 128
Lemann, Nicholas 70
Lemley, Mark 46
Le Pen, Jean-Marie 60
Le règle du jeu (1939) 63
Les glaneurs et la glaneuse (2000) 18
Lessig, Lawrence 47-8
Letter to Jane (1972) 106
Let There Be Light (1946) 60-1

Le vent d'est (1969) 105
Lewis, Joseph 41
Lewis, Juliette 111
Lewis, Mark 62-4
Lewis, Sinclair 118
Lewton, Val 123
Lidz, Franz 116-17
Lillington, Karlin 47
Lilo & Stitch (2002) 32
Limey, The (1999) 34
Lindlaw, Scott 129
Lion King, The (musical) 98
Lippert, Robert 123
Liquid Audio 53
Lisbon (1956) 42
Little Mermaid, The (musical) 97
Litvak, Anatole 63
Livent Productions 98
Loach, Ken 19
Loneliness of the Long Distance Runner, The (1962) 21
Looney Tunes 12
Lord of the Rings: The Fellowship of the Ring (2002) 10
Losey, Joseph 66
Los Olvidados (1950) 31
Lost Continent (1951) 123
Lost Weekend, The (1945) 42
Lost World: Jurassic Park (1997) 72
Loud, Lance 55-6
Lucas, George 10-11, 13, 31, 99
Ludlum, Robert 18
Lupino, Ida 111
Lyman, Rick 12, 25-7
Lyne, Adrian 11
Lyne, Susan 95

Mackey, Robert 13
Mackintosh, Cameron 98
MacLachlan, Kyle 45
Maguire, Toby 4
Malanga, Gerard 141-2
Malick, Terrence 75
Malle, Louis 20
Man Alone, A (1955) 42
Mani di pietra (1986) 138
Man Made Monster (1941) 138
Mann, Anthony 41
Mann, Delbert 6
Mannion, Steve 49
Man Who Haunted Himself, The (1970) 9
marketing, aggressive 41; niche 33
Markoff, John 124-5
Marks, Peter 97-8
Mars Attacks! (1996) 96
Marshall, Tonie 31, 110, 112
Martha Stewart Living (magazine) 103
Martin, Dean 12
Marty (1955) 14
Mary Poppins (musical) 98
Match Girl (1966) 140
Matsubayashi, Shuei 6
McCarthy, Joseph 114
McCarthy, Todd 14, 136
McClintock, Pamela 93-4
McGirk, Tim 79
McKinney, Cynthia 88
McLaglen, Victor 14

media, access to 2; alternative 46-7; bans 82; circumvention of controls by 53; conglomerates 15; control by 82, 97; corporate 53; corporate control of 2; dissent in 35; homogenization of news by 114; hyperconglomerization of 34-5, 47, 83; megaconglomerate 105; monopolies 15; propaganda 69-70; radio 46-7; saturation 54
mediocrity principle 131
memorials 37-8
Men in Black (2002) 5
Men Must Fight (1933) 122-3
Messier, Jean-Marie 30
Meteor (1979) 6
Metropolis (1927) 2
Meyer, Andrew 140-3
MGM Studios 12, 115, 122
Middle East Broadcast Center 69-70
Miéville, Anne-Marie 107
Milestone, Lewis 75
Milius, John 71
Milland, Ray 41-2, 65
Mill of the Stone Women (1960) 41
Minority Report (2002) 18
Miramax 12-13, 74
Miranda, Carmen 64
Mission: Impossible (1996) 26
Mission: Impossible II (2000) 26
Mr. Deeds (2002) 5, 59
Mr. Deeds Goes to Town (1936) 5
Mitchel, Mary 42
Mohr, Gerald 137
Monogram Studios 5
Monroe, Marilyn 6, 141
Monsters Inc. (2001) 32
Monster Zero (1970) 7
Monstrosity (1964) 138
Moore, Michael 129
Moore, Roger 9
Morley, Robert 143
Morris, Vincent 89
Morrison, Toni 100, 101
Moseley, Roy 6
Mothra (1962) 7
Motion Picture Association of America 33, 93
Mouthpiece, The (1932) 117
Movie, A (1958) 49-50
Movin' Out (musical) 98
MPO Productions 39
Mulhare, Edward 22
multiculturalism 91-2
multilateralism 91
multinational corporations 90
Mummy Returns, The (2001) 26
Murderers Among Us, The (1946) 61
Murder Game, The (1965) 123
Murdoch, Rupert 15
Murray, Alan 86-8
Murray, Bill 45
music, control of 46-7; "mash-up" 48, 50; MP3 downloads 53; radio 46; satellite 82; underground 48
My Life to Live (1962) 105
My Mother-in-Law is an Atomic Bomb (1952) 138
My Son, the Hero (1963) 21
My Son John (1952) 67
Mysterians, The (1957) 49

Naish, J. Carrol 76
Napster 53
Nathalie, agent secret (1959) 138
National Research Group 28
National Rifle Association 42
Natural Born Killers (1994) 111-12
Nelson, Ralph 41
Nelson, Robert 49
Némero Deux (1975) 106
Nesselson, Lisa 109
Neumann, Kurt 41
New Guy, The (2002) 8, 17
New Line Cinema 12, 52
New World Pictures 22, 142
Nicholson, Jack 96, 115, 119
Nicholson, James 25
Nicol, Alex 22
Nielsen Media Research 29
Nielsen NetRatings 29
Night and Fog (1955) 139
Night of the Cobra Woman (1972) 142
Night Porter, The (1974) 139
Night to Remember, A (1958) 24
Night Train to Paris (1964) 123
Nine Inch Nails 132
Nippon chinbotsu (1973) 142
Nixon, Richard 15, 16-17
Nolan, Christopher 18
No Man's Land (2002) 75
Norris, Chuck 124
Nose Bleed 72
NTT DoMoCo Inc. 54
Nuit et brouillard (1955) 139
Numan, Gary 48

O, The Oprah Magazine 102-3
Oboler, Arch 8
Odets, Clifford 67
O'Donnell, Rosie 103
Oh, Woe is Me (1993) 107
O'Hara, Maureen 14
O'Herlihy, Dan 137-8
Olbrych, Grazyna 104
Oliveira, Manoel de 31
O No Coronado (1992) 49
On the Beach (1959) 6
On the Beach (2000; television) 8
Open City (1945) 21
Openlaw: Eldred v. Ashcroft (website) 43
Oprah's Book Club 99, 100-3
ORG-MARG 28
Orient, Jane 82
Osborne, Lawrence 105-7
Osbournes, The (television) 51, 55-8
Outbreak (1995) 72
Outrage (1950) 111
Ozzman Cometh: Greatest Hits, The (album) 57

Pace Theatrical Group 98
Pacino, Al 18
Paisan (1946) 61
Palme d'Or 31
Paltrow, Gwyneth 120
Panic in the Year Zero! (1962) 42-3
Paramount Communications 94
Paramount Pictures 13

Parker, Dorothy 67
Pasolini, Uberto 19
Patch Adams (1998) 116
Path to Paradise: The Untold Story of the World Trade Center Bombing (television) 70-1
Pay It Forward (2000) 116-17
Payne, Alexander 118
Peacemaker, The (1997) 72
Pearl Harbor (2001) 26, 74
Penn, Sean 115
Perry, Matthew 119
Peter Pan 13
Pham, Alex 126
piracy 25, 27
Place Vendôme (1998) 112
Planet of the Apes (2001) 26-7
Planet of the Vampires (1965) 23
Platoon (1986) 60, 75
Playmates (1941) 64
Pledge, The (2001) 115
Plummer, Christopher 98
Police Tapes, The (1977) 55
political disintegration 92
Populuxe films 39
Porky's (1981) 108
Post coitum animal triste (1997) 112
Powell, Corey 133
Powerpuff Girls 18
PRC Studios 5
Predator (video surveillance) 127
Prelinger, Rick 38-40
Preminger, Otto 8
Producers, The (musical) 98
production, boutique 116; in Canada 29; digital 47; globalization of 29
publishing 98-105
Punch-Drunk Love (2002) 31

Radley, Gordon 11
Raimi, Sam 4
Ramis, Harold 119
Random House 101
Rape Me (2001) 111-12
Rat (1960) 77
Raymond, Alan 55-6
Raymond, Susan 55
Ray, Satyajit 22
R.D.A.F. Nuclear Defence: H Hour Now (1959) 138
Real Player 53
Red Dance, The (1928) 71
Red Danube (1949) 71
Red Dawn (1984) 71
Red Dragon, The (1945) 71
Red Menace, The (1949) 71
Red Planet Mars (1952) 71
Red Rock West (1992) 8
Red Salute (1935) 71
regional coding enhancement (RCE) 52
Renoir, Jean 41, 63-4, 141
Republic Pictures 5
research, market 28-29, 127-8
Resnais, Alain 139
Return to Castle Wolfenstein (video game) 125
Revenge of the Radioactive Reporter (1991) 138
Reznor, Trent 132
Rhames, Ving 73

Rhodes, Richard 130
Ricard, René 141
Rich, Robert 67
Ricks, Thomas 127
Riff-Raff (1990) 19
Riley, Terry 50
Rio Grande (1950) 14
RKO-Pathé 38, 136
RKO Pictures 13, 66, 123, 135
Robbins, Tim 95
Roberts, Julia 4, 107, 120
Robson, May 122
Rock, The 12
Rodan (1956) 7
Rohmer, Eric 13-14, 107, 113
Rollerball (1975) 24
Rollins, Henry 132
Roma, città aperta (1945) 21
Romance (1999) 112
Rooney, David 122
Rose Hobart (1936) 49-50
Rosenbaum, Jonathan 28
Rosie (magazine) 103
Rossellini, Roberto 61
Rossen, Robert 67
Rothapfel, Samuel Lionel 9
Rothman, Wilson 37
Roüan, Brigitte 110, 112
Rove, Karl 93-4
Rules of the Game (1950) 63
Rumsfeld, Donald 86-8
Rush Hour (1998) 13
Rush Hour 2 (2001) 13, 26
Rushin, Steve 116-17
Russian Ark (2003) 31

S.A.-Mann Brand (1933) 139
Safecracker, The (1958) 42
salaries 119-20
Sally Jesse Raphael (television) 51
Samaha, Elie 115-16
Sandler, Adam 18, 31
San Francisco (1936) 133
Sarandon, Susan 95
saturation booking 25
Saving Private Ryan (1998) 61, 75
Schallert, William 137
Schirach, Baldur von 139
School for Scoundrels (1960) 41
Schreiber, Liev 45
Schulberg, Budd 67
Schuller, Robert 36
Schumacher, Thomas 97
Schwarzenegger, Arnold 114
Schwimmer, David 119
Scientology 115-16
Sciuscià (1946) 61
Scooby-Doo 33-4
Scorpion King, The (2002) 8, 12
Scorsese, Martin 31, 109
Scott, A.O. 9-10
Scott, Ridley 75
screen tests 16
Sears, Fred 41
Season's Beatings (1999) 112
Secret Garden, The (Burnett) 44, 45

security concerns 59; facial recognition technology 84-5; political right and 60; surveillance 83-6
Sekai daisenso (1961) 6
Sergeant York (1941) 64
Serial Metaphysics (1972) 50
Serling, Rod 113
Seven Samurai, The (1954) 12
Seventh Victim, The (1943) 123
Sex and the City (television) 72
Sexy Boys (2002) 108-9
SFX entertainment 98
Shades and Drumbeats (1964) 140
Shamberg, Michael 143
Sharp, Don 123
She Had to Say Yes (1933) 118
Shelby, Richard 89
Shepard, Sam 45
Sherlock Holmes series 5
Shoeshine (1947) 61
shows, Broadway 97-8
Shrek (2001) 26, 31-2
Shyamalan, M. Night 18
Sidewalks of New York (2002) 72
Siege, The (1998) 71-2
Signs (2002) 18
Simone (2002) 36
Singer, Bryan 5
Skarsgård, Stellan 18
Sky Pirate, The (1970) 141
Skyscraper Souls (1932) 118
Slansky, Paul 16
Smith, Anna Nicole 58
Smith, Art 67
Smith, Dennis 95
Smith, Will 120
Smultronstället (1957) 110
Snow Dogs (2002) 8, 32
social, culture 2; trends 89; values 110, 132
Soderbergh, Steven 109-10
Sokurov, Aleksandr 31
Sominage 107
Sonbert, Warren 142
Sondergaard, Gale 67
Sonic Outlaws (1995) 49
Sonny Bono Copyright Term Extension Act 43-8
Sony Productions 12
So Proudly We Hail (1943) 64
Sora no daikaijû Radon (1956) 7
Spacey, Kevin 115
Spartacus (1960) 66
Spectres of the Spectrum (1999) 49
Spencer, Diana 60
Spider-Man (2002) 4, 26
Spider-Man 2 (2004) 4
Spielberg, Steven 18, 61, 75, 106, 109, 116
Spirit: Stallion of the Cimarron (2002) 31-2
Spitz, Bob 120
Springsteen, R.G. "Bud " 41
Spy Kids 2: The Island of Lost Dreams (2002) 18
Stallone, Sylvester 116
Stander, Lionel 67
Stanwyck, Barbara 71
Star Wars: Episode II - Attack of the Clones (2002) 5, 9-11, 31
Star Wars: Episode One - The Phantom Menace (1999) 99
Star Wars: Episode VI - Return of the Jedi (1983) 26

Star Wars series 12
Staudte, Wolfgang 61
Steele, Danielle 102
Steel Helmet, The (1951) 123
Stewart, James 95
Stewart, Martha 103
Stewart, Patrick 5
Stoller, James 141
Stone, Lewis 122
Stone, Oliver 75, 111
Story of Gilbert and Sullivan, The (1953) 45
Strange Death of Adolf Hitler, The (1943) 64-5
Strange Impersonation (1946) 41
Strasberg, Paula 67
Strauss, Neil 48-9
Stuart Little 2 (2002) 5
Sub-Mariner 5
Sugababes 48
Sum of All Fears, The (2002) 8, 74, 138
Suna no onna (1964) 21
Superman 5, 12
Surf Nazis Must Die (1987) 116
Surprise Attack on America (2001) 73
Survival Under Atomic Attack (1951) 77, 138
Survivor (television) 51

Talbot, Lyle 118
Tarantula (1955) 18
Taste of Others, The (2001) 112
Taylor, Elizabeth 67, 142
Taylor, Quinn 95
Taylor, Robert 67
Taylor, Nelson Sofres 29
Taymor, Julie 98
Tecnica per un massacro (1967) 138
Teenage Catgirls in Heat (1997) 116
Teenage Research Unlimited 127-8
telescreens 1
television, advertising 32; cable 20; hypersurveillant 51; pay 22; propaganda on 69-70; reality 51, 55-6; trash talk shows 51
Tengoku to jigoku (1963) 21
Terminator 3: Rise of the Machines (2003) 114
Terminator series 12
Terrore nello spazio (1965) 23
terrorism 59, 67-8, 70-1, 78, 132; counterprogramming to further war on 93; fears of 86-9; international 90; spread of 90; "War on Terror" 91
Tetzlaff, Ted 41
Texas Chainsaw Massacre, The (1974) 12, 131
That Darn Cat (1965) 50
That Touch of Mink (1962) 6
Thelma & Louise (1991) 111
Them! (1954) 18
Thin Red Line, The (1998) 75
This Island Earth (1954) 49
This Is Not a Test (1962) 77
Thomas, J. Parnell 66
Thompson, Danièle 112-13
Thoroughly Modern Millie (musical) 98
Tidal Wave (1973) 142
Tierney, Gene 8-9
Till the End of Time (1946) 61
Time Machine, The (2002) 8, 72
Timeslip (1956) 138
Titra Sound Studios 21

Toback, James 14
Toho 7
Tom Jones (1963) 21
Toomey, Regis 118
Topsy-Turvy (1999) 45
Townsend, Prescott 141
Tracy, Spencer 120
Trailers 127
Travolta, John 115-16
Tribulation 99: Alien Anomalies Under America (1999)
  49
Trinh Thi, Coralie 111
Trinity and Beyond (1995) 138
Troma Pictures 116-17
Tromeo and Juliet (1996) 116
Truffaut, François 107, 113
Trumbo, Dalton 66
Tucker, Chris 120
Tuttle, Frank 67
Tuxedo, The (2002) 18
24 Hour Party People (2002) 31
Two Girls and a Guy (1997) 14
Tyson, Cicely 143

Ullman, Tracey 119
Under Siege (1995) 72
Unfaithful (2002) 11
Unfaithful Wife, The (1969) 11-12
United Dutch Publishers 28, 29
Universal Pictures 12, 32
Unknown Pleasures 31
Unreal Tournament (video game) 126
Usai, Paolo Cherchi 140
Usual Suspects, The (1995) 8

Valenti, Jack 33, 93
values, indigenous 110; social, 110, 132
Varda, Agnès 18-19, 107, 110
Vaucher, Andrea 30-1
Vaughn, Robert 67
Venus Beauty Institute (2000) 112
Verenigde Nederlandse Uitgeversbedrijven 28-9
VHS format 51
Vidor, King 75
Virilio, Paul 9, 97
Viskningar och rop (1972) 22
Vivendi Universal 15, 30
Vivre sa vie: Film en douze tableaux (1962) 105
Voice of America 70

Wagner, Natasha Gregson 14
Walker, Robert 67
Wallace, Edgar 22
Wallace, George 15
Wallace, Randall, 60-2
Wall Street (1987) 73
Walt Disney Company 44
War Game, The (1965) 7-8, 78

Warhol, Andy 16-17, 58, 117, 141-2
Warner, Jack 67
Warner Books 101
Warner Bros. 12, 52, 63, 115
Warner Home Video 52
"War on Terror" 91
Warriors, The (1979) 13
Waters, John 98
Watkins, Peter 7, 78
Wayne, John 5-6, 14, 67
Weekend (1967) 105
Welles, Orson 16, 41
Westworld (1973) 12
We Were Soldiers (2002) 8, 60-2, 75
When Worlds Collide (1951) 134
When You Wish (musical) 98
Whirlpool (1949) 8, 9
White, E.B. 17, 37
Whole Nine Yards, The (2000) 116
Wilder, Billy 42, 110
Wild Strawberries (1959) 110
Wild Things (1998) 8
Wilkerson, Kevin 127
William, Warren 117-18
Willis, Bruce 116, 120
Wind from the East (1969) 105
Windtalkers (2002) 74
Winfrey, Oprah 99-101
Winterbottom, Michael 31
Wiseman, Frederick 117
Witchcraft (1964) 123
Witherspoon, Reese 118-19
Wizard of Oz, The (1939) 118
Wolk, Douglas 82
Woman in the Dunes (1964) 21
Wood, Michael 128
Woodstock Festival 131-2
World War III 72
Wright, Jeffrey 45
Wright, Lawrence 95
Wright, Will 65
Wyler, William 61
Wynyard, Diana 122

X2 (2003) 5

Yardley, Jonathan 99-100
Yeoh, Michelle 120
Yojimbo the Bodyguard (1962) 21
You Can Beat the A-Bomb (1950) 77
Young, Loretta 118
Young, Robert 122
Young and the Damned, The (1950) 31

Zhangke, Jia 31
Zubaydah, Abu 73
Zugsmith, Albert 135
Zulu (1964) 75-6

ABOUT THE AUTHOR

Wheeler Winston Dixon is the James Ryan Endowed Professor of Film Studies; Chair of the Film Studies Program; Professor of English at the University of Nebraska, Lincoln; Series Editor for the State University of New York Press Cultural Studies in Cinema/Video; and the Editor-in-Chief of the *Quarterly Review and Film and Video.* His many books include *Straight: Constructions of Heterosexuality in the Cinema* (State University of New York Press) and *Experimental Cinema: The Film Reader* (Routledge), co-edited with Gwendolyn Audrey Foster.